Women's History at the Cutting Edge

This book considers the promise of women's and gender history for revolutionizing our understanding of the past while also acknowledging the current national political, financial, and other contextual realities that can (and do) constrain or promote the possibilities for researching and writing women's history. The editors assert that women's and gender history is a cutting edge field of research, "a revolutionary development in the politics of historical scholarship," essential for understanding the human past. Further, they argue for the inseparability of women's history and gendered analytical approaches.

The contributors to the volume address questions including the following: What have been the achievements of women's and gender history over the past two decades? To what extent has it succeeded in making women's history an integral part of historical study rather than an optional specialist area? What impact has the study of manhood, masculinities, and men's gendered power had on our understanding of women's lives? What is the relationship between gender studies and new critical histories of colonialism and empire, contact zones, cross-cultural encounters, and racialization? How is new work on cultural geography and spatial categories impacting on our historical understandings of bodily difference?

This book was originally published as a special issue of *Women's History Review*.

Karen Offen is a Historian and Independent Scholar, affiliated as a Senior Scholar with The Clayman Institute for Gender Research at Stanford University, USA. She publishes on the history of modern Europe, especially France and its global influence, from a women's and gender history perspective. She holds a PhD from Stanford University, USA.

Chen Yan is a Professor and the Vice-Chair of the History Department at Fudan University, Shanghai, China and the Co-Director of the UM-Fudan Joint Institute for Gender Studies. She specializes in the modern history of China, especially women's and gender history.

Women's History at the Cutting Edge

Edited by
Karen Offen and Chen Yan

Routledge
Taylor & Francis Group

LONDON AND NEW YORK

First published 2019
by Routledge
2 Park Square, Milton Park, Abingdon, Oxon, OX14 4RN, UK

and by Routledge
52 Vanderbilt Avenue, New York, NY 10017, USA

Routledge is an imprint of the Taylor & Francis Group, an informa business

British Library Cataloguing-in-Publication Data
A catalogue record for this book is available from the British Library

ISBN13: 978-0-367-02907-4

Typeset in Minion Pro
by codeMantra

Publisher's Note
The publisher accepts responsibility for any inconsistencies that may have arisen during the conversion of this book from journal articles to book chapters, namely the possible inclusion of journal terminology.

Disclaimer
Every effort has been made to contact copyright holders for their permission to reprint material in this book. The publishers would be grateful to hear from any copyright holder who is not here acknowledged and will undertake to rectify any errors or omissions in future editions of this book.

Contents

Citation Information

The chapters in this book were originally published in *Women's History Review*, volume 27, issue 1 (February 2018). When citing this material, please use the original page numbering for each article, as follows:

Introduction
Karen Offen and Chen Yan
Women's History Review, volume 27, issue 1 (February 2018) pp. 1–5

Chapter 1
Women's History at the Cutting Edge: a joint paper in two voices
Chen Yan and Karen Offen
Women's History Review, volume 27, issue 1 (February 2018) pp. 6–28

Chapter 2
The Dangers of Complacency: women's history/gender history in Canada in the twenty-first century
Catherine Carstairs and Nancy Janovicek
Women's History Review, volume 27, issue 1 (February 2018) pp. 29–40

Chapter 3
The History of Women and Gender: French perspectives on the last twenty years
Françoise Thébaud (translated from the French by Karen Offen)
Women's History Review, volume 27, issue 1 (February 2018) pp. 41–47

Chapter 4
From Invisibility to Marginality: women's history in Romania
Maria Bucur
Women's History Review, volume 27, issue 1 (February 2018) pp. 48–57

Chapter 5
Women's History at the Cutting Edge in Japan
Rui Kohiyama
Women's History Review, volume 27, issue 1 (February 2018) pp. 58–70

Chapter 6
Women's and Gender Studies of the Russian Past: two contemporary trends
Natalia Pushkareva and Maria Zolotukhina
Women's History Review, volume 27, issue 1 (February 2018) pp. 71–87

Chapter 7
'A Glass Half Full'? Women's history in the UK
June Purvis
Women's History Review, volume 27, issue 1 (February 2018) pp. 88–108

Chapter 8
Women's History in Many Places: reflections on plurality, diversity and polyversality
Joanna de Groot
Women's History Review, volume 27, issue 1 (February 2018) pp. 109–119

For any permission-related enquiries please visit:
http://www.tandfonline.com/page/help/permissions

Notes on Contributors

Maria Bucur is the John V. Hill Professor of History and Gender Studies at Indiana University, USA. Her recent publications include *Heroes and Victims: Remembering War in Twentieth-Century Romania* (2009) and *The Century of Women: How Women Have Transformed the World Since 1900* (2018).

Catherine Carstairs is the Department Chair and a Professor of History at the University of Guelph, Canada. She is the author of *Jailed for Possession: Illegal Drug Use, Regulation, and Power in Canada, 1920–1961* (2006) and the Co-Editor of *Feminist History in Canada: New Essays on Women, Gender, Work, and Nation* (2014). She was the President of the Canadian Committee on Women's History (2011–2012).

Joanna de Groot is a Senior Lecturer in the History Department at the University of York, UK. Her main academic interests are in gendered approaches to histories of societies in the Middle East, especially Iran, since c.1800; imperial and colonial relationships and cultures since c.1700; and historical practices and theories.

Nancy Janovicek is an Associate Professor who teaches at the University of Calgary, Canada. She is the author of *No Place to Go: Local Histories of the Battered Women's Shelter Movement* (2007) and the Co-Editor of *Feminist History in Canada: New Essays on Women, Gender, Work, and Nation* (2014). She was the President of the Canadian Committee on Women's History (2012–2013).

Rui Kohiyama is a Professor of American History and Gender Studies at Tokyo Woman's Christian University, Japan. She is the former President of the Gender History Association of Japan, Tokyo, Japan; the former Vice-President of the Japanese American Studies Association; and the current Vice-President of the Society of Historical Studies of Christianity, Japan.

Karen Offen is a Historian and Independent Scholar, affiliated as a Senior Scholar with The Clayman Institute for Gender Research at Stanford University, USA. She publishes on the history of modern Europe, especially France and its global influence, from a women's and gender history perspective. She holds a PhD from Stanford University, USA.

June Purvis is an Emeritus Professor of Women's and Gender History at the University of Portsmouth, UK. She has published extensively on women's education in nineteenth-century England and on the suffragette movement in Edwardian Britain. She is the Founding and Managing Editor of *Women's History Review* and also the Editor for the Routledge book series *Women's and Gender History*.

Natalia Pushkareva is a Professor and Leading Research Fellow in, and the Head of, the Women's and Gender Studies Department in the Institute of Ethnology and Anthropology at the Russian Academy of Sciences, Moscow, Russia. She is also the Chief Editor of the Yearbook, *Social History* and the President of the Russian Association for Research in Women's History (since 2002).

Françoise Thébaud is a Professor Emerita at the University of Avignon, France and is currently an Affiliated Researcher in the Institute of Gender Studies at the University of Geneva, Switzerland. She is the Founder and Co-Editor of the women's history journal *Clio: Femmes, Genre, Histoire* (previously called *Clio: Histoire, Femmes et Sociétés*), from 1995 until 2012.

Chen Yan is a Professor and the Vice-Chair of the History Department at Fudan University, Shanghai, China and the Co-Director of the UM-Fudan Joint Institute for Gender Studies. She specializes in the modern history of China, especially women's and gender history.

Maria Zolotukhina is an Assistant Professor of Social Anthropology in the Department of Sociology and Advertising and Communications at Moscow State University of Design and Technology, Russia and an Assistant Professor in the Department of Theology at the National Research Nuclear University (Moscow Engineering Physics Institute), Russia.

Introduction

Karen Offen and Chen Yan

ABSTRACT

This Special Issue on women's and gender history consists of substantially revised papers that were initially presented at the XXII International Congress for the Historical Sciences, held in August 2015 in Jinan, China, which met jointly with the International Federation for Research in Women's History. A number of commentators respond to a position paper on 'Women's History At the Cutting Edge', presented by Chen Yan and Karen Offen, noting the existence of contextual and political specificities that condition (and constrain or promote) the possibilities for researching and writing women's history in their respective countries.

The position paper by Chen Yan and Karen Offen, followed by seven commentaries from leading historians of women and gender from around the world, was originally written for the XXII International Congress of Historical Sciences (ICHS/CISH), sponsored by the Shandong University and the Chinese Academy of Social Sciences and held in Jinan (Shandong Province), China, in August 2015. Nearly 3,000 persons registered for the international congress (the first to be held in Asia) and the various sessions were very well-attended. Complementing the excellent organization of the congress, our Chinese hosts provided visitors with a sumptuous display of cultural events, including dance, orchestral presentations (both Chinese and Western music), and excellent food. Women's and gender history topics appeared on the program in a quantity never before seen at the ICHS congresses, which take place only every five years. The next congress will be held in 2020 in Poznan, Poland.

Our Round Table, 'Women's History at the Cutting Edge,' took place in two sessions, one under the auspices of the main program of the ICHS and the second as the opening session of the joint conference of the International Federation for Research in Women's History (IFRWH/FIRHF), both scheduled sequentially on Thursday, 27 August. Each presentation has been revised and updated for publication in the *Women's History Review*.

The first session began with recognition of China's most famous female poet: Li Qingzhao (pronounced Lee Ching Joe in English), whose poetry is still read by schoolchildren in China today. She was born in 1084 (ad) in Shandong Province during the Sung (Song) dynasty. There are four memorials to her in China (three in Shandong Province alone), including one in downtown Jinan's Leaping Spring Park, which includes a large statue of her, along with portraits and excerpts from her writings. According to the *Encyclopedia Britannica*, this poet 'produced seven volumes of essays and six volumes of poetry, but

1

most of her work is lost except for some poetry fragments.' She was a master of ci poetry, which was a lyrical song form, and she also produced a critical scholarly study on this art form. For us, as historians of women & gender, it seemed particularly significant that her poetry was not only 'noted for its striking diction' but also 'for her focus on relating her personal experiences, giving her work more emotional intensity than that of her peers … ' . It 'reflects the dramas of her lifetime, with the earlier works marked by a carefree vitality and the pieces that she wrote after her husband's death [1129] and her exile reflecting a sombre, grief-stricken tone.'[1] Thus, Li Qingzhao speaks to us in an authentically female voice from over 900 years ago.

Chen Yan and Karen Offen dedicated the round table to the memory of Li Qingzhao, following which Chen Yan read one of Li's poems in Chinese.

Chen Yan's and Karen Offen's joint position paper is written in two voices, reviewed and edited by both authors. It raises five questions for review by the commentators to consider, and each of the respondent's essays speaks, in its own way and from the standpoint of the author's particular background, to the opportunities and/or constraints in which the sexual politics of knowledge play out on the ground as concerns the possibilities for the development and impact of women's and gender history.

Not surprisingly, in a number of countries, the opportunities for and restrictions on research and publication in women's and gender history are the indirect (but sometimes direct) result of governmental policies at the national level, which control and constrain research funding possibilities, and in certain cases, opportunities for publication as well. As these policies shift, or governments change, one finds that the possibilities for research and publication in women's and gender history can fare quite well, as is currently the situation in France and Japan; equivocally, as is the case in Canada and the United Kingdom; or with restrictions (both implicit and explicit), as is the case in Russia, Romania, and in the People's Republic of China. A number of these commentaries speak, implicitly or explicitly, to restrictions, both formal and informal, on freedom of speech, of the press, and of association—in a word, to a lack/absence of civil liberties as those are understood in the West.[2] But state policy is not the sole determinant; the possibilities are also inflected by self-censorship, by the reading public's notions of what is considered 'sayable' and what should be 'silenced' in a given society. Thus, some topics concerning women and gender continue to remain off limits, notably when they question the normativity of heterosexuality.

With the exception of Joanna de Groot's remarkable think-piece, 'reflections on plurality, diversity, and polyversality,' most of the commentators discuss the politics and production of women's and gender history that focus internally on the women (and, to some degree, the men) of a specific nation. Already in the early 1990s, in volume 5 of the influential *History of Women in the West*, Françoise Thébaud pointed to 'The Nationalization of Women':

> most European countries swept aside old distinctions between private and public, family and government, individuals and the state. Governments of every stripe—from social-democratic Sweden to the fascist and Nazi dictatorships, and including first republican and later Vichy France—attempted to 'nationalize' their female citizens. Their methods were more authoritarian in some countries, less so in others.[3]

The consequences of this nationalization continue to affect historiography in all areas, and those who research and write about women's/gender history are as entrapped by this 'nationalization' as any others. It is not only the nation-state, however, that entraps historians, but also language itself. The increasing world hegemony of the English language is a reality, but we still encounter deep pockets of resistance, including in the historical professions of smaller or linguistically distinctive nations. We can see this in the international congresses of the ICHS/CISH, where French was once hegemonic, as well as in the IFRWH/FIRHF.

Some of our contributors do mention the existence of publications by historians in their country who do not focus on their own national history. For instance, the contribution by the Canadian historians Catherine Carstairs and Nancy Janovicek (from bi-lingual Canada) makes an effort to include the work of scholars in both English and French, as well as point to research and publication being done by scholars in their countries on other countries or regions. In addition to singling out the productive English-language scholarship in the UK and the Japanese-language scholarship in Japan, both June Purvis and Rui Kohiyama do acknowledge (to some degree) the publications of historians based elsewhere who explore the women's/gender history of their respective countries. Nevertheless, it is difficult for those 'other' historians and their contributions to find space or voice in what have become overpoweringly national, unilingual historiographies. Natalia Pushkareva and Maria Zolothukina speak to the rapid expansion of women's and gender histories in post-Soviet Russia, especially in the various widespread regions of the country, and point to their efforts to organize a community and hold conferences over such distances. Their publications are almost exclusively in Russian, and only a few works by outsiders have been translated into Russian. This last point concerning translation is, as Chen Yan points out, the case in China as well. Our French colleagues, on the contrary, benefit from extensive internal organization and increasing acceptance during the last decade by governmental research organizations, as Françoise Thébaud attests. (The growing women's and gender history community in France has also become much more open to the research of outsiders and its members increasingly look beyond their own borders for research opportunities or are establishing provocative transnational initiatives.)

Maria Bucur-Deckard frames her remarks with reference to several broader issues, including the tenuous state of the humanities more generally, especially in the USA where she teaches, and the great expansion in the numbers of women studying in colleges and universities, where she sees untapped opportunities for teaching the history of women and gender. Among other things, she proposes refocusing mainstream histories on alternative 'big' topics, such as study of the peace movement, that lend themselves to a focus on women's activism. She then turns her attention to Romania (her own area of research specialization, no doubt influenced by her Romanian family roots) and to indigenous contributions to the development of Romanian women's history within the context of that nation's rapidly evolving political situation since 1989 and other conditions on the ground.

Joanna De Groot, whose research has focused primarily on the Middle East and Iran, provides a thoughtful analysis of the intrinsic interconnections of women's history and gender(ed) history, providing multiple examples of excellent analytical work by Anglophone scholars in a variety of world settings (excluding continental Europe). In particular, she underscores the extent of conceptual work being published, especially as concerns the history of empire and global contact zones.

Virtually all these papers speak to the dramatic influence of Joan Scott's germinal article, 'Gender as a Category of Analysis,' originally published in 1986 in the *American Historical Review*, included in her book in 1988, and translated into a variety of languages.[4] But that influence seems to have had varied effects from one country to another, as these papers suggest. 'Gender' as concerns the politics of history is differently understood in different national contexts.

Admittedly, one cannot cover all the bases or answer all the questions with these relatively short essays, but it is clear that readers of this special issue are in for a treat. If one compares these essays with their predecessors in IFRWH's 1991 publication, *Writing Women's History: International Perspectives*, it will not be difficult to recognize that in many respects women's and gender history remains on the 'cutting edge' of historical scholarship, but that in different settings its trajectory as a field of research has taken very different paths.[5]

Notes

1. All quotations in this paragraph come from https://www.britannica.com/biography/Li-Qingzhao
2. In the USA the state does not 'control the production of historical knowledge;' far from it! Indeed, the closest we have come to this is a twenty-year-long series of arguments about proposals for historical standards for teaching history (i.e. old-fashioned, male-centered political history), especially in the secondary schools, and any such proposals have been hotly disputed. Curriculum in the schools is the prerogative of the fifty states. True, there are federal grants to be had for research from the National Endowment for the Humanities and the National Endowment for the Arts, and, occasionally, for topics in the sciences ('historical sciences' don't count) via the National Science Foundation. But these are not the only grants available; others come from the private sector, or as with the ACLS (American Council of Learned Societies), consortia of other scholarly organizations, or from within the research universities. This flexibility is not the case elsewhere, as several of our commentators make clear.
3. Georges Duby & Michelle Perrot (Eds) (1991–1992) *Histoire des femmes en Occident*, 5 volumes (Paris: Plon). Originally published in Italian (1990–1992) as *Storia Delle Donne in Occidente* (Rome-Bari: Laterza); in English (1992–1994) as *A History of Women* (Cambridge, MA: Harvard University Press). Volume editors are Pauline Schmitt Pantel (I: Antiquity); Christiane Klapisch-Zuber (II: Middle Ages); Natalie Zemon Davis & Arlette Farge (III : 16th–18th centuries); Michelle Perrot & Geneviève Fraisse (IV: 19th century); Françoise Thébaud (V: 20th century). This landmark work has been translated into a number of other languages, including Spanish, Dutch, German, Russian, etc., with chapters added by local historians to flesh out the historical context. The quote from Thébaud appears in volume five of the English edition, p. 17. Her theme of 'The Nationalization of Women' comprises both the title and subject-matter of Part I.
4. See Joan W. Scott (1986) Gender: a useful category of historical analysis, *The American Historical Review*, 91 (5), pp. 1053–1075; republished in Joan W. Scott (1988) *Gender and the Politics of History* (New York: Columbia University Press), pp. 28–50.
5. See Karen Offen, Ruth Roach Pierson, & Jane Rendall (Eds) (1991) *Writing Women's History: International Perspectives* (Bloomington: Indiana University Press; London: Macmillan).

Women's History at the Cutting Edge: a joint paper in two voices

Chen Yan and Karen Offen

ABSTRACT

This is, as the subtitle indicates, a joint paper in two voices. Each author has worked with her counterpart to revise what began as their position paper for the Round Table 'Women's History at the Cutting Edge' at the International Congress for the Historical Sciences, held in August 2015 in Jinan, China, which met jointly with the International Federation for Research in Women's History (IFRWH). Chen Yan explains her perplexity about the reticence of Chinese historians (based in China) to embrace topics in women's and gender history, using her own case as an example. She then poses five questions in the paper to stimulate reflections from the commentators, drawing on their varied experiences as historians of women and gender in other countries. Her particular objective is to 'jump-start' research and publication in these areas in China, where a variety of obstacles dissuade scholars from pursuing this path. Karen Offen's contribution builds out from that of Chen Yan, arguing that women's and gender history is at the cutting edge of historical research precisely because it offers 'a revolutionary development in the politics of historical knowledge'. No historian can be considered 'up-to-date' in the field of history without taking its findings into account. Offen addresses each of the five questions, making provocative arguments and rehearsing some of the achievements in providing an organizational structure that welcomes historians from many lands through the IFRWH. She emphasizes the vast expansion of publications in the field during the last twenty-some years in many languages besides English and addresses the controversies of the 1990s concerning the 'turn' to gender history and to theoretical analyses. Offen then proposes thinking about 'women' and 'gender' as two focal points along the continuum of the same project, using the analogy of the 'zoom lens'. Making women's history an integral part of historical study requires a 'gendered analysis' of any historical topic, but it also requires deeper thinking about communication strategies that can bring the findings of our research to the general public.

Chen Yan

Sixteen years ago, when I was preparing the research proposal for my doctoral dissertation, my professor refused my naïve idea of choosing some female traitors during the anti-Japanese War (1931–1945) as the subjects of my thesis. He said earnestly that: Perhaps it's an interesting topic, but we have many more important and meaningful topics that deserve your attention. In the end, I wrote my doctoral thesis on the diplomatic system of the Chinese government during the anti-Japanese War, which is a classic topic of 'male-centered' history, dealing with government affairs.

In 2015, I received a refusal letter from a top Chinese historical journal concerning my submission of an article that addressed questions of masculinity in the anti-Japanese war. I was told that one of the anonymous referees thought my article was 'interesting', but he preferred me to do some other more meaningful topics. My article investigated two items of gossip that spread like wildfire in Chongqin (the wartime capital of China 1937–1945) in the 1940s, and went on to discuss the complex and specious 'affairs—Chinese first couples, some American special envoys' and 'relationships—between the Chinese and American government'. Already in 1970 we had learned that the personal is political, so how could it be that items of gossip and affairs would still be considered marginal topics in Chinese history?

Based on my personal experience, I realize that the study of women's and gender history in China has stalled, so I proposed this roundtable, initially titled 'What's New for Women's History? After Gender', hoping for more feedback from Chinese and global historical circles, in order to locate (and possibly dislodge) the bottleneck in China. Dr Karen Offen from Stanford University became the co-organizer of this roundtable later, and we revised the title to 'Women's History at the Cutting Edge'. The irony is that the Chinese organizing committee of the CISH's 22nd International Congress initially translated the title into Chinese and published it on their website as: '边缘中的妇女史—the Marginalized Women's History'. I was shocked by the translation at first sight, then realized that our Chinese organizing committee could only understand this roundtable as 'marginal'. In fact, it is definitely not a marginal topic, and we received many proposals for commentators from around the world, including some of the 'founding mothers' of women's history in other countries. I still remember how excited I was to post the news on my Wechat (Chinese Facebook) when I received the application e-mail from Prof. June Purvis, founder and editor of the *Women's History Review* in England.

In the final draft of our proposal for this roundtable, Dr. Karen Offen and I have raised five questions:

(1) What have been the achievements of women's and gender history over the past two decades?
(2) To what extent has it succeeded in making women's history an integral part of historical study rather than an optional specialist area?
(3) What impact has the study of manhood, masculinities and men's gendered power had on our understanding of women's lives?
(4) What is the relationship between gender studies and new critical histories of colonialism and empire, contact zones, cross-cultural encounters and racialization?
(5) How is new work on cultural geography and spatial categories impacting on our historical understandings of bodily difference?

I can't find any clues to answer these five questions, except for the first one. In her landmark article, 'Gender: A Useful Category of Historical Analysis', the American historian Joan Scott said that, in its simplest recent usage, 'gender' had become, for some, a synonym for 'women'.[1] And she tried to provide a more sophisticated understanding of 'gender'. In fact, any number of books and articles whose subject is women's history had substituted 'gender' for 'women' in their titles, and this is still going on today. Joan Scott criticized the use of this misapplied synonym, but unfortunately it still describes today's reality in Chinese historical circles. In the 1990s, accompanying the organization of the 1995 World Conference on Women in Beijing, the notion of 'gender as a category of analysis' was introduced into Chinese academia; at the same time, some Chinese historians, especially a group of women historians began to try 'engendering' Chinese history. But to date, this effort has not ushered in a gender turn for Chinese history.[2]

In 2008, Prof. Du Fangqin, one of the pioneer historians in women's history, reviewed the development of Chinese women's & gender history research. She divided the last thirty years into three periods: she characterized 1978 to 1989 as the revival period; 1990 to 1999 as the climax period; and from 2000 to the present as the practicing period. She also pointed out that, even though there are more research resources and external financial support available to historians in the twenty-first century, the development of theory lagged well behind the production of low-quality localized case studies.[3]

I agree in substance with Prof. Du's points, so in my part of this article, I will focus on asking why, in China during the last twenty years, has women's and gender history been turning in circles, becoming no more than a kind of self-entertainment.

I have to admit that, in China, gender history is still equated with women's history, and that women's history is still stuck, more or less, in the stage of 'separate spheres': women's writing, family, marriage, famous women, elite men's thoughts about women's emancipation. There is little dialogue between women's history and the mainstream (or the male-stream) of Chinese historical research. The published research results of women's history in China seldom gets feedback from mainstream scholars. What's more, we have not yet established an effective dialogue with global gender history. If the 1995 conference on 'Engendering China: Women, Culture and the State', held at Harvard University, opened the eyes of Chinese women's historians, today, twenty years later, the historical study of women's history is still blocked in a difficult start-up stage, with little or no momentum behind it. We need to analyze why that might be, and how we might gain momentum.

Sexuality studies and the history of sexuality, one of the important foundations and now a very lively field in gender studies in western academic circles (the relations of sexuality studies and gender studies is a long story, which I can't go into here) is still absent in China. In an important article published in the United States in 2000, Prof. Susan Mann has analyzed why research on Chinese women did not stimulate much interest in the subject of men or male culture in Chinese history; one reason seems to be the absence of sexuality studies. Mann argues that:

> In point of fact, historians of China have yet to develop a sustained interest in the study of sexuality, which has been the starting point for work on the history of men and of masculinity in European and North American studies.[4]

Prof. Mann does note some exceptions including the work of Keith McMahon, Frank Dikotter and Charlotte Furth. More recently, see the publications of Matthew Sommer.[5] However, we cannot find any comparable results in the Chinese historical publications of the last fifteen years.

Some work has been published by writers outside of the historical profession. For example, Prof. Li Yinhe's new book, *Sexual Discourse Studies in People's Republic of China* (2014)[6] proposed five reasons for the refusal of sexuality studies in China. The first reason is the still cautious respect for Chinese traditional culture, the masses being usually more conservative in this regard than the educated elites. The second reason is that as a revolutionary party, the Chinese Communist Party (CCP) keeps to the sexual 'normal' formed in the pioneer days. The third reason is that Chinese cling to the old idea that 'Food is the first thing for people', sex is only a luxury. What is more, she says, the Chinese still believe that sex is for birth, not for happiness. Finally, Li Yinhe concludes that the control of sex has become the key means to control Chinese society.

Li Yinhe is China's most famous sexologist and the love story of her and her transgender partner enlightens the commonsense of LGBT in Chinese mass media, but her findings are still subject to question. As a historian, I venture to disagree with his/her second reason in particular. Some historians, including Christina Gilmartin and Patricia Stranahan, have revisited the sexual relationship and women's liberation in the CCP before 1949. Based on their research, it seems clear that the pioneer generation of the CCP were, in fact, engaging in more overt sexual behavior that, already in the 1920s, was seen as symbolic of liberation and revolution.[7] But I couldn't agree more with Lin Yinhe's final conclusion, which sounds almost like a conspiracy theory. If sex, the most personal and (presumably) private activity of human beings, is under the control of CCP, then nothing that pertains to the state will be out of control. In recent years, it seems that the CCP have done just that. And, if this is indeed the case, it absolutely cries out for a historical analysis from a gendered perspective.

We historians also face some problems with publication, which have blocked the dissemination of research findings. During the last two decades, a series of books and articles in women's and gender history have been translated from foreign languages, mostly from English, such as those in the Jiangsu People Press series, 'Oversea China Book Series-Women Studies' (海外中国研究丛书·女性系列), whereas there have been far fewer high-quality publications by Chinese scholars. *The Introduction to Women and Gender History* (妇女与社会性别史导论课程阅读文选, 2005) published by the Center of Women Studies of Tianjin Normal University is still the sole textbook to introduce the theories and case studies of gender studies on the edge. *The Readings on Women's History* (中国妇女史读本, 2011) is a good textbook edited by three distinguished professors from mainland China, Taiwan and United States. Among these readings, over 50% of the articles are translated from English, and most of the Chinese authors are from Taiwan. Among the nineteen essays of the Readings, only three were written by historians in mainland China.[8] We had to admit that in mainland China we have made less progress. Even compared to the situation of ten years ago, Chinese feminist scholars confront more troubles in publishing and circulating their findings. The translation into Chinese of the special issue of *Gender and History: translating feminisms in China*[9] has been completed for three years, but the publishing house delays publication again and again due to issues concerning the 'correct political orientation'. *Translating feminism in China* presents critical examinations of both nationalism and feminism in Chinese history. Feminist historians are trying to redefine and remake both women's history and women's liberation, an intellectual project that will challenge those still-dominant narratives of modern Chinese history that center on party history, nationalism, and modernization.

We have to admit as well that, in recent years, China's leaders are tightening controls in publishing. Accordingly, the publishing houses have become simultaneously more calculating and more cautious.

These reasons do not entirely explain the blockage in the development of Chinese women's & gender history. I am even more concerned that some of my former colleagues have abandoned women's studies altogether. In the last twenty years, Chinese scholars have benefitted from many more resources within the Party-State System than did their predecessors. We have many more female professors in history than ever before, but—compared with when I was a graduate student a dozen years ago—they seem reluctant to mentor undergraduate and graduate students to explore new, micro, gender issues.

Finally, the question of how to cater to the ever-changing tastes of the Party and State has preoccupied many Chinese scholars, in history as in other academic disciplines. Unfortunately, in China, the issues surrounding women and gender, including their history, are still marginalized. I am not sure we can push forward if we can't promote sexuality studies, but this is how it seems. I am also uncertain as to when or how China's authorities will loosen their grip on ideology, mass media, and social movements.

Here is some good news and some bad news. Fortunately, I succeeded in publishing the stories of those female 'traitors' in my new book,[10] the dream of a graduate student finally realized after fifteen years. Unfortunately, five young feminist activists were arrested on 8 March 2015 in China. It is particularly ironic that these anti-domestic violence activists lost their freedom on International Women's Day.

In sum, and despite this sense of stagnation, coupled with cautious optimism about the future of women's & gender history in China, we await your feedback and suggestions. Will women's & gender history soon move to the 'cutting edge' of historical writing in China? Only time will tell.

Karen Offen

My contribution to this paper is less pessimistic than that of Chen Yan, which you have just read above.[11] Perhaps this is because I see the potential of women's and gender history in a larger framework, as a revolutionary development in the politics of historical knowledge—or, to be more precise, a quintessential case-study in the sexual politics of historical knowledge. Precisely because of its potential as a revolutionary development, it first met with considerable resistance from traditionalists and skeptics, who insisted that it lacked interest and/or that there were no sources. In some countries, however, it has overcome that resistance through extraordinary research and thousands of publications, and even former adversaries now acknowledge its importance. The American editors of a recently-published collection express their confidence 'that the writing of women's and gender history is here to stay'.[12] Indeed, a knowledge of its now-vast historiography and its findings seems essential for any historian who claims to be 'up-to-date' in his or her field.

It bears remembering that the current phase of women's history sprang from and is intimately related to a vast and relatively recent sociopolitical movement—the women's movement—which is at once local, national, inter-national, and transnational in scope. Women's history is an integral aspect of the development of 'women's studies', which, in fact, began as a self-help movement in higher education, as young women began to realize what they had not learned—or were not learning—in the then male-oriented colleges and universities: information that directly pertained to their own lives. 'When women ask the questions', as Marilyn J. Boxer has put it in the title of her book on the creation of women's studies in America, everything looks different, including the past. Her title echoes a line from a poem by Adrienne Rich: 'We are not "the woman question" asked by somebody else; we are the women who ask the questions.'[13] Women's studies is predicated on the asking of new questions, the formulation of new perspectives, even new theoretical understanding of women's status, the relations of the sexes over time and in the present; these new questions and perspectives had their source in women's lived experience. It encouraged, indeed demanded that women's lives and changes over time in their status and perceptions be taken seriously. In the beginning, it was akin to exploring the dark side of the moon.

To be sure, women's studies and women's history practitioners were asking many new questions, which could only be answered by seeking new information, often long-buried information that had to be uncovered, made visible, in a quest to understand how and why women had been held back, and to get a handle on what could be done in the present to advance their situation in the future. In short, it was a knowledge quest directly related to and designed to inform activism and change. It was not about fantasy but about action in real time. And in this quest, women's history and the histories of feminisms took on added significance; how could one know where women could go, unless one knew where they had come from, and how they had fought against, struggled against, centuries of subordination to men.

My colleague Chen Yan queries whether the history of sexuality (and in particular a focus on constructions of masculinity) might provide a key to advancing women's & gender history in China. In the western countries where women's & gender history already has a substantial foothold, it should be noted that this approach has come as a subsequent development (influenced in great part by the male-centered history of sexuality championed by the French philosopher Michel Foucault). One can certainly attest that the history of sexuality *per se* grabs people's attention. Certainly it is less easy to ignore or push to one side. But it is accompanied by risk. An exclusive focus on constructions of masculinities (without reference to their intertwining with femininities) can have the effect of reinforcing rather than contesting that time-worn masculine perspective that women are equated with sex, that indeed they are 'the sex'. Whether the introduction has resulted in greater opportunity to inflect the so-called 'discipline' of history by expanding its perspective to encompass women as well as men remains to be seen.

Is, then, women's history at the cutting edge? Overall, I would say 'yes', even though it may not yet be perceived as such either by defenders of convention in the historical establishment or by the general public in every society. And here is why I think so.

Several years ago I was invited to write the article on the 'history of women' for *The Oxford Encyclopedia of Women in World History* (edited by my colleague Bonnie G. Smith) in which I provided the following synopsis of 'what women's history is'.[14] I stand by this summary paragraph today:

> Women's history encompasses the history of humankind, including men, but approaches it from a woman-centered perspective. It highlights women's activities and ideas and asserts that their problems, issues, and accomplishments are just as central to the telling of the

human story as are those of their brothers, husbands, and sons. It places the sociopolitical relations between the sexes, or gender, at the center of historical inquiry and questions female subordination. It examines the closely intertwined constructions of femininity and masculinity over time in one or more cultures, looking for evidence of continuities and changes. It also exposes and confronts the biases of earlier male-centered historiography, asking why certain subjects and choices of themes for study were favored over others and posing new questions for investigation. Women's historians have expanded the scope of research on women and gender both temporally, from prehistory to the present, and geographically, from dealing only with the West to encompassing the globe.

Based on some forty years of investigation and wide reading in the field, I think this statement encapsulates what our field is about. Note that under the rubric of women's history, I include history focused solely on women, but I also include what is now called 'gender history', or I think more accurately, 'gendered history' or, also, the history of gender—the changing relations of women and men across time and how they are perceived. Taken together, these two aspects provide a revolutionary approach to investigating the past, to writing a history of humanity that encompasses far more than the recounting the deeds of 'great men' or the intricacies of diplomacy, war, or works of art by great male painters, or the ideas of great male philosophers, physicians, or political theorists. Or as Jane Austen put it in her novel *Northanger Abbey* (1803/1817): 'The quarrels of popes and kings, with wars or pestilences, in every page; the men all so good for nothing, and hardly any women at all—it is very tiresome.'

It is not surprising that, even today, women's history meets with resistance in some cultural settings; knowledge revolutions of this magnitude take time to take effect. Chen Yan's portion of this article attests only too well to the extent of resistance that exists in the People's Republic of China, and not only, as she indicates, among academic historians, but also among publishers. The question we all need to consider is how to identify and implement the best strategies to surmount such resistance. It should hardly be necessary to convince others of the legitimacy of a field of investigation that has now produced such an extensive bibliography in the world's major languages; the length of that bibliography and the quality of the items it contains, speaks for itself.

The prospectus for this round table posed five questions, which Chen Yan has restated above, and which I will address here, at greater or lesser length.

Let us begin with question 1, which queries **the achievements of women's and gender history over the past two decades.** First, let me say that the achievements have been very considerable, even astounding overall, even though results vary widely from one country to another, due to a variety of local circumstances. As concerns the West, I would suggest extending the period under consideration to at least three decades, or even four. But only since 1985 did concerted plans finally materialize to institutionalize women's history in the historical profession at the international level via the founding of the (now thirty-year-old) International Federation for Research in Women's History/Fédération Internationale de Recherche en Histoire des Femmes, hereafter IFRWH/FIRHF.[15] IFRWH has been affiliated with CISH since 1987 and hosted its first small, albeit groundbreaking conference at the Rockefeller Center in Bellagio in 1988. IFRWH hosted its first major public conference at the 1990 CISH meeting in Madrid. Since then IFRWH has organized a conference at each CISH meeting—this conference in Jinan will be its sixth; but it has also organized other, more extensive interim conferences which are much bigger, the most recent one having taken place in 2013 at Sheffield Hallam University in the UK. Our conference here in Jinan is the first conference held in Asia. IFRWH welcomes this opportunity to meet and discuss findings in and approaches to women's & gender history with colleagues from every part of the world.

The achievements of women's history, and note that, as I mentioned above, I do use this term to include the history of gender and gendered analysis, are well documented in the Newsletters of the IFRWH, in the scholarly journals that have been founded by women's historians in a number of languages, and in the many publications—books, articles, bibliographies—that have appeared in many world languages besides English. In certain countries, it is a field of research whose growth has been nothing short of phenomenal. Despite the initial skepticism of some male colleagues as to the existence of sufficient source material, women's historians are discovering more sources every day. Some consist of hand-written or (since the invention of printing) published documents; others are ethnographic or embedded in material culture (these sources allow us to explore women's history and embark on analysis of gender relations very far back in time). Oral histories now provide additional material for analysis for more contemporary historical studies.

Let me say a few words about 'gender' and 'gendered history'. In my view (and here I confess, I am a contrarian), I do not accept the argument, frequently made, that there exists an intrinsic 'progression' from women's history, which focuses on the activities, words, and actions of women, to 'gender history', which I understand as an approach to the past that (a) 'places the sociopolitical relations between the sexes, or gender, at the center of historical inquiry and questions female subordination' or (b) 'examines the closely intertwined constructions of femininity and masculinity over time in one or more cultures, looking for evidence of continuities and changes'. These are two aspects of the same project, even though some think that 'gender history' is somehow more acceptable to 'mainstream' historians. The metaphor of the 'double-Helix', as developed by Margaret and Patrice Higonnet in the multi-authored work, *Behind the Lines* (1987) provides an excellent way of thinking about 'gender systems', about the way in which femininity and masculinity are deeply intertwined and mutually construct each other.[16] I do think, though, that 'gender' itself has a history, and would recommend the insights of R. W. Connell, the Australian sociologist, on this matter.[17]

But in the early 1980s, another, more complex, understanding of 'gender' entered the scene––a move in the direction of conscious theorizing, and what has since been labeled as 'post-modern' or 'critical' theory. 'Gender' no longer referred simply to 'the social construction of sex' (much less a synonym for women, as some took it to be) but was contemplated as a 'category of analysis' comparable to 'class' and 'race'. Indeed, those who promoted this 'gender turn' insisted on the necessity of achieving a heightened theoretical sophistication in order to lend 'respectability' (in mainstream academic circles, that is) to the project of women's history. As our prospectus for this round table indicated, Joan Scott's contribution to understanding gender as both a category of analysis and a signifier of power has influenced many academics,[18] and not only those who write histories: 'Gender analysis', we stated, 'has contributed both to more sophisticated understandings of women's lives in the past and to a reconfiguring of historical research as a whole'. But its reception has varied widely in different cultural settings. Chen Yan has reminded us that in China, where no word existed to express the 'social construction of the sexes', Scott's formulation of gender as a category of analysis has been extremely influential. It remains to understand just what about it has been the most influential, in other words, just how it has been understood and used. The fact is that there are many world languages, for example German and Swedish, in which the concept of gender is wholly encompassed in the concept of sex (the same word is used to signify both), and the word 'gender' (in English) has been adopted to connote the social construction aspect. In French, the concept of social construction of sex has been around for centuries, and has even been called *genre masculin/genre féminin*, to refer to human gender as well as to grammatical constructs.[19]

Some historians have since claimed superiority for the post-modern formulation, which has tended to spawn a jargon (some would say 'vital critical vocabulary') of its own: 'discourses' and 'representations' abound, as do alleged 'paradoxes' and 'contradictions'. Others have gone on, in the spirit of certain social sciences, to examine evidence through the lens of 'theory' (which seems to limit some researchers to 'seeing' only the evidence that supports the theory); others, like myself, prefer to let the theoretical statements develop (or to test a given theory) after a careful consultation of a wide range of evidence, within the framework of the context that produced it. It may be true that 'theorizing' is necessary to achieve status in the still conservative academy, but it seems fair to say that the general reading public could care less. Women's historians need to decide whom they are attempting to reach. Not all historians, even in the West, concern themselves with 'categories of analysis' … they just want to tell interesting stories, and in particular, in the case of women's historians, stories that can serve to empower women, while also challenging conventional wisdom. Women's historians ask 'new', often unsettling questions of the past.

In any event, the rush in the 1990s to theorize gender and to claim its superiority led critics such as the co-founder of the *Journal of Women's History*, Joan Hoff, to categorize the 'turn' to gender as a 'category of paralysis' in a time when the investigation of women's history was barely getting underway, for example in eastern European countries well outside the Anglo-American or Western European parts of the world. Others debated the gender turn in the first issue of *Rethinking History*.[20] Subsequently, Scott herself has backed away from 'gender', turning for her inspiration to psychoanalysis, with its notions of fantasy and imagination.[21] And finally, she has moved to arguing, as she did in 2008: 'I want to insist that the term gender is useful only as a question.'[22] But this goes beyond the intellectual terrain that most historians—of any denomination—occupy, and into the cloud-land of critical theory, with its practice of constantly pulling-apart, tearing down, deconstructing, and destabilizing categories, including 'experience' and 'women'. Some of us who are more empirically-minded perceive this exercise as philosophical game-playing, while others think it is 'good to think with'. But in any case, this is a different enterprise. Most of us here are not 'doing' critical theory —or 'challenging the fundamentally dualistic and oppositional paradigms of science'— we are interested in excavating and illuminating the history of real embodied women and of the construction of gender relations (in the more conventional sense, which was irrefutably dualistic) through time, and in showing how its inclusion broadens and deepens our understanding of the human experience, past and present.

It's not only a question of what women's history can do for feminist theory, but perhaps more importantly what it can do to add a gendered dimension to sister disciplines, notably those in the social sciences, which even today, although they do address questions about women and gender, characteristically lack historical depth and consciousness of change over time. But it is also true that women's history has much to offer not only to the social sciences, but also to the study of philosophy, languages and literatures, art and music, science, etc. and has, certainly in the West, convincingly challenged the academic 'canons' of 'great books' and great works of all kinds. Decentering the male paradigm takes a lot of effort. And interdisciplinary work in addressing the sexual politics of knowledge requires additional time and energy.

To return to an earlier point, it seems clear that writing the history of women and analyzing gender constructions over time has led us to some very important insights. It does not seem terribly helpful to claim that either 'gender' trumps 'women', or vice versa; no one approach is definitively 'better' than another. Each approach can add to our cumulative knowledge of the past of humankind—a past in which we can 'see' women as historical actors just as we have seen men as historical actors, and in which we can render visible the sexual politics of knowledge. Ultimately, the interlinked combination of women's and gender histories offers a rich variety of approaches. Different topics lend themselves to different combinations, and an either/or choice between 'women' and 'gender' is not really an option. At the American Historical Association in 2000, the historian Susan Pedersen asserted that it is:

> an argument neither side should ever win .... Women's history isn't a stage that we move through as we struggle toward gender history, for gender history itself sends us endlessly back to women. And both inquiries have transformed our historical work and understanding.[23]

What is important for us as practitioners of women's and gender history is to recognize not only that each historian has a 'standpoint' (for most of us it is a feminist standpoint), but also, to draw on a metaphor from photography, each historian must understand the characteristics and manipulability of the instrument she or he is using to investigate. 'Through the lens of ...' is a familiar statement by academic historians, but it says nothing about the lens itself. The historian must consciously choose the magnifying capacity of the lens being looked through, and to indicate whether it is a wide angle lens, good for capturing breadth and the big picture (regional, national, transnational, even global) or a close-up lens with a sharp focal point that allows the investigator to look more closely at a single woman, clusters of women, a couple, a family, a 'tribe' or 'nation', an activity, a publication or clusters of publications. This is what macrohistory and microhistory are all about; one is not 'better' than the other. If we assume that the objective of historical research is a richer understanding of the human experience in its myriad manifestations, then we must examine it through lenses of varying magnification, as we focus on specific times and places, and examine change over time. Of course, no historian can 'see' all of the past of humanity; that is why historians deal with specific topics, with pieces of the whole that they think may illuminate the whole, or at least a substantial part of the complexities—and diversity—of the human species.

What the analysis of gender relations through historical time has brought us is the opportunity to revisit and rethink many basic male-centered 'master narratives', such as the Renaissance, the rise of capitalism in England and Europe, the 'gender' of nation-states and of notions of citizenship, the parameters of war, the history of medicine, science and the arts, the causes and consequences of sociopolitical movements, etc.; virtually any topic, however important or obscure, can be examined and illuminated from the perspective of 'gender' analysis. Historians have addressed, variously, the gender of skill, the gender of civilization, the gender of poverty, and the gender of genocide. For the modern and contemporary eras alone, we have *Gendered Nations: nationalisms and gender order in the long nineteenth century*, edited by Ida Blom, Karen Hagemann and Catherine Hall (Berg, 2000), for example, or *Chinese Femininities, Chinese Masculinities*, edited by Susan Brownell and Jeffrey N. Wasserstrom (University of California Press, 2002); *Gendering Modern Japanese History*, edited by Barbara Molony and Kathleen Uno (Harvard East Asian Studies, 2005); *Gendering Jewish History*, edited by Marion A. Kaplan and Deborah Dash Moore (Indiana UP, 2011); or *Gender History in a Transnational Perspective*, edited by Oliver Janz and Daniel Schonpflug (Berghahn, 2014), which honors the work of one of IFRWH's first board members, Gisela Bock, whose groundbreaking articles and books on gender and history are not as well known in the Anglophone world as they should be. We can also point to path-breaking articles, such as Ann Taylor Allen's transnational analysis, 'Feminism, Social Science, and the Meanings of Modernity: The Debate on the Origin of the Family in Europe and the United States, 1860–1914' (1999) and Mrinalini Sinha's feminist re-reading of the political history of India through a gendered lens that reveals the centrality of feminist arguments in producing the child marriage prohibition law of 1929, a campaign that lies at center of constructions of citizenship in the context of Indian 'community' claims.[24]

In the grand 'global' macrohistories that are currently in fashion in the West, even individuals disappear, and certainly their sex becomes irrelevant; 'processes' and 'systems' (generally male-centered) take over. Conversely, when one zooms in on 'women' (or femininity, fertility, and motherhood, or family structures and dynamics, or even a divorce or infanticide case that can illuminate a bigger picture) one moves much closer to the earth's surface and thus, to the objects of analysis that are situated in the complexities of daily life; when one shifts the lens that focuses on women sideways, or backs it out a bit, 'men' appear, first in the margins, and then side-by-side with women (or in some cases, above them, which immediately illuminates the sexual hierarchies and highlights conflicts over power and authority). When one shifts the lens to the male side, women's historians zoom in on 'men' and on 'masculinity;' this allows for analysis of many developments that were heretofore taken for granted, even 'erased' from view, by those earlier generations of male historians who in the nineteenth century established History with a capital H as an academic discipline. This use of the 'zoom lens' limited its focus to particular male-centric subjects such as government, war, and diplomacy, business deals, and military campaigns.[25] But even grand 'global' macrohistories, telescopic views, can reveal evidence of important woman-centered phenomena, such as the rise throughout the twentieth century and into our own, of a worldwide women's movement, an expansive movement toward women's emancipation. A Francophone team of women's and gender historians has labelled this *'le siècle des feminismes'*, the century of feminisms.[26] One might also look at the flip side and say that it has spawned a century of antifeminisms, or pushbacks against women's challenges to masculine domination. Such movements for and against gender equality are, of course, complicated by many factors (or as some would say, 'categories') including race, religion, and class; we speak here of 'intersectionality'. These are also complicated and conditioned by differential access to resources, not the least of which is money. Historically speaking, does money have a gender? Certainly, access to money is gendered.

This brings us briefly to the notion of 'feminist history'. Is there such a thing? The introduction to the volume *Feminist History in Canada*, edited by Catherine Carstairs and Nancy Janovicek (2013) proudly puts this term front and center; there is no trace here of 'fantasy'. Jocelyn Olcott promotes the notion of 'transnational feminist history'. Presumably, this term means writing women's & gender history from a feminist perspective. Does it matter—or not—whether we call our project 'women's history', 'history of women', or 'feminist history'? Does it matter (and to whom does it matter) whether we talk about 'women's studies' or 'feminist studies'? The editorial statement of the *Women's History Review* (April 2013), for example, refers simply to 'the expanding field of *women's history*' and welcomes 'contributions from a wide range of disciplines … that further *feminist knowledge, theory, consciousness, action and debate* about women's history and/or *gender relations in history*'.

Not everyone agrees with using the terminology of 'feminist history'. The French philosopher and historian Geneviève Fraisse insists that there is no such thing as 'feminist research, only individuals who are feminists who do research'; she categorizes herself as a feminist who researches women and gender, not as a researcher who does feminist history.[27] This distinction is worth pondering. Is this simply a strategic choice, based in a differing sociopolitical and cultural context? That we are even discussing such terminological distinctions is, in my view, a sign of the success of women's and gender history as a global project. There is no question that a good many historians of women & gender would identify themselves as feminist historians, but do we/they 'do' 'feminist history'? Certainly (and we can cite examples of this), it is possible to 'do' women's and even gender history without being particularly committed to its revisionist goals—or, for that matter, to feminist goals. Food for thought! As for 'feminism's history', many of us have engaged in researching and writing the history of feminisms (in the plural), which as I have claimed in print, in *European Feminisms* (and elsewhere) is 'women's political history'.[28]

Now to question 2. To what extent has it succeeded in making women's history an integral part of historical study rather than an optional specialist area? This is a more practical question.

In my view it is not yet possible to answer this question; the local, regional, and national contexts still differ too much. In some countries, notably in the Anglophone world, women's history has already become an integral part of historical study. But we cannot yet claim victory. The implications of women's & gender history for 'history in general' are indeed revolutionary, and, as has been noted earlier, have aroused considerable resistance. Doing women's history does mean rethinking the priorities of our predecessors and of most of our graduate advisors, developing the sensibilities of many of our colleagues, in and outside the universities, and educating the public. I will defer further discussion of this question to the end of this article.

Question 3 shifts our focus in yet another direction. This too is a practical question. It asks **'what impact has the study of manhood, masculinities and men's gendered power had on our understanding of women's lives?'** It seems clear that the study of manhood, masculinities, and men's gendered power—i.e. shining a spotlight, especially historically, on the development and change over time, promises to illuminate much that has been taken for granted or assumed by the old conventional history. The disadvantage is that this newer focus on masculinity and manhood can have the unintended consequence of relegating women to the shadows once again—to the dark side of the moon. Should it be a primary focus, or an auxiliary focus, for historians of women and gender? Should the study of manhood, masculinities, and men's gendered power trump the study of womanhood, femininities, and women's gendered influence and quest for authority? Should we cede this terrain just because some individuals are uncomfortable with woman-focused projects, even though these can and do also illuminate gender relations? It bears pointing out that some men are entirely comfortable with woman-focused projects: one notable example in my own field is my colleague Steven C. Hause who has written about the history of the women's suffrage campaigns in France and produced an excellent biography of Hubertine Auclert, one of the foremost French advocates of women's vote.[29]

'What', asks question **4**, 'is the relationship between gender studies and new critical histories of colonialism and empire, contact zones, cross-cultural encounters and racialization?' The short answer to this question is that, of course, there is a necessary, even inextricable relationship. Each of these newer areas of specialization has a gendered component, simply because in colonies and empires, in contact zones, in cross-cultural encounters, and in questions about racialization (critical race studies), there are women as well as men both as actors and acted-upon and there are gendered elements to each. It bears remarking that historians of women and gender were already addressing these issues in the later 1980s and that these fields are already indelibly marked by the insights of feminist historians, especially those in countries which developed extensive colonial empires. Historians of women and gender have addressed such topics early on; indeed 'colonialism and empire' was among the subjects of discussion by delegates to our IFRWH founding meeting in 1989. Since then, let me cite, in particular, the proceedings of the IFRWH conference and grand theme at the 1995 CISH congress in Montreal, published as *Nation, Empire, Colony: historicizing gender and race*, edited by Ruth Roach Pierson and Nupur Chaudhuri (Indiana UP, 1998). Contributors to this volume include women's historians from Australia, Austria, India, Japan, New Zealand, Mexico, Ireland, the UK, and Canada. Many of the contributors came to these topics through their national histories, while others (including one of our round table participants here, Joanna de Groot) work on topics concerning other cultures. To pick another example, the essays in a slightly earlier book, *Western Women and Imperialism: complicity and resistance*, edited by Nupur Chaudhuri and Margaret Strobel (Indiana UP, 1992) investigate cultural encounters between the women of the colonizers and women of the colonized in a number of different parts of the world. One could cite many more examples. In short, gender analysis as well as attention to women has been and continues to be important for these new critical histories.

Another aspect of this question concerns the national/transnational dimension. Most histories of women & gender are still written within a national framework, for obvious reasons having to do with legal, economic, social, and cultural particularities, access of historians to sources and funding resources, etc. But what we now refer to as transnational analyses were already being attempted in the later 1970s and early 1980s by historians of women. Here I will cite two early, co-authored documentary works in which I played a significant role: *Victorian Women* (1981) which examined the comparative history of women in England, France, and the United States during the nineteenth century; and *Women, the Family, and Freedom* (1983, 2 vols) which reconstructed aspects of the woman question debates in Western Europe and across the Atlantic. Remember, though that the stellar collections, *Becoming Visible: women in European history*, edited by Renate Bridenthal and Claudia Koonz (1st edn, Houghton-Mifflin, 1977), and *Connecting Spheres: women in the western world, 1500 to the present*, edited by Marilyn J. Boxer and Jean Quataert (Oxford UP, 1987) both represent efforts at transnational coverage; even 'Europe' is a transnational space, and does not consist merely of Britain, France, and Germany.[30] One could say the same for 'Latin America', a 'neo-Europe' in which there are many nation-states but a dominant common Spanish language (the notable exception being Brazil, where Portuguese prevails).[31] Historians such as Susan Zimmermann (based in Budapest and Vienna), have also challenged the 'national' framework, certainly as it influenced the organization of the international women's movement, by probing the complications introduced by empire, in this case the multinational, multi-ethnic Austro-Hungarian Empire, into a narrative and an organizational structure based on national membership. The venerable Ottoman Empire offers similar complexities.

Several new collections of articles continue this effort to move women's history beyond the 'national metanarrative' into a transnational dimension: *Making Women's Histories: Beyond National Perspectives* (2013; previously mentioned) does just that in its last section, which includes articles that examine a convergence between history of gender and sexuality and world history in the field of Latin American studies, cross-cultural exchanges between US and Chinese participants with respect to women & gender, in the context of the medical arts, and claims about the 'recent union of transnational and feminist history'[32]; in this version of 'transnational', which is inspired by the recent proliferation of NGOs and favors non-state actors, the emphasis is neither comparative nor inter-national. To what extent this will help us understand women's history prior to the twentieth century is an important question. Is 'transnational', like 'transformative', simply the 'flavor of the week' for twentieth-century history? Or can it serve us in the twenty-first century to illuminate the *longue durée*?

Question 5 asks: **'How is new work on cultural geography and spatial categories impacting on our historical understandings of bodily difference?'** To some degree this question is an extension of Question 4. I am going to leave it to our commentators on this round table—and the audience—to address (or rephrase) this question, which in terms of 'new work' extends beyond my competence. But bear in mind that since the very beginning of women's history, spatial categories, their assignment and often arbitrary distribution (notably of 'private/public' spaces) has been a longtime concern for researchers in women's history. Already in 1987, for example, the author/editors of the landmark volume, *Connecting Spheres*, announced (in their preface)[33] that:

> The connections between the so-called separate spheres of women and men must be traced and their mutual dependency revealed. Broken links between women's lives in different places must also be connected and bridges built between the sexes and the peoples of the many continents.

Since then, questions concerning spatial categories have hardly been absent. Note the publication in France in 2004 of a collection of articles, edited by Christine Bard, entitled *Le Genre des territoires; féminin, masculin, neutre* (The Gender of Territories: feminine, masculine, neuter).

In the last thirty to forty years, women's historians have done excellent work in demonstrating—and insisting on—the interpenetration of (rather than hard boundaries between) public and private in various cultures. What these spaces are like and, in particular, *who decides—who is doing the assigning of women to particular spaces—and why—*(and how women's spaces are ranked relative to men's spaces) are important questions that embrace everything from menstrual huts and the taboos on women that their use implies, to enforced claustration ranging from the convent to the institution of the women's quarters or 'Hareem' or 'Terem' in polygamous societies, to the binding of young Chinese women's feet (which severely restricted their mobility), to encumbering French and English dress (corsets and weighty skirts), or to imposing the burka (blinders), to efforts to dissuade women from riding bicycles or from driving automobiles (which vastly increase their mobility), to illiteracy and/or deliberate campaigns to exclude women from institutionalized places of primary, secondary or higher education, or the sanctuaries where the lucrative male professions (not to mention political authority) were and are practiced, and not least, to the constraining circumstances of poverty through laws that have concentrated wealth and resources in the hands of men, whether by depriving women in marriage of dowries and propertied assets, or by depriving employed women from equal pay for equal work. 'Separate spheres' were long treated by historians as descriptive; what we have since learned is that this language of separate spheres is utterly prescriptive. These are realities against which women (and male allies) in a variety of cultures have fought back, and are still fighting back: their struggle is concisely summarized by an American political bumper sticker which reads: 'A Woman's Place is in the House--and in the Senate'. Obviously, there are many other examples that could—and should—be cited.

A sixth question, implied by our prospectus, asks **'what new categories, methodologies and directions are currently emerging in the fields of women's studies and women's history, and what is their relationship to broader global trends in historical research?'** I would surmise that the answers to this double-jointed question will vary from one commentator to another, based on their experience as historians who have operated primarily in national contexts. A corollary to this question would be: what are the implications of 'global history' for women's and gender history, and conversely, what do researchers in women's and gender history bring to the formulation of global history? How do we keep questions concerning the ever-morphing 'social relations of the sexes' in the foreground when writing history on this scale? It seems to me that one way to approach this is to reiterate the importance of several of the truly global issues concerning women that have emerged in the last several centuries: the education of girls; the legal status of married women, the treatment of mothers, and particularly interesting corollaries that have arisen since the later nineteenth century—the question of married women's nationality; the comparative study of prostitution (in and outside of marriage) and government-established and regulated brothels and the development of a cross-border international traffic in women for purposes of prostitution; the cluster of issues concerning women's employment and the difficulty of achieving equal pay for equal work; the problem of making maternity safe and assuring appropriate social and cultural conditions for the raising of children—the future citizens of every extant society. These are *transnational* issues—issues that could only be, and can only be, addressed effectively at a regional or even global level, and that call for feminist insights and comparisons.[34] The struggles that have brought them to the transnational level for consideration have often been fierce, and their history is important to know about. The claim that women's rights are human rights did not arise out of a vacuum, but out of centuries of indigenous women's rights movements across the globe. And by 'indigenous', I do not mean only 'brown women' but simply those women who live in a particular place and time and who challenge the restrictions that men have placed on their lives and opportunities or restrictions imposed by circumstances outside their immediate control.

One new emerging category that has arisen comes from the field of bioethics. What bioethical concerns arise from female biology and women's historical condition of subordination? What bioethical questions does the new biotechnology pose? Does women's subordination and the concomitant lack of knowledge of women's history mask bio-ethical issues? Marilyn Boxer would argue that these questions matter. 'To the extent that ethical considerations require attribution of personhood and personal agency to every human being,' she writes:

> ethical behavior toward women calls for disclosure and discussion of the full record of women in history. It demands that women define their own positions within specific and changing contexts and exercise choices that encompass the full range of their human attributes.

And, she adds, in conclusion, 'It calls for major societal change'.[35]

Here I want to return briefly to **question 2** ... that of **making women's history an integral part of historical study rather than an optional specialist area.** At the risk of preaching to the choir, here is my response: in the best of all possible worlds, all historians now and in the future—in whatever society they live—would integrate a gendered analysis into their thinking and writing about the past. They would 'see' that women are historical actors just as are men, that the work they do is just as valuable, that their perspectives have great merit. However, we are still far from that point—as the books and articles published today in English, French, German, Dutch, Swedish, Spanish, Portuguese, Turkish, Japanese, Korean, Chinese, and other languages certainly attest. Just look through any journal, any book catalog, and you will see that even when topics seem to us to cry out for the inclusion of women and/or gender analysis, it is often absent. This is because publishers, editors, and manuscript reviewers do not insist on its inclusion—or they have a 'series' for women's and gender studies, but do not actively encourage their other authors to address such issues. And because of the continuing male monopoly and manipulation of the politics of knowledge, not least in academic history departments, those who wish to do it can, even today, encounter discouragement or dissuasion. The insistence of male graduate advisors on 'safe' or conventional male-centered topics (topics that can more easily land one a teaching position) can still damp down the impulse for graduate students of either sex to explore these still-pioneering topics. The story told by Chen Yan of her graduate advisor's response to her proposed research topic offers a case in point. Was it the notion of 'traitors' or the fact that they were female that inspired his response? Sometimes it only seems possible, especially for women scholars, to engage with pioneering topics once they have achieved tenure and full professorships; one of my American colleagues in French history (Christine Adams) is currently investigating the political history of beauty in France—e.g. women's use (primarily in the history of the royal courts prior to the Revolution and during the Revolution) of their beauty as a 'power tool'. Such a topic would have been deemed unacceptable just a few decades ago.

In some countries, more than in others, our colleagues in the history profession have begun to understand the promise of women's history and gender analysis; some have come around to understanding why women's history is important and are investigating it themselves. With others there is a lot of work still to do, practical advocacy work. For example, it took forty years—from 1975 to 2015—to succeed in getting a substantial amount of women's & gender history into the program for this 2015 CISH congress in Jinan. It happened because CISH now has women historians on its Bureau and on the Program committee; the president of CISH (2010–2015) is a woman historian from Finland, Marjatta Hietala, who has published research on women in towns. Most members of the newly-elected Bureau (2015–2020) are sympathetic to women's & gender history.[36] But this friendly environment could change, and fast, if advocates of women's history do not continue to insist on its inclusion, to ensure that women's historians are among the national and organizational delegates to the CISH General Assembly, and to make a deliberate effort to keep IFRWH active under the CISH umbrella. CISH's congresses bring historians together from all parts of the world, and it is here that we can demonstrate to the world's historians, even to the skeptics among them, the myriad ways in which scholarship in women's history remains on the 'cutting edge'. Here we can demonstrate why it is that every historian needs to take women's history findings into account in order to be 'up-to-date'.

That women's & gender analysis is 'cutting edge' seems obvious to those of us who do it, and we are passionate about our research and our findings. We do think that what we do can change not only the discipline of history, by expanding its scope, but that it can also affect people's minds and inform their actions in the present. Findings in women's history can help us understand and resolve current dilemmas, and can inspire young women to action. The question is how.

Having said that, we need to do a better job of explaining our field, our findings, and our passion to skeptics—and of promoting the significance of what we do in graduate history programs—and in teacher training schools. We need to do a better job of explaining what we do to teachers in high schools and middle schools, and enabling them (through seminars and teacher education) to understand the realities we are uncovering as well as the inspiration that women's history can provide to students. We need still to identify ways to incorporate our findings into the curricula of the schools below the university level—without 'dumbing them down'. We need to add salient questions about women's history on examinations at all levels. Only in these ways can we overcome the persistent phallocentrism of academic history, the inadequate training of many history teachers in the schools—and the indifference of the general public.

Like global climate change, women's history is here and now. Women are well over 50% of the world's population; their stories, their concerns, their actions, their changing relationships with men and with one another, and their own perspectives, must inform the histories we research and write. Historically speaking, the social relations of the sexes, the contributions of women as well as men, the patterns of male dominance and female subordination have been foundational to the organization and operation of human societies. But as societies have urbanized, modernized and industrialized, these relations have been changing. Despite great resistance from established authorities, religious and secular, despite persisting and deeply-entrenched pockets of sexism, the historical imbalance of power between the sexes is slowly on the way to being righted. Women's history can help to set the record straight, as well as to inspire change. But, of course, societal change is always a work-in-progress.

We need more historical research and writing that documents—and that attempts to explain—these changes in the relations of the sexes over time, in every society. We need more books and articles that revise previous work based on new findings, such as the path-breaking revisionist articles by leading historians of feminisms around the world that are reproduced in *Globalizing Feminisms, 1789–1945* (2010).[37] We need more books that rewrite national histories, like those published by teams of women's historians in Australia and Canada, and in the United States, and that do examine transnational questions and women's collaborations across borders. We need more women's history journals like *Arenal*, in Spain, *Clio* in France, *Geneses* in Italy, *L'Homme* in Vienna, and like the path-breaking *Aspasia*, which focuses on women's & gender history in the region of central, eastern, and southeastern Europe. And we need more review essays that examine production in women's/gender history from a transnational perspective.[38] We need more books like Françoise Thébaud's extraordinary comparative synthetic study, *Écrire l'histoire des femmes et du genre* [Writing the History of Women and Gender] which forcefully clinched the case for women's history in the Francophone world.[39] And we also need more 'blogs' that convey our passion for history and historical understanding to internaut (online) audiences. It is not a question of 'either/or' but of 'all' these approaches.

We need more books like *A History of Women's Political Thought in Europe, 1400–1700* by the Australian historians of political thought Jacqueline Broad and Karen Green (Cambridge University Press, 2009), which make explicit their contextualized methodology that allowed them to 'not begin with the modern paradigm of political thought, with the aim of then looking back into the past and including only those works that fall within its purview', but 'by considering the actual political traditions of late-medieval Europe—traditions derived from ancient Greek and Roman sources, and heavily modified by Christian doctrine—and then moved forward to the early modern era' which allowed them to find 'a greater number of women political thinkers than some historians have hitherto acknowledged'.[40] 'We have come to the conclusion that women's thought fits rather badly into these standard chronologies, and should not be represented as defective because it fails to fit the contours of the history of men's ideas.'[41] We need wider circulation for landmark works in translation by women such as those in the University of Chicago series, 'The Other Voices in Early Modern Europe', edited by Margaret L. King and Albert Rabil, Jr., just to mention two substantive examples from English-language publications.

We need more books like Trisha Franzen's recent revisionist biography of the valiant American suffragist Anna Howard Shaw, who for decades had been virtually ignored by scholars of suffrage who had taken their cue from Eleanor Flexner's influential book, *Century of Struggle*,[42] which was enthusiastic about the radical suffragette wing led by Alice Paul but cast the mainstream leadership into the shadows. We need more works like the collective work in French on the Japanese women's publication *Seitô*, edited by Christine Lévy, which brings not only interpretations but also translations of the documents themselves to the attention of an audience outside of Japan.[43] We need more evocative books like those of the pioneering French scholar Yvonne Knibiehler on the history of motherhood and fatherhood, and the sweeping survey of women's history in Russia 'from the tenth to the twentieth century' by Natalia Pushkareva.[44] The list can go on and on … and it doubtless will go on and on. There is so much still that we don't know—and so many questions about the past that remain unanswered.

Women's & gender history offers the possibility of giving currency to the extraordinary stories of women in every part of the world, of acknowledging the politics that foster evolution in relations between the sexes over time, and of providing the sources and the tools for comparisons and for further transnational historical analyses. When women ask the questions and when those questions challenge conventional wisdom, the past begins to look much different. And that is why women's & gender histories, and more generally women's studies, will continue to perch on the 'cutting edge', with the potential to revolutionize everyone's understanding of the past and its implications for women—and men —in the present and the future. Without a knowledge of, or better yet, expertise in, women's and gender history, no historian can pretend to be 'up to date' in the field of history.

Notes

1. Joan W. Scott (1986) Gender: A Useful Category of Historical Analysis, *The American Historical Review*, 91 (5), pp. 1053–1075; republished in Joan W. Scott (1988) *Gender and the Politics of History* (New York: Columbia University Press). The Chinese version of this essay can be found in Wang Zheng & Zhang Yin (Eds) (2012) *Masculinity Studies* (Shanghai: Sanlian Press), pp. 3–34.
2. For more information, see also Gail Hershatter & Wang Zheng (2008) Chinese History: a useful category of gender analysis, *The American Historical Review* 113 (5), pp. 1404–1421.
3. Du Fangqin & Wang Xiangxian (2008) *Women's and Gender Studies in China: 1978–2008* (Tianjin: Tianjin People's Press).
4. Susan Mann (2000) The Male Bond in Chinese History and Culture, *The American Historical Review* 105 (5), pp. 1600–1614.
5. Exceptions are Keith McMahon (1995) *Misers, Shrews, and Polygamists: sexuality and male-female relations in eighteenth-century Chinese fiction* (Durham, NC: Duke University Press); Frank Dikotter (1995) *Sex, Culture and Modernity in China: medical science and the construction of sexual identities in the Early Republican period* (Honolulu: University of Hawaii Press); Charlotte Furth (1999) *A Flourishing Yin: gender in China's medical history, 960–1665* (Berkeley & Los Angeles: University of California Press). Also, Matthew H. Sommer (2000) *Sex, Law, and Society in Late Imperial China* (Stanford: Stanford University Press), and (2015) *Polyandry and Wife-Selling in Qing Dynasty China: survival strategies and judicial interventions* (Berkeley & Los Angeles: University of California Press).
6. Li Yinhe (2014) *Sexual Discourse Studies in People's Republic of China* (Shanghai: Shanghai Social Sciences Academia Press).
7. Christina Kelley Gilmartin (1995) *Engendering the Chinese Revolution: radical women, communist politics, and mass movements in the 1920s* (Berkeley & Los Angeles: University of California Press). See also Gail Hershatter (1986) *The Workers of Tianjin* (Stanford, CA: Stanford University Press); Christina K. Gilmartin (1989) Gender, Politics, and Patriarchy in China: the experiences of early women communists, 1920–27, in Sonia Kruks, Rayna Rapp & Marilyn B. Young (Eds) (1989) *Promissory Notes: women in the transition to socialism* (New York: Monthly Review Press), pp. 82–105; Patricia Stranahan (1983), *Yan'an Women and the Communist Party* (Berkeley & Los Angeles: University of California Press).
8. Deng Xiaonan, Wang Zheng & You Jianming (2011) (Eds) *The Reading on Chinese Women's History* (Beijing: Peking University Press).

9. Dorothy Ko & Wang Zheng (2006) (Eds) Special Issue: translating feminisms in China, *Gender and History* 18 (3) (November).

10. Chen Yan (2014) *Gender and War: Shanghai 1932–1945* (Social Sciences Academic Press).

11. Karen Offen would like to acknowledge the insights and stimulating publications of many colleagues, too numerous to mention here. She would especially like to thank her long-time friend and colleague Marilyn J. Boxer, historian and pioneer in the development of a historically informed women's studies in the United States. Boxer's book (1998) *When Women Ask the Questions: creating women's studies in America* (Baltimore: Johns Hopkins University Press) appeared in a Chinese translation by Mingping Yu in 2006 (Tian Jin, China: Tian Jin People's Publishing House).

12. See Jocelyn Olcott, 'A Happier Marriage? feminist history takes the transnational turn,' in Pamela S. Nadell & Kate Haulman (Eds) *Making Women's Histories: beyond national perspectives* (New York: New York University Press), p. 12.

13. Adrienne Rich (1986) Notes toward a Politics of Location, in A. Rich (Ed.) *Blood, Bread, and Poetry: selected prose, 1979–1985* (New York & London: W. W. Norton), p. 216.

14. See Karen Offen (2008) History of Women, in Bonnie G. Smith (Ed.) *The Oxford Encyclopedia of Women in World History*, 4 vols (Oxford & New York: Oxford University Press).

15. An earlier effort was made at the 1980 Bucharest congress of the ICHS, with the inclusion of several important reports on women's history in response to its absence in 1975 at the San Francisco congress, but this did not lead to immediate institutionalization. On this earlier history, see Karen Offen (2009) 'Parallels and Intersections: The International Federation for Research in Women's History in Comparative Historical Perspective, a Plenary Address presented at the Twentieth Anniversary Conference, Sofia, Bulgaria, August 2007', *Women's History Review*, 18(3) (July), pp. 355–371. Also see Karen Offen (2011) 'Founding the International Federation for Research in Women's History, 1987–2007', *Women's History Review*, 20(4) (September), pp. 491–495, in the Special issue 'Gender and the Cultural Production of Knowledge,' edited by Krassimira Daskalova, Mary O'Dowd, & Daniela Koleva.

16. See the Higonnets' essay (1987) From Margins to Mainstream, in Margaret Randolph Higonnet, Jane Jenson, Sonya Michel & Margaret Collins Weitz (Eds) *Behind the Lines: gender and the two world wars* (New Haven: Yale University Press), pp. 4–6.

17. See R. W. Connell (2002) *Gender* (Cambridge, UK: Polity Press).

18. Most notably, Scott, 'Gender: A Useful Category of Historical Analysis'. This project was, however, framed earlier, at a conference held in 1984 at Harvard University: see Scott, 'Rewriting History', *Behind the Lines*, pp. 21–30.

19. See my article, Karen Offen (2006) Le *gender* est-il une invention américaine? *Clio: Histoire, Femmes et Sociétés*, no. 24, pp. 291–304.

20. See Joan Hoff (1994) Gender as a Postmodern Category of Paralysis, *Women's History Review*, 3 (2), pp. 149–168, and the subsequent exchange among British historians of women: Penelope J. Corfield (1997) History and the Challenge of Gender History, *Rethinking History*, no. 1, pp. 241–258, followed by June Purvis & Amanda Wetherell (1999) Playing the Gender History Game, *Rethinking History*, no. 3, pp. 333–338, and Corfield's rejoinder (1999), From Women's History to Gender History: a reply to 'playing the gender history game', *Rethinking History*, no. 3, pp. 339–341.

21. I have discussed the critical reception of Scott's essay in Karen Offen (2003) French Women's History: retrospect (1789–1940) and prospect, *French Historical Studies* 26 (4), pp. 727–767, in n. 37 (p. 756), adding that: 'It is less well-known than it should be among historians of France that Scott, moving even deeper into theoretical territory during the 1990s, has recently repudiated gender as a category of analysis (because it is too often seen—by others—as synonymous with "women"), in favor of inquiring [through psychoanalytic theory] into fantasy and the imaginary, on grounds that "gender" has failed to challenge the fundamentally dualistic and oppositional paradigms of science. This renunciation is embedded in Scott's introduction to the 2nd edition of *Gender and the Politics of History* (1999) and it made quite a splash in Switzerland in December 1999, during an endowed lecture for

which, ironically, Scott was being honored for her contributions to *women's* history; see the article on Scott by Martine Chaponnière (2000) in *Femmes en Suisse*, no. 1438, p. 13'; see also the conference proceedings: Caroline Arni & Claudia Honegger (Eds) *'Gender': Die Tücken einer Kategorie. Joan W. Scott, Geschichte und Politik, Beiträge zum Hans-Sigrist-Symposium 1999 an der Universität Bern* (Zürich: Chronos Verlag, 2001). In one of her recent publications, Scott remarked that the title of her influential article on gender as a useful category of analysis was originally intended to end with a question mark.

22. In 'AHR Forum: Unanswered Questions', *American Historical Review*, 113 (December 2008), p. 1422. On the evolution of Scott's thinking and question asking, see the collection Judith Butler & Elizabeth Weed (Eds) (2011) *The Question of Gender: Joan W. Scott's critical feminism* (Bloomington: Indiana University Press), especially the editors' introduction.

23. Susan Pedersen (2000) The Future of Feminist History, *AHA Perspectives* 38 (7), pp. 1, 20–25; quotation, p. 20. Susan Pedersen is professor of history at Columbia University.

24. See Ann Taylor Allen (1999) Feminism, Social Science, and the Meanings of Modernity: the debate on the origin of the family in Europe and the United States, 1860–1914, *American Historical Review*, 104 (4), pp. 1085–1113; reprinted in Karen Offen (Ed.) (2010) *Globalizing Feminisms, 1789–1945* (London: Routledge); Mrinalini Sinha, Historically Speaking: gender and citizenship in colonial India, in Butler & Weed, *The Question of Gender*, pp. 80–101.

25. See Bonnie G. Smith (1998) *The Gender of History: men, women, and historical practice* (Cambridge, MA: Harvard University Press), and her many other publications and edited volumes.

26. See Eliane Gubin, Catherine Jacques, Florence Rochefort, Brigitte Studer, Françoise Thébaud & Michelle Zancarini-Fournel (Eds) (2004) *Le Siècle des féminismes* (Paris: Editions de l'Atelier).

27. See Geneviève Fraisse (2012) *La Fabrique du féminisme: textes et entretiens* (Paris: Éditions le passager clandestin), p. 245.

28. In *European Feminisms, 1700–1950: a political history* (Stanford University Press, 2000), and perhaps more visibly in Offen (2011) The History of Feminism IS Political History, *AHA Perspectives on History*, 49 (5), pp. 22–24. My claim here is to establish that the history of feminisms must be effectively understood as political history, not (as previously understood) as a purely a subject of social history. This is not to claim that it is the sole manifestation of women's political history, as women have long been actively engaged in men's political history in a variety of ways, though without challenging its parameters on behalf of their sex.

29. Steven C. Hause with Anne R. Kenney (1984) *Women's Suffrage and Social Politics in the French Third Republic* (Princeton, NJ: Princeton University Press), and Steven C. Hause (1987) *Hubertine Auclert: the French suffragette* (New Haven, CT: Yale University Press).

30. Marilyn J. Boxer and Jean Quataert (Eds) (1987) *Connecting Spheres: women in the western world, 1500 to the present* (New York & Oxford: Oxford University Press).

31. Other pioneering examples of transnational women's history would include Ian Tyrrell's (1991) *Woman's World, Woman's Empire: the Woman's Christian Temperance Union in international perspective, 1880–1930* (Chapel Hill, NC: University of North Carolina Press), as well as Margaret McFadden's and Bonnie Anderson's studies of early (nineteenth-century) transnational feminist networks, respectively titled (1999) *Golden Cables of Sympathy* (Lexington, KY: University of Kentucky Press) and (2000) *Joyous Greetings!* (New York: Oxford UP). Two early works explored transnational feminisms in Latin America: Francesca Miller's (1991) *Latin American Women and the Search for Social Justice* (Hanover, NH: New England UP) and Asunción Lavrin's (1995) *Women, Feminism, and Social Change in Argentina, Chile, and Uruguay, 1890–1940* (Lincoln, NB: University of Nebraska Press). Leila J. Rupp probed the culture of the three initial organizations comprising the international women's movement in (1997) *Worlds of Women: the making of an international women's movement* (Princeton, NJ: Princeton University Press). As this sample of titles suggests, the 'transnational turn' in women's history and the history of feminisms began several decades ago.

32. Jocelyn Olcott, 'A Happier Marriage? feminist history takes the transnational turn', *Making Women's Histories*, p. 237.
33. Boxer and Quataert, *Connecting Spheres,* cited above.
34. See Anne Cova (2006) *Comparative Women's History: new approaches* (Boulder, CO: Social Science Monographs/Columbia University Press). This work has since been translated into Spanish, Portuguese, and French.
35. See Marilyn J. Boxer (2014) Women, Historical and Cross-Cultural Perspectives, in Bruce Jennings et al. (Eds) *Bioethics,* 4th edn (Farmington Hills, MI: Macmillan Reference USA), vol. 6, pp. 3186–3195; quote, p. 3193. NB: the first three editions of this work appeared under the title *Encyclopedia of Bioethics,* ed. Warren T. Reich.
36. Note that the Bureau and officers of the CISH have changed for the 2015–2020 term.
37. See Offen, *Globalizing Feminisms,* cited above.
38. *Aspasia* began publication in 2007. See the jointly authored review essay by Krassimira Daskalova & Susan Zimmermann (forthcoming 2017) Women's and Gender History, in Irina Livezeanu, & Arpad von Klimo (Eds) *The Routledge History of East Central Europe since 1700* (London: Routledge).
39. See Françoise Thébaud (1998) *Écrire l'histoire des femmes* (Paris: ENS Éditions Fontenay/Saint-Cloud); the revised second edition (2007) is entitled *Écrire l'histoire des femmes et du genre* (Lyon: ENS Éditions).
40. Jacqueline Broad & Karen Green (2009), *A History of Women's Political Thought in Europe, 1400–1700* (Cambridge, UK: Cambridge University Press), p. 289.
41. Ibid., p. 291.
42. Trisha Franzen (2014) *Anna Howard Shaw: the work of woman suffrage* (Urbana: University of Illinois Press); Eleanor Flexner, *Century of Struggle* (Cambridge, MA: Harvard University Press, 1959; New York: Athenaum 1968).
43. Christine Lévy (Ed.) (2014) *Genre et modernité au Japon: la revue Seitô et la femme nouvelle* (Rennes: Presses Universitaires de Rennes). See also Barbara Molony & Kathleen Uno (Eds) (2005) *Gendering Modern Japanese History* (Cambridge, MA : Harvard East Asian Monographs).
44. Yvonne Knibiehler & Catherine Fouquet (1980) *L'Histoire des Mères du moyen-âge à nos jours* (Paris: Editions Montalba); Natalia Pushkareva (1997) *Women in Russian History: from the tenth to the twentieth century,* trans & ed. Eve Levin (Armonk, NY: M. E. Sharpe).

The Dangers of Complacency: women's history/gender history in Canada in the twenty-first century

Catherine Carstairs and Nancy Janovicek

ABSTRACT

Our contribution will focus on some of the intellectual developments occurring in gender history/women's history in Canada in the twenty-first century, while also drawing attention to the decline of women's history outside of the university environment. In the mid-1990s there was a vigorous debate over the merits of gender history vs. women's history. Over the past decade, these debates have quieted along with a growing recognition that gender history and women's history have many common goals. Today, biography and recent history (post 1945) figure among the strong trends in Canadian women's and gender historiography. But the impact of government funding cuts under the previous decade-long Conservative government has seriously handicapped federal institutions such as museums and archives. So far, the current Liberal administration is moving in a more positive direction.

Women's history and/or gender history has a long history in Canada. The first women's history courses emerged in the early 1970s, and our leading organization, The Canadian Committee on Women's History, founded in 1975, now has the largest membership of any sub-committee of the Canadian Historical Association. Gender and women's history has a comfortable place on the curriculum at most universities and in English, there are now two excellent textbooks serving the field: Rethinking Canada: the promise of women's history (now in its 7th edition) as well as the more recent Gender History: Canadian perspectives.[1] In the French language, L'histoire des femmes au Québec depuis quatre siècles (1992) and Brève histoire des femmes au Québec (2012) provide excellent historical overviews.[2] While this paper addresses Canadian women's and gender history, there are also women's and gender history classes that focus on women in other parts of the world, as well as a large number of feminist historians doing research on places outside of Canada including Europe, the United States, China, Vietnam, and South Africa.[3] The Studies in Gender and History series at University of Toronto Press has been extremely successful, publishing one to three volumes per year. The other Canadian presses also have substantial lists in gender history and women's history. And yet, there are some worrying trends on the horizon. Some of these are specific to women's history/gender history and some have to do with the status of women in the profession.

The journalist, Catherine Porter, recently pointed out that women authored only 34 of the 132 Canadian history books published last year.[4] Over the past five years, only one woman has won the John A. Macdonald Prize for the best book in Canadian History, although numerous books authored by women received honorable mentions.[5] The decline in tenure-track positions in history in Canadian universities has meant that there are few hires being made in women's history/gender history. History departments appear to be focusing their limited hires in the fields of global history, the history of science and technology, and or even business history, as universities strive to globalize, and humanities departments struggle to convince policymakers and students that their fields are relevant. Concurrently, the progress that was being made in hiring women for all faculty positions appears to have stalled.[6] Secondly, the Conservative federal government, led by Stephen Harper from 2006 to 2016, encouraged public institutions to focus on the history of Canada's involvement in military conflicts (with relatively little space being devoted to women), political and economic history and the history of sport, especially hockey. Since we presented this paper in Jinan, a Liberal government has been elected. This government is more receptive to commemorating women's contributions to history, but it will take time to change the male-centered history that has taken root in federal museums. Our contribution in this article will focus on some of the intellectual developments occurring in gender history/women's history in Canada. We also draw attention to the decreasing interest in women's history that we have seen in government agendas and major museums over the past decade. Even so, feminist community-based initiatives demonstrate that there is still enthusiastic interest in women's history.

A quick note about gender history vs. women's history in the Canadian context. In the mid-1990s there was a vigorous debate over the merits of gender history over women's history. Over the past decade, these debates have quieted along with a growing recognition that gender history and women's history have many common goals. As Karen Offen mentioned in her paper, we chose to call our recent collection *Feminist History*, as a way of recognizing the many shared political commitments of those who do gender history and women's history.

One of the marked intellectual trends in Canadian gender history is the ongoing popularity of biographical approaches. As in many countries around the world, women's history in Canada began by telling the important stories of Canada's first women doctors, lawyers, and heroines.[7] In the 1980s and the 1990s, amidst growing concern about the classism and racism in the women's movement, and in the field of history more generally, there was a move towards telling the stories of more marginalized women: women workers, women who got caught up in the law, recent immigrants to Canada etc.[8] Currently, there is a return to biographical approaches, often of elite or professional women. One of the long-time leaders in our field, Veronica Strong-Boag, has recently published *Liberal Hearts and Coronets: the lives and times of Ishbel Marjoribanks Gordon and John Campbell Gordon, the Aberdeens*.[9] This book provides a collective biography of Ishbel Gordon, the founder of the National Council of Women of Canada, and her husband, the Governor General of Canada, John Gordon. It also reflects recent trends in the field by not confining itself to Canada: instead Strong-Boag traces their careers across the empire, especially in Ireland, bringing a larger lens and broader understanding of how this powerful Scottish couple envisaged Canada, Ireland and the British Empire. Similarly, Adele Perry's most recent work, *Colonial Relations: the Douglas-Connolly family and the nineteenth century imperial world* employs a collective biographical approach in her history of James Douglas (born in Guyana of a free black woman and

Scottish father) and his wife, Amelia Connolly (born of an indigenous mother and an Irish-Canadian father).[10] Both of these books pay careful attention to class and race, but both ultimately focus on the lives of elite men and women, a topic that many women's historians, who have traditionally been closely allied with working-class historians in Canada, have shied away from. But as Strong-Boag makes clear, these elites played a vital role in constructing Canada's sense of itself as a nation. And, as Perry argues, studying colonial elites from indigenous families allows her to bring 'historiographies of dispossession, migration and gender into conversation and mapping gender, kinship and intimacy on a close and revealing scale'.[11] Another interesting aspect of these works is that they draw upon and contribute to almost twenty years of scholarship on the history of masculinity in Canada.[12] These are just two books in a spate of biographically focused work, some of which makes use of collective biographies (such as Jean Barman's *French Canadians and Indigenous Women in the Making of the Pacific Northwest*, which won the award for the best book published in Canadian history in 2014, and Bettina Bradbury's *Wife to Widow: lives, laws, and politics in nineteenth-century Montreal*, which won the award for the best book published by a Canadian over the past five years), and others which explore the lives of less well-known figures (such as Suzanne Morton's recent biography of the social worker Jane Wisdom).[13]

Another strong trend in Canadian History, including gender history and women's history is the heavy focus on recent history, especially the period after World War II. This may be because these topics have obvious political connections to the present. The history of sexuality continues to attract strong attention from historians, including a few who are trying to make their work accessible to a broader public by making it available on the web.[14] Disability history is a relatively new area of interest that has been greatly enriched by gender history. This is another field in which historians have reached out to a larger public through the internet.[15] The focus on relatively recent topics may reflect the presentist thinking of our funding councils, which ask scholars to demonstrate the immediate relevance of their work and are prizing large-scale research projects with web-based knowledge-translation components.[16] It may also have to do with the growing complexity of studying earlier time periods. What was once defined as Pre-Confederation Canadian History (i.e. the period before 1867 when parts of current-day Canada officially became a nation), no longer seems like a useful category to many working in the field, who prefer to define themselves as colonial historians, as early North Americanists, or as indigenous historians, reflecting the fact that Canada, as we know it today, did not exist in the nineteenth century. Colonial historians are now interested in the complex web of relationships and boundaries that existed in the seventeenth, eighteenth and nineteenth centuries among the various European powers, European immigrants, and the many indigenous peoples who populated North America. This requires a complex training in ethnographic research methods, as well as language and paleography skills: this depth of education is hard to achieve when graduate funding is hard to obtain and usually lasts no more than a few years.[17] While important work is still being in done in gender history/women's history in these earlier time periods, there are relatively few tenured or tenure-track faculty for students to study with, and many of the most prominent women's historians in this area have retired, or are on the verge of retirement, suggesting that this trend is unlikely to be rectified any time soon.[18]

Canada defines itself as a nation of immigrants, and from almost the very beginning gender and women's historians have been interested in the intersectionality of identities. In the 1970s and 1980s, immigration history and the histories of ethnic groups in Canada emerged as a dynamic field that challenged progressive narratives of Canada as a multicultural nation that celebrated diversity. Feminist historians have played an important role in these debates from the beginning by ensuring that immigration history addressed the unique experiences of women and their contributions to family economies, cultural preservation, and community building. They also introduced important challenges to women's and gender history and feminism more generally by exploring how discrimination against racialized women and migrants from Eastern and Southern Europe created economic and social hierarchies among women in Canada.[19] More recently, influenced by transnational history, migration histories examine the interconnectedness of immigrant families living in different parts of the world. While establishing themselves in their new home, women continued to contribute to family economies in their country of origin.[20] Another encouraging development is new work on women of colour including African-Canadian and Muslim women, although it is disappointing that there is still so little being done and that the current impasse in the job market may prevent some of the work from ever reaching publication.[21]

Canadian women's historians have had a long interest in the history of indigenous people. In the 1980s groundbreaking books by Sylvia Van Kirk and Jennifer Brown showed that women had played a vital role in the fur trade economy.[22] In recent years, exciting new work has emerged in indigenous women's history, much of it done by a new generation of indigenous scholars.[23] Other work has been done in collaboration with female indigenous elders.[24] But as Mary Jane McCallum underlines, there are still shockingly few indigenous scholars working in Canadian history departments, and there is an ongoing tendency to ignore or discount the work of indigenous historians.[25] In response to the Truth and Reconciliation Commission, which reported in December 2015, many post-secondary institutions have initiated strategies to indigenize the university.[26] Hiring indigenous scholars is a priority in these strategies, which we hope will provide more opportunities for the growing number of indigenous scholars completing their doctoral degrees. The discipline itself must also change to value different kinds of indigenous scholarship. Community-based research, which many indigenous historians do to establish relationships or as a political obligation to their communities, tends to be less valued for merit pay and promotion than a single-authored monograph published by a university press and publication in established scholarly journals. There is still a perception that community-based research, which is sponsored and published by indigenous communities rather than university presses, is not rigorous scholarship because it does not go through academic peer-review. Historians who collaborate with community members to develop public history projects go through a review process that requires researchers to respond to criticisms from within the community. Indigenous colleagues explain that community-based research is far more difficult because it requires good relationships with elders and the community. Establishing working relationships takes time and is itself a form of evaluation that is dictated by indigenous protocols and conforms to indigenous ways of gathering and disseminating knowledge.[27]

Another ongoing challenge in our field is integrating Francophone and Anglophone historiographies. Language is a barrier for many scholars, even though English-speaking students of Canadian history are generally expected to demonstrate reading skill in French as part of the requirements for the PhD degree. Books that are not regionally specific usually include 'in English-speaking Canada' in their titles to acknowledge that the specific cultural and legal traditions in the province of Quebec have resulted in unique historical experiences for Québecoise women. The maintenance of the French Civil Code alongside English Common Law in British North America meant that women had different economic and political rights than women in the English-speaking colonies. The strong influence of the Roman Catholic Church in government and society in the first half of the twentieth century played a role in delaying provincial suffrage in Quebec until 1940 and also accounts for distinct developments in the social welfare state and programs for mothers and children in Quebec. While the literature on Quebec women is rich, the influence of the independence movement has made it more challenging for women's history to find a secure place in the national narrative. Quebec historiography has attempted to explain the exclusion of French-Canadians from political and economic power or how Quebec followed economic and social trajectories that were similar to other places in North America. Feminist historians Denyse Baillargeon and Micheline Dumont criticize these nationalist narratives because they ignore women's experiences.[28] Dumont argues that women have not been integrated into the national narratives because these conservative male historians do not consider feminism a legitimate political movement and consequently do not think it is necessary to incorporate women into political and economic histories. While Anglophone historians have not provided a comparable analysis for popular histories of English-speaking Canada, a similar critique could be made, as many of the best-selling history books in Canada focus on sport, wilderness and war, topics that have often paid little attention to women.[29] Canadian newspapers and magazines continue to promote the 'great men of history' narratives of 'the rise of the Canadian nation' rather than more complicated histories that include the contributions of women, indigenous peoples, and other marginalized communities.[30] Australian feminist historians have criticized similar trends in their country.[31]

Indeed, things have been much more discouraging on the public history front. From the beginning there has been a close relationship between feminist activists and feminist scholars. Community-based writing groups and publishers, most notably the Canadian Women's Educational Press/Corrective Collective published widely read history books, some of which were taken up in school curriculums.[32] To ensure that the history of the second wave was preserved, grassroots activists founded the Canadian Women's History Archives, initially located in a house in downtown Toronto and now part of the University of Ottawa Library and Special Collections.[33]

Inspired by the proliferation of new publications in women's history, historians working in museums and cultural heritage institutions began to interrogate how to include women into museum exhibitions and public commemorations in a meaningful way, but this has been a challenge due to a lack of government funding and resources.[34] A further problem is that most of the women who are included in museums and who are commemorated are white. Interpreting the rich and vibrant field of women's and gender history was additionally challenging when the Conservatives assumed power. The Conservative Harper government promoted an outdated interpretation of Canadian history that focused on military victories and Canada's British heritage.[35] In the history section of *Discover Canada: the rights and responsibility of citizenship*, a guide to help new Canadians prepare for their test to become citizens, twenty of the thirty events celebrate battles and wars.[36] Only five images are of women, and only two of the images are of actual historical figures. With the exception of Mary Ann Shadd Cary, a Black anti-abolitionist and publisher of *The Provincial Freeman*, all of the women are discussed in the context of war.[37] In 2012, the same year that deep cuts to heritage institutions began, the federal government invested $28 million dollars in commemorations of the 200th anniversary of the War of 1812, arguing that this 'decisive moment' in the development of the nation has been overlooked for too long.[38] The current Liberal government has amended the Culture, Heritage, and Sport website to underscore the importance of the advancement of human rights, cultural diversity, and gender equality to Canadian identity and society.[39] Nevertheless, the website for the upcoming celebration of Canada's 150th birthday, again highlights military history and male politicians.[40] Until recently, it has been difficult for feminist historians, working in both academic and in public institutions, to demand that gender be a central category in exhibitions and commemorations, although this may change with the election of the new government, which also made a point of ensuring gender parity in the ministerial cabinet.

During the decade that it was in power, the Conservatives replaced women with symbols that celebrate traditional political power. For example, in 2012, they replaced images of the Famous Five, Alberta women who fought for the right to be recognized as 'persons' in 1929, and Thérèse Casgrain, a key Québecoise suffrage organizer, with an Arctic icebreaker on the $50 bill.[41] In 2011, the federal government changed the Thérèse Casgrain Volunteer Award to the Prime Minister's Volunteer Award.[42] The Liberal government has now reversed this decision. It has restored the Thérèse Casgrain Lifelong Achievement Award.[43] The Bank of Canada launched a campaign inviting Canadians to nominate 'an iconic woman' to appear on a commemorative banknote in 2017 as part of the celebration of the 150th anniversary of Confederation.[44]

We will have to wait to see whether the Liberal government can reverse the impact of the deep cuts to Heritage Canada, Library and Archives Canada (LAC), and other federal cultural institutions under the previous government. The cuts under the Conservative government have created a crisis in Canadian heritage preservation with serious implications for women's and gender history. In the 2012/13 budget, the Conservative government laid out a three-year plan to reduce spending in heritage institutions. At LAC, spending fell by 18% from 2012/13 to 2015/16.[45] As a result, there were moratoriums on purchased acquisitions and LAC lacked the resources necessary to systematically collect records. One consequence of these cuts was the elimination of the National Archival Development Program, a fund on which many local and regional archives depended. These archives are repositories for local family histories and the records of regional organizations, collections that have been rich sources for women's history. With fewer resources, we are concerned that the records of women's groups will not be a priority.[46] There have been positive announcements under the new government. The March 2016 federal budget introduced additional funding to major national museums, including a 16.7% increase to LAC.[47] LAC has recently announced the National Heritage Digitization Strategy. Working in collaboration with regional libraries and cultural institutions, the strategy aims to make collections more accessible to Canadians by developing a cohesive national plan.[48] A new programme has been established to fund local archives.[49] Finally, Parks Canada has the commemoration of the centennial of partial suffrage of Canadian women as a priority for the celebration of the 150th anniversary of Confederation as well as new initiatives to reflect indigeneity in heritage places.[50]

To end on a positive note, we are encouraged that the link between feminist activists and historians continues. In Vancouver and Toronto, 'Herstory' cafes bring women's and gender history to a broader audience.[51] Merna Forster's popular books on Canadian heroines continue to generate large sales and a passionate readership.[52] Although we are concerned about the declining enrolments in the humanities, and in history in particular, women's history and gender history continues to be popular among students. Graduate enrollments in gender history also appear to be healthy. In 2015, at the Canadian Historical Association, women won the François-Xavier Garneau Medal for the best book in Canadian history published over the past five years, The Sir John A. Macdonald Prize for the best scholarly book in Canadian history published in the last year as well as fourteen of the twenty-two smaller prizes.[53] While we need to recognize (and challenge) the ongoing systemic barriers that women face, both within and outside of the historical profession in Canada, we have achieved a great deal over the past half century.

Notes

1. Lara Cambell, Tamara Myers & Adele Perry (Eds) (2016) *Rethinking Canada: the promise of women's history* (Toronto: Oxford University Press); Willeen G. Keough & Lara Campbell (2014) *Gender History: Canadian perspectives* (Toronto: Oxford University Press).
2. Collectif Clio (1992) *L'Histoire des femmes au Québec depuis quatre siècles* (Montreal: Le Jour); Denyse Baillargeon (2012) *Brève histoire des femmes au Québec* (Montreal: Boréal). Both of these books have been translated into English.
3. Just a few of the prominent women's historians in Canada who focus on other parts of the world include: Mary Lynn Stewart (1989) *Women, Work and the French State: labour protection and social patriarchy, 1879–1919* (Montreal and Kingston: McGill-Queen's University Press); Mary Lynn Stewart (2001) *For Health and Beauty: physical culture for Frenchwomen, 1880s–1930s* (Baltimore: John Hopkins University Press); Annette Timm & Joshua Sandborn (2016) *Gender, Sex and the Shaping of Modern Europe: a history from the French Revolution to the present day*, 2nd ed. (London: Bloomsbury Academic); Joy Dixon (2001) *Divine Feminine: theosophy and feminism in England* (Baltimore: John Hopkins University Press); Jennifer Spear (2011) *Historicizing Gender and Sexuality* (Oxford: Wiley-Blackwell); Jennifer Spear (2009) *Race, Sex and Social Order in Early New Orleans* (Baltimore: John Hopkins University Press); Susan Smith (1995) *Sick and Tired of being Sick and Tired: black women's health activism in America, 1890–1950* (Philadelphia: University of Pennsylvania Press); Michelle Murphy (2012) *Seizing the Means of Reproduction: entanglements of feminism, health and technoscience* (Durham: Duke University Press); Nhung Tuyet Tran (2012) Women as Nation: tradition and modernity narratives in Vietnamese histories, *Gender and History*, 24(2), pp. 411–430; Joan Judge (2015) *Republican Lens: gender, visuality and experience in the early Chinese periodical press* (Berkeley & Los Angeles: University of California Press); Norman Smith (2007) *Resisting Manchukuo: Chinese women writers and the Japanese occupation* (Vancouver: UBC Press). The 2016 winner of the CCWH Book Prize was Susanne M. Klausen (2015) *Abortion under Apartheid: nationalism, sexuality, and women's reproductive rights in South Africa* (Toronto: Oxford University Press). The list could go on.
4. Her statistics come from a search of BookNet Canada, which counts sales of books in Canada. Catherine Porter, 'Ask why Canadian history is written by men', *Toronto Star*, 8 April 2016, http://www.thestar.com/news/canada/2016/04/08/ask-why-canadian-history-is-written-by-men-porter.html

5. 'John A. Macdonald Prize', http://www.cha-shc.ca/english/what-we-do/cha-prizes/the-sir-john-a-macdonald-prize.html#sthash.goZ57wyk.dpbs (accessed 26 April 2016). For a discussion, see Elise Chenier, Lori Chambers & Anne Frances Toews (2015) Still Working in the Shadow of Men? An analysis of sex distribution in publications and prizes in Canadian history, *Journal of the Canadian Historical Association/Revue de la Société historique du Canada*, 26(1), pp. 291–318.

6. As of 2013–2014, the percentage of women in Assistant Professor positions was 43%. This compares to 43% of women at the Associate Professor rank and 24% of women at the rank of Full Professor: *CAUT Almanac of Post-Secondary Education in Canada* 2013–14 (2014) (Ottawa: CAUT).

7. Mary Quaile Innis (1967) *Clear Spirits: twenty Canadian women and their times* (Toronto: Canadian Federation of University of Women/University of Toronto Press); Carlotta Hacker (1974) *Indomitable Lady Doctors* (Toronto: Clark Irwin); Byrne Hope Sanders (1958) *Famous Women: Carr, Hind, Gullen* (Toronto: Clark Irwin).

8. See for example: Joan Sangster (1995) *Earning Respect: the lives of working women in small-town Ontario, 1920–1960* (Toronto: Toronto University Press); Ruth Frager (1995) *Sweat-shop Strife: class, ethnicity, and gender in the Jewish labour movement of Toronto* (Toronto: University of Toronto Press); Pamela Sugiman (1994) *Labour's Dilemma: the gender politics of auto workers in Canada, 1937–1979* (Toronto: University of Toronto Press); Nadia Fahmy-Eid & Lucie Piché (1987) *Si le travail m'était conté autrement: Les femmes dans la Confédération des syndicates nationaux depuis 1920* (Montreal: CSN); Sylvie Murray (1990) *À la jonction du mouvement ouvrier et du mouvement des femmes: La ligue auxiliaire de l'Association international des machinists Canada 1903–1980* (Montreal: Regroupement des chercheurs-chercheures en histoire des travailleurs et travailleuses du Québec); Meg Luxton (1980) *More Than a Labour of Love: three generations of women's work in the home* (Toronto: Women's Educational Press); Denise Baillageron (1991) *Ména-gères au temps de la crise* (Montreal: Éditions de Remue-Ménage); and Marjorie Griffin Cohen (1988) *Women's Work, Markets, and Economic Development in Nineteenth-Century Ontario* (Toronto: University of Toronto Press); Jean Burnet (Ed.) (1986), *Looking into my Sister's Eyes: an exploration in women's history* (Toronto: Multicultural History Society of Ontario); Carolyn Strange (1995) *Toronto's Girl Problem* (Toronto: University of Toronto Press); Joan Sangster (2001) *Regulating Girls and Women: sexuality, family and the law in Ontario, 1920–1960* (Oxford: Oxford University Press).

9. Veronica Strong-Boag (2015) *Liberal Hearts and Coronets: the lives and times of Ishbel Mar-joribanks Gordon and John Campbell Gordon, the Aberdeens* (Toronto: University of Toronto Press).

10. Adele Perry (2015) *Colonial Relations: the Douglas-Connolly family and the nineteenth century imperial world* (Cambridge: Cambridge University Press).

11. Perry, *Colonial Relations*, ix.

12. See for example: Joy Parr (1990) *The Gender of Breadwinners* (Toronto: University of Toronto Press); Steven Penfold (1994) 'Have You No Manhood In You?': gender and class in the Cape Breton coal towns, 1920–1926, *Acadiensis*, 23(2), pp. 21–44; Robert Rutherdale (1999) Fatherhood, Masculinity and the Good Life during Canada's Baby Boom, *Journal of Family History*, 24, pp. 351–373; Christopher Dummitt (2007) *The Manly Modern: masculi-nity in the postwar years* (Vancouver: University of British Columbia Press); Craig Heron (2006) Boys Will Be Boys: working-class masculinity in the age of mass production, *Inter-national Labor and Working-Class History*, 69(1), pp. 6–34.

13. Jean Barman (2014) *French Canadians, Furs and Indigenous Women in the Making of the Pacific Northwest* (Vancouver: University of British Columbia Press); Bettina Bradbury (2011) *Wife to Widow: lives, laws and politics in nineteenth century Montreal* (Vancouver: University of British Columbia Press); Suzanne Morton (2015) *Wisdom, Justice and Charity: Canadian social welfare through the life of Jane B. Wisdom* (Toronto: University of Toronto Press).

14. See for example, the Archives of Lesbian Oral Testimony (http://www.alotarchives.org/) which was founded by Elise Chenier.

15. See the eugenics archives: http://eugenicsarchive.ca/; Out from Under: http://www.ryerson.ca/ofu/; and A Wheelchair History of Disability http://www.mobilityhistories.ca/

16. Much of the funding for historical work in Canada comes from the Social Sciences and Humanities Research Council of Canada. The federal government appoints the members of the council that governs SSHRC. In Quebec, there is also funding available from Fonds de Recherche du Québec.

17. The Canadian Historical Association hosted a very interesting panel in 2015 on this phenomenon. We are grateful to the presenters and participants. 'Who Killed Pre-Confederation Canadian History? The place of early-Canada in an interdisciplinary and transnational historiographical environment', Canadian Historical Association, 3 June 2015. We are especially grateful to Beatrice Craig who shared her presentation notes with us.

18. For example, Sylvia Van Kirk and Jennifer Brown, who published pioneering studies of indigenous women in the fur trade retired a few years ago. Jane Errington and Margaret Conrad who published important studies of women in British North America have both retired, although they both continue to publish.

19. Burnet, *Looking into my Sister's Eyes*; Franca Iacovetta & Marlene Epp (Eds) (2004) *Sisters or Strangers? Immigrant, ethnic and racialized women in Canadian history* (Toronto: University of Toronto Press).

20. Elizabeth Jane Errington (2007) *Emigrant Worlds and Transatlantic Communities: migration to upper Canada in the first half of the nineteenth century* (Montreal & Kingston: McGill-Queen's University Press); Donna R. Gabaccia & Franca Iacovetta (2002) *Women, Gender, and Transnational Lives: Italian workers of the world* (Toronto: University of Toronto Press); Marlene Epp (2008) *Mennonite Women in Canada: a history* (Manitoba: University of Manitoba Press); Karen Flynn (2011) *Moving Beyond Borders: Black Canadian and Caribbean women in the African Canadian diaspora* (Toronto: University of Toronto Press); Noula Mina (2013) Taming and Training Green 'Peasant Girls' and the Gendered Politics of Whiteness in Postwar Canada: Canadian bureaucrats and immigrant domestics, 1950s–1960s, *Canadian Historical Review*, 94(4), pp. 514–539.

21. Flynn, *Moving Beyond Borders*; Funke Aladeljebi is writing about African-Canadian educators; Deirdre McCorkindale is working on educational and intelligence testing of African-Canadian children and Melissa Shaw is working on the history of Black Social Activism in Ontario. Nadia Lewis (2008) Iraqi Women, Identity and Islam in Toronto: reflections on a new diaspora, *Canadian Ethnic Studies*, 40(3), pp. 131–147.

22. Sylvia Van Kirk (1980) *Many Tender Ties: women in fur trade society in Western Canada, 18670–1870* (Winnipeg: Watson & Dwyer); Jennifer S. Brown (1980) *Strangers in Blood: fur trade families in Indian country* (Vancouver: University of British Columbia Press).

23. Mary Jane Logan McCallum (2014) *Indigenous Women, Work and History, 1940–1980* (Winnipeg: University of Manitoba Press); Kim Anderson (2011) *Life Stages and Native Women: memory, teachings and story medicine* (Winnipeg: University of Manitoba Press); Kim Anderson (2000) *A Recognition of Being: reconstruction native womanhood* (Toronto: Sumach/Canadian Scholars Press); Brenda Macdougall (2010) *One of the Family: Metis culture in nineteenth-century Northwestern Saskatchewan* (Vancouver: University of British Columbia Press); Jan Hare & Jean Barman (2006) *Good Intentions Gone Awry: Emma Crosby and the Methodist mission on the Northwest coast* (Vancouver: University of British Columbia Press); Brittany Luby (2016) *Nizaabaawe/Drowned: Anishinabek economies and activism during the post-war hydroelectric boom, 1950–1975* (PhD thesis, York University); Sarah Nickel (2015) '*United We Stand, Divided We Perish': identity, community, and the politics of activism in the union of BC Indian chiefs, 1969–1980* (PhD thesis, Simon Fraser University).

24. Elsie Paul in collaboration with Paige Raibmon & Harmony Johnson (2014) *Written As I Remember It: teachings (?ems ta?aw) from the life of a Sliammon Elder* (Vancouver: University of British Columbia Press); Leslie Anne Robertson & the Kwagu'l Gixsam Clan (2012)

Standing up with Ga'axsta'las: Jane Constance Cook and the politics of memory, church, and custom (Vancouver: University of British Columbia Press).

25. McCallum, *Indigenous Women*, pp. 225–240.

26. The Truth and Reconciliation Commission of Canada was charged to investigate the injustices experienced by indigenous peoples who attended residential schools and to provide a space of healing in order to move toward reconciliation. Many of its calls to action focus on education: http://www.trc.ca/websites/trcinstitution/index.php?p=3

27. Thanks to Heather Devine for explaining the complexities of community-based research. It should also be noted that not all indigenous graduate students focus on indigenous history/studies. Moreover, many non-indigenous historians who work on indigenous studies also focus on establishing strong relationships with communities.

28. Micheline Dumont (2013) *Pas d'histoire, les femmes! Réflexions d'une historienne indigénée* (Montreal: Les Éditions du remue-ménage).

29. For a sampling of recent bestsellers see: Roy McGregor (2015) *Canoe Country: the making of Canada* (Toronto: Random House); Tim Cook (2014) *The Necessary War: Canadians fighting the Second World War, 1939–1943* (Toronto: Allen Lane); Bobby Orr (2013) *My Story* (Toronto: Viking).

30. Conrad Black, 'From Champlain to Carleton to St Laurent and Howe, Conrad Black's Civitas speech tracks Canadian history and what should come next, *Maclean's*, 2 May 2016, http://www.macleans.ca/news/canada/for-the-record-conrad-black-on-canadas-tradition-of-greatness/ (accessed 7 May 2016). Black was an influential newspaper publisher and has written popular histories that celebrate great men. For example, see his (2016) *Rise to Greatness: the history of Canada from Vikings to the present* (Toronto: McClelland & Stewart).

31. Ann Curthoys (1999) Expulsion, Exodus and Exile in White Historical Mythology, *Journal of Australian Studies*, 23(61), pp. 1–19.

32. Corrective Collective (1971) *And She Called It Canada Because That Is What It Was Called* (Vancouver: Press Gang); Corrective Collective (1974) *Never Done: three centuries of women's work in Canada* (Toronto & Vancouver: Corrective Collective/Canadian Women's Educational Press). Feminist anthologies also included sections on early feminist writing. Margret Andersen (1972) *Mother Was Not a Person* (Montreal: Black Rose Books).

33. Stacey Loyer (2006) *Preserving Records, Creating Memories, Shaping Research: inside the Canadian Women's Movement Archives* (MA dissertation, University of Ottawa). Some members of the CWMA Collective have recently launched an initiative to create a digital archive of the women's movement entitled *Women Rise Up: feminist activism in the 1970s and 1980s*.

34. Krista Cooke (2009) Representing Women at Canada's Public History Sites, *Women and Social Movements in America, 1600–2000*, http://asp6new.alexanderstreet.com.ezproxy.lib.ucalgary.ca/wam2/wam2.object.details.aspx?dorpid=1002869393.

35. Ian McKay & Jamie Swift (2012) *Warrior Nation: rebranding Canada in an age of anxiety* (Toronto: Between the Lines), 9. The most well-known revanchist history is J. L. Granatstein (1998) *Who Killed Canadian History?* 1st ed. (Toronto: HarperCollins).

36. McKay & Swift, *Warrior Nation*, 15.

37. At the time of publication, this is still the study guide recommended to New Canadians to prepare for the citizenship test. Department of Citizenship and Immigration (2009) *Discover Canada: the rights and responsibilities of citizenship* (Ottawa: Government of Canada), http://www.cic.gc.ca/english/resources/publications/discover/download.asp. The women are: Laura Secord (War of 1812); the section on women's suffrage added to a discussion of WWI has a portrait of a nurse and picture of Agnes McPhail, the first woman MP; and detail from a Red Cross fundraising poster from WWII featuring a female nurse. For a critical response to the new citizenship guide, see Esyllt Wynne Jones & Adele Perry (Eds) (2011) *People's Citizenship Guide: a response to Conservative Canada* (Winnipeg: Arbeiter Ring).

38. 'Conservatives draw fire for War of 1812 spending', *CBC News*, 15 June 2012, http://www.cbc.ca/news/politics/conservatives-draw-fire-for-war-of-1812-spending-1.1265851 (accessed 24 June 2015).

39. Government of Canada, 'Canadian Identity & Society', http://canada.pch.gc.ca/eng/1446836 048006 (accessed 7 May 2016).

40. Government of Canada, 'Canada 150', http://canada.pch.gc.ca/eng/1342792785740/1342793 251811 (accessed 7 May 2016).

41. 'New $50 bill: Out, women's rights, UN Charter; in, Arctic icebreaker', *Globe and Mail*, 26 March 2012, http://www.theglobeandmail.com/news/national/new-50-bill-out-womens-rights-un-charter-in-arctic-icebreaker/article534411/ (accessed 24 June 2015). The icebreaker symbolizes Canadian sovereignty in the Arctic.

42. 'Thérèse Casgrain, feminist icon, quietly dropped as federal award namesake', *CBC News*, 28 July 2014, http://www.cbc.ca/news/canada/montreal/th%C3%A9r%C3%A8se-casgrain-feminist-icon-quietly-dropped-as-federal-award-namesake-1.2719588 (accessed 24 June 2015).

43. Dean Beeby, 'Liberals restore name of feminist icon Thérèse Casgrain to volunteer award', ·*CBC News*, 11 April 2016, http://www.cbc.ca/beta/news/politics/therese-casgrain-award-name-restored-1.3530320 (accessed 12 April 2016).

44. 'A Bank NOTE-able Canadian woman', Bank of Canada, http://www.bankofcanada.ca/banknotes/banknoteable/ (accessed 12 April 2016).

45. Library and Archives Canada (2014) Report on Plans and Priorities 2014–15, http://www.bac-lac.gc.ca/eng/about-us/report-plans-priorities/rpp-2014-2015/Pages/rpp-2014-15.aspx#_Toc378592495 (accessed 22 August 2016); Library and Archives Canada (2016) Report on Plans and Priorities 2016–17, http://www.bac-lac.gc.ca/eng/about-us/report-plans-priorities/rpp-2016-2017/Pages/rpp-2016-17.aspx (accessed 22 August 2016).

46. CAUT, 'Backgrounder—Canada's Past Matters', *electriccanadian.com*, 31 May 2012, http://www.electriccanadian.com/lifestyle/Backgrounder.pdf (accessed 22 August 2016); 'One month later: how the 2012 federal budget impacts the arts', *Art-Threat*, 2 May 2012, http://artthreat.net/2012/05/one-month-later-how-the-2012-federal-budget-impacts-the-arts/

47. Elizabeth Thompson (2016) 'Trudeau government spending plans provide clues to budget, priorities', *iPOLITICS*, https://ipolitics.ca/2016/03/22/trudeau-government-spending-plans-provide-clues-to-budget-priorities/ (accessed 22 August 2016).

48. Library and Archives Canada (2016) 'Librarian and Archivist of Canada Announces National Heritage Digitization Strategy Collaboration', http://www.marketwired.com/press-release/librarian-archivist-canada-announces-national-heritage-digitization-strategy-collaboration-2131227.htm (accessed 22 August 2016).

49. Library and Archives Canada (2016) 'Library and Archives Canada Announced $1.5 million in Funding to Help Local Archives Preserve Canada's Documentary Heritage', http://www.marketwired.com/press-release/library-archives-canada-announces-15-million-funding-help-local-communities-preserve-2134258.htm (accessed 22 August 2016).

50. Parks Canada (2016) '2016–17 Report on Plans and Priorities', http://www.pc.gc.ca/eng/docs/pc/plans/rpp/rpp2016-17/index.aspx (accessed 22 August 2016).

51. The Herstory Café in Vancouver can be found here: https://herstorycafevancouver.wordpress.com/; The Toronto equivalent can be found here: http://herstoriescafe.com/upcoming-cafes/.

52. Merna Forster (2004) *100 Canadian Heroines: famous and forgotten faces* (Toronto: Dundurn); (2011) *100 More Canadian Heroines: famous and forgotten faces* (Toronto: Dundurn). Reviews from readers can be found on amazon.ca: https://www.amazon.ca/product-reviews/1550025147/ref=pd_sim_14_cr_1?ie=UTF8&refRID=ZG1RF1TQT39T5H 4A3XZS (accessed 26 April 2016).

53. 'CHA Prizes', http://www.cha-shc.ca/english/what-we-do/cha-prizes/cha-prizes.html#sthash.3kWl5v39.Ip4yQwsa.dpbs (accessed 26 April 2016).

The History of Women and Gender: French perspectives on the last twenty years

Françoise Thébaud (translated from the French by Karen Offen)

ABSTRACT

This presentation sketches the slow growth of acceptance for and ultimate success of women's & gender history in French academic circles. In order to briefly evoke the French situation, the author regroups her responses to the five questions posed by Chen Yan and Karen Offen by examining realizations to date (questions 1 & 2) and emerging themes for research (questions 3 to 5). The author concludes with a final remark about a new category of analysis—gender regimes—recently introduced by women's historians of the medieval and early modern periods. An important recent development in the production of women's history in France is its widening out from the 'national' to a more expansive view that includes empire and comparative history, and new media initiatives such as bilingual journal publications in French and English, and e-journals.

In order to briefly evoke the French situation, I will regroup my responses to the five questions posed by Chen Yan and Karen Offen: the first two questions having to do with the realizations to date, and questions 3 to 5 concerning themes for research, and I will make a final remark about a new category of analysis.

In France, the history of women has long found itself in a paradoxical situation.[1] Publications have been numerous since the 1970s, thanks to the impulsion of a pioneering generation born in the 1920s (in particular, Michelle Perrot and Yvonne Knibiehler) when history was, along with sociology, the dominant discipline in women's studies. Moreover, at the end of the 1980s it was a French team that directed a first synthesis of research in the most important Western countries (USA, England, Germany, Italy, and France): the five volumes of the *Histoire des femmes en Occident*, some 3,000 pages (in French we added 'in the West').[2] This five-volume series written by seventy-four authors, of which 15% were men and 35% were from other countries outside France is one of the series the most globalized in its area of research, less by its content (the West and not all the West, and not the empires), but by its circulation: the volumes were translated into seven languages, including English, Spanish, and Japanese,[3] and subsequently stimulated parallel enterprises in other countries, most recently the *Historia de las mujeres en España y América latina*.[4]

Despite that, the French academic milieu long expressed its reserves, even hostility toward the history of women. With notable exceptions such as Alain Corbin who saw in it a 'laboratory of innovations',[5] most French researchers perceived these works as 'particulariste', unscientific, even militant. For these colleagues 'the politics of knowledge' was a concept without meaning: in their eyes, there were only good and bad works.[6] As Karen Offen has underscored, in France we did not use the term 'feminist history', for theoretical reasons, as Genevieve Fraisse has explained, but also for strategic reasons: the researcher, or more pointedly the female researcher [*chercheuse*]—in fact the majority were women— who worked in women's history was usually feminist and hoped that her research would have feminist effects (on the place and identity of women in our own time) but the history that he or she wrote was just as scientific as any other and pretended equally to universality. Another remark that for me seems to characterize France: the sex of the historian has always been less of a problem (except for attaining the most prestigious positions) than the theme of research, with an increasing feminization of the discipline, including the recruitment of women who were also mothers of families. However, the history we call 'contemporary', prestigious and closely linked to the affirmation of the French nation, is less feminized than that of earlier periods.[7]

To become recognized and to influence the historiography more generally, the history of women has had to carry on a struggle for legitimacy, both intellectual and institutional. The first was acquired early in the twenty-first century, as is demonstrated for example by the introduction of chapters on the subject (of women's and gender history) in the manuals on historical writing for students. Institutional legitimacy was only acquired around 2010, some forty years after the first researches, when the CNRS (Centre National de la Recherche Scientifique) created an Institute on Gender (Institut du Genre)[8] to make visible and promote research in this domain; when the access to fellowships for doctoral students is becoming easier and there are positions for young post-docs in this field; when the CNRS is giving a subvention to the French journal of women's history *Clio: Femmes, Genre, Histoire* for the purpose of translating its articles into English and distributing them online on Cairn international and possibly other anglophone sites. This review publishes at least half its articles on non-French topics, whether or not written by French scholars, but we hope, by the translation into English, to broaden the audience for this research, inasmuch as French is now little spoken beyond France, Belgium, Switzerland, Quebec, and some western African states. In order to assure that this translation experiment will continue, we have need of everyone's support, for the subsidy is temporary.[9]

How can we explain this success story? For one thing, the publishers in France have always welcomed the history of women, for a reading public beyond the academy has always existed. The history of women has resonance and allows readers to better understand what is going on in the contemporary world, which in France during the last twenty years, has been marked by the struggle for parity in politics. Young people have grown up in a context where parity in politics but also in employment and in the family has been (much) discussed. Today, to include women and questions of gender in a historical study seems to have become self-evident, even a necessity, for the greater number of young researchers of either sex. The second factor, doubtless the most important: the perseverance of researchers and the institutionalization of the research field with the example of, and in contact with, international developments in the field. We have always continued to produce and publish in history of women, to form students in several universities; in this respect, my book *Écrire l'histoire des femmes* (1998)—then its revised edition, *Écrire l'histoire des femmes et du genre* (2007)[10]—was intended to be an vehicle for the transmission of what I call an intellectual and political adventure.

After the publication of *Histoire des femmes en Occident*, which has sold more than 20,000 copies in France alone, and at the moment in which, following the United States, scholarly journals in women's history were born in Europe, in 1995 we founded, without support other than volunteer labor, the review *Clio: Histoire, Femmes et Sociétés* (the principal title Clio [the classical muse of History] to state that we were writing accomplished history and good history; the subtitle in triptyque to imitate the prestigious journal *Annales: Économies, Sociétés, Civilisations*. In 1995 it seemed difficult to use in the title the word 'gender/genre', which was still largely unknown or misunderstood.) We also created associations for historical research, such as Mnémosyne (Association for the development of women's and gender history, named for the classical goddess of Memory) which is the French affiliate of IFRWH,[11] the SIEFAR (Société Internationale pour l'Étude des Femmes de l'Ancien Régime), to investigate the history of women during the old regime, and the Archives du Feminisme to preserve the sources for the history of feminism in France.[12] We also wanted to distribute the research results in secondary education by producing a manual for teachers at the secondary level, a manual that incorporated both women and gender (it is called *La place des femmes dans l'histoire: Une histoire mixte*).[13] Finally and lastly, the impulse coming from outside: European funding designated for programs of research in gender studies, participation of French historians in colloquia in other countries where they discovered that the history of women & gender was by no means marginal, the role of French historians of England and the United States who understood the importance of gender studies in the countries they studied. One of them, highly placed at the CNRS, helped to facilitate the creation of the Institut du Genre.

As for my responses to questions 3, 4, and 5? I would say, first of all, that in France, we used the expression 'history of women and gender' (as has our association Mnémosyne, the French section of IFRWH, the subtitle of which is: 'association pour le développement de l'histoire des femmes et du genre') to underscore the continuity and overlapping of an approach centered on women and a more gendered approach. There is no progression toward something 'better', even if the non-specialists or beginners speak of a history of gender that seems to them more 'scientific.' The term in its French translation was not used before the last decade (2000–2010) but today one must speak 'gender' to get financing. Another remark: in France, by comparison with the English-speaking countries, there was no polemic between post-structuralists and social historians in the 1990s, but rather a slow acclimatation to gendered approaches, accepted in their diversity. In my book, I was thus able to distinguish a number of uses of gender, none of which excluded the others.

I will invoke four of these approaches here. First, the cultural and political usage proposed by Joan Scott and connected to the linguistic turn was certainly important: gender invited one to analyze the principle of partition between masculine and feminine and the significations of power in this principle of partition.[14] But this is not the sole possible use of gender. A more social, more anthropological approach investigates all forms of relations between men and women; gender thus invites the historian to write a 'mixed' history, to propose a sexed re-reading of events and historical phenomena, to understand, as Cécile Dauphin and Arlette Farge have written, 'the infinite nuances of the encounter between men and women',[15] an encounter which is not marked solely by domination. Third use:

the study of the construction of identities, masculine and feminine: the history of women has thus called forth a history of masculinities. Fourth use: the articulation of gender with other categories of analysis, initially, to take account of the differences between women and between men—who do not constitute homogenous groups, but also to account for what sociologists and political scientists call the intersectionality of power relations (relations of gender, class, race, etc.). Our journal *Clio: Histoire, Femmes et Sociétés* (since 2013, *Clio: Femmes, Genre, Histoire*) bears witness to this opening to pluralism: each thematic issue proposes different approaches, opens its columns to foreign researchers, and to male researchers as well as female researchers.[16]

Over these last twenty years new themes have developed, with a nod to international research—of which a part is translated—and to advances in general history, under the impetus as well of contemporary social and political interrogations. For example, the history of masculinities and virility—the value of affirming masculinity—which in France does not seem to me to be linked to the history of sexualities, but more to the history of education, to the history of the worker's movement which presented itself as 'viriliste', and to the history of war. Concerning this subject, one French historian has cleverly titled an article 'masculine identity and the fatigues of war'.[17] Such a history of masculinities is interested both in the modes of domination of men but also in their sufferings. This theme has produced a recent synthesis and a public international colloquium.[18]

Another recent theme: that of sexualities and of the articulation of sex, gender, and sexuality. This theme has produced numerous works in history, sociology and even political science, because the doctoral students want to engage with these new subjects, which are much debated in contemporary society: notably homosexualities, transsexuals, and transgender. 2009 witnessed the launch of a new online transdisciplinary journal entitled *Genre, sexualité & société*.[19]

For a long time, research by French historians was largely focused on the French nation, or as we say 'franco-centrique' and not only that, but on a continental France that was envisioned without its empire. This is paradoxical for a country which has been both a land of extensive immigration and a great colonial power. Women researchers on Africa have finally succeeded in shifting this view; in 2012, they organized a large colloquium in Paris, which they put online.[20] The journal *Clio* has also published an issue on 'Colonisations' and another one entitled, in the plural, 'Amériques métisses' (hybrid Americas). For her part, Linda Guerry has studied the gender of immigration and naturalization in France in the interwar period;[21] today she is internationalizing and globalizing her approach by studying an international women's association for aid to migrant women and the politics of the League of Nations. For historians in France as for others, the global and transnational approaches that go beyond mere comparison and interest themselves in what circulates and what mixes (both persons and ideas) have become familiar. This is very interesting for the history of women and gender, notably for the history of feminism, which is, as Karen Offen has always underscored, an important and long overlooked component of the political history of nations and of international engagement. Concerning this theme, in France as elsewhere, what a long way we have come since the rediscovery in the 1970s of the militant texts of our foremothers! Today research privileges, beyond the diversity of movements, the analysis of those national and international networks that provide a space for pursuit of the advancement of women's cause. That said, it is also true that to write the political history of women is to render visible the less positive/edifying (to our eyes) figures on which recent work has focused (conservative women on the right, and on the extreme right, women guards in the Nazi camps, collaborating women in the German occupation of France during the Second World War, the women of the Phalange who supported Franco in Spain, etc.). My own current work attests to such a broadening of perspectives: after a master's and a doctoral thesis that focused on France—on the women workers in the munitions factories during the war of 1914–1918 and on the medicalization of maternity during the interwar period—after a comparative approach in the *Histoire des femmes en Occident* and my work on historiography in women's history, I now employ a global and transnational perspective. I am currently writing the biography of Marguerite Thibert, a French woman and historian who spent her professional life as an international civil servant with the International Labour Organization and became a true world citizen. I also belong to a gender research team—well financed (we are now integrated into the mainstream!) called EHNE (*Écrire une Histoire Nouvelle de l'Europe*)—to write a new history of Europe.[22] Our activities include conferences (the last one in November 2015 was on the 'gender of the construction of Europe') and an online encyclopedia which will appear both in French and in English.[23]

Here I come to my final remark, in response to the sixth question posed by Chen Yan and Karen Offen. Although the category 'gender system' seems to me highly useful for examining modern history (from 1789 to the present, according to English-language usage), the historians of ancient, medieval, and 'early modern' history have proposed a new category, 'regimes de genre' or gender regimes. On this subject they have published an issue of the *Annales*, a mainstream historical journal that is also being subsidized for English translation.[24] By this notion they wish to, first, insist on the necessity of historicizing the binarity of the sexes and the categorization of persons; second, to be attentive 'more to manners of acting and to situations than to identities', and third, to underscore that a variety of gender regimes can co-exist at the same time in the same society. Gender is indeed a useful category for historical analysis and its uses continue to engender and to stimulate our thinking.

Notes

1. I would like to thank Chen Yan and Karen Offen for organizing this round table and writing an interesting and comprehensive text. Thanks also to Karen Offen for translating my commentary.
2. Georges Duby & Michelle Perrot (Eds) (1991–1992) *Histoire des femmes en Occident*, 5 volumes (Paris: Plon).
3. In English, by Harvard University Press (1992–1994).
4. Isabel Morant (Ed.) (2005–2006) *Historia de las mujeres en España y América latina* (Madrid: Cátedra).
5. See Corbin's preface to Françoise Thébaud *Écrire l'histoire des femmes* (Paris: ENS Éditions Fontenay/Saint-Cloud, 1998), p. 10, and to the revised second edition, *Écrire l'histoire des femmes et du genre* (Lyon: ENS Éditions, 2007), p. 9. Corbin, at the time France's most prominent social historian, repeatedly referred to this new field of research as innovative, even qualifying the history of women as 'one of the most fascinating attempts at innovation in the discipline of history.'
6. On this subject, see Françoise Thébaud (2011) Politiques du genre en sciences humaines. L'exemple de la discipline historique en France, in Alexandre Duchêne & Claudine Moïse (Eds) *Langage, genre et sexualité* (Montréal: Nota Bene), pp. 27–47; Michèle Riot-Sarcey

(2000) L'historiographie française et le concept de 'genre', *Revue d'histoire moderne et con-temporaine*, 47 (4), pp. 805–814.

7. See Françoise Thébaud (2003) Histoire des femmes, histoire du genre et sexe du chercheur, in Jacqueline Laufer, Catherine Marry & Margaret Maruani (Eds), *Le travail du genre. Les sciences sociales du travail à l'épreuve des différences de sexe* (Paris: La Découverte), pp. 70–87; André Burguière & Bernard Vincent (Eds) (2014) *Un siècle d'historiennes* (Paris: éditions des femmes-Antoinette Fouque). See, for the situation in 2012–2013: http://cache.media.enseignementsup-recherche.gouv.fr/file/statistiques/01/0/Demographie_ Enseignants-chercheurs_2012-2013_CNU_corps_sexe_384010.pdf

8. See http://institut-du-genre.fr/

9. Until 2016, the English language version of the journal Clio could only be consulted on the French academic journals website CAIRN at http://www.cairn-int.info/revue-clio-femmes-genre-histoire.htm. Beginning in 2017, however, it will also be available on JSTOR, along with the French edition.

10. Françoise Thébaud, *Écrire l'histoire des femmes et du genre*, p. 10.

11. The IFWRH semi-annual bulletin provides a very useful link between the affiliated sections. For a long time Karen Offen provided the bibliography of new books and articles in French. Today this is managed by Rebecca Rogers, the French correspondent with IFRWH and member of the editorial board of the journal *Clio: Femmes, Genre, Histoire*.

12. See http://www.mnemosyne.asso.fr/mnemosyne/; http://siefar.org/; http://www.archivesdu feminisme.fr/

13. Geneviève Dermenjian, Irène Jami, Annie Rouquier & Françoise Thébaud (Eds) (2010) *La place des femmes dans l'histoire. Une histoire mixte* (Paris: Belin-Mnémosyne).

14. Joan Wallach Scott (1988) Gender as a Useful Category of Historical Analysis, in Joan Wallach Scott, *Gender and the Politics of History* (New York: Columbia University Press), pp. 28–50. A new French translation of Scott's important article appears as one of the chapters in Joan W. Scott (2012) *De l'utilité du genre* (Paris: Fayard).

15. Cécile Dauphin & Arlette Farge (Eds) (2001) *Séduction et sociétés. approches historiques* (Paris: Seuil), p. 8.

16. For the full collection (forty-three issues to the spring of 2016), see https://clio.revues.org/

17. Luc Capdevila (2002) L'identité masculine et les fatigues de la guerre, *Vingtième siècle: revue d'histoire*, no. 75, pp. 97–108.

18. Alain Corbin, Jean-Jacques Courtine & Georges Vigarello (Eds) (2011) *Histoire de la virilité*, 3 volumes (Paris: Le Seuil); Anne-Marie Sohn (Ed.) (2013) *Une histoire sans les hommes est-elle possible? Genre et masculinités* (Lyon: ENS éditions).

19. See https://gss.revues.org/

20. Colloque 'Femmes et genre en contexte colonial, XIXè–XXè siècle,' organized by Pascale Barthélémy, Christelle Taraud & Anne Hugon. See http://genrecol.hypotheses.org/

21. Linda Guerry (2013) *Le genre de l'immigration et de la naturalisation* (Lyon: ENS Éditions).

22. See https://genreurope.hypotheses.org/

23. See http://ehne.fr/ EHNE is the acronym for the research laboratory *Écrire une histoire nouvelle de l'Europe* (mentioned above) as well as for the encyclopedia its members are producing —the online *Encyclopédie pour une histoire nouvelle de l'Europe*.

24. *Annales. histoire, sciences sociales*, juillet–septembre 2012. In English: 'Gender Regimes'. See http://www.cairn-int.info/numero.php?ID_REVUE=E_ANNA&ID_NUMPUBLIE=E_ ANNA_673

From Invisibility to Marginality: women's history in Romania

Maria Bucur

ABSTRACT

This essay enhances the broad context in which Karen Offen's argument is framed by addressing the question of how the humanities are faring today in relation to academic research and learning. I explore what that context means specifically for women's history and vice-versa into the future. Secondly, I provide a historical overview of how women's history in Romania has developed since 1989. My analysis highlights the slow and uneven shift from complete invisibility to some interest and a small number of excellent books in several areas of research, from demographic to political history of the modern period.

Karen Offen's description of the history and scholarly trends in women's history in this forum offers a great starting point for developing a narrative about similarities and differences at more localized levels. My focus below is twofold. To begin with, I want to enhance the broad context in which Offen's argument is framed by adding a new dimension, the question of how the humanities more broadly, and not just women's history as a particular field of inquiry, are faring today in relation to academic research and learning. I want to explore what that context means specifically for women's history and vice versa into the future. Secondly, I will provide a historical overview of how women's history in Romania[1] has developed since 1989, because before the fall of communism we cannot really speak about anything other than sparse and disconnected attempts to write about some women, rather than focusing on women as a category of historical actors.

Women's History and the Crisis in the Humanities

As a historian teaching at a public university in the United States, over the past decade I have seen the level of interest among undergraduate students as well as among younger readers diminish significantly.[2] History as an academic discipline is in danger of becoming irrelevant. While this makes me concerned on a personal level in terms of my livelihood, it worries me even further as a humanist. What does it mean for our children and students to have lost interest in understanding where humanity comes from as a fundamental aspect of what we are as individuals, as communities, and where we are heading? It basically means that we are losing our common roots and with them, our moral compass. Because of these concerns, I consider women's history particularly important today.

The impact that historical narratives have on future generations depends on our ability to connect the questions we ask and our framing of the answers with big existential questions for these younger generations.

Today, more women than men are attending universities the world over. The percentages of women pursuing graduate degrees have also increased significantly and will soon surpass those of men, especially in the humanities.[3] We have larger numbers of women before us than ever before in the history of humanity as the next generation of leaders.[4] This is an extraordinary opportunity for gender historians to make ourselves more relevant than ever and to shape the world—the problem solvers, the dreamers, the critical thinkers, the activists—to a greater extent than any other generation of feminists before us. But those opportunities arise in a world that has become more and more fragmented even though we are permanently connected, and in which post-feminism co-exists with many types of feminism.[5] So the fundamental question for us is: how do we grab and hold on to the attention of our audiences in this increasingly cluttered landscape of information? How do we make the past relevant to a population that is more likely to tweet and take selfies than read extended analyses of what the world was like a hundred years ago? Though this may be a secondary question of strategy for some, for me it is a fundamental, even existential one in terms of how we retain the importance of studying the past into the future.

The stakes are high, and the questions we must ask need to become equally bold. I believe that in the next decade, our profession will become radically altered due to changes in funding for the humanities, in universities as well as through other types of funding available for humanities research projects that necessitate multiple years of work in the archives.[6] New technologies and the political forces that control them are also radically altering access to sources. Because of this, I want to call on all of us to renew our commitment to writing histories that highlight the specific qualities, achievements, failures, and overall contributions that women have made to humanity as a core element of how we understand our past, not only as something we may be personally passionate about or that is 'just' women's history. To our growing audience of women, as well as to the men in the classroom, gaining a comprehensive understanding of how women have shaped history and been shaped by gender regimes is an essential intellectual tool that will help our students and future generations around the world relate both appreciatively and critically to the past.

The Century of Women

We have come a long way, as Karen Offen pointed out in her opening essay, but we have a long way to go, and new departures are necessary in dealing with the larger issues posed by the contemporary flattened and globalized world of knowledge and academic encounters. My own research focuses on the recent past, the twentieth century, so the following remarks focus on this period of time. I limit myself to the twentieth century also because of the much greater potential for rewriting the history of the recent past in a way that can be rendered relevant to the younger women whom I want to see become future active citizens and leaders. The history of the twentieth century offers unparalleled opportunities for critiquing patriarchy and sexism, which is one foundation of doing feminist history.[7] This is also a period of time richly documented regarding women's public activities, which enables us to develop an appreciative and at the same time critically inflected picture of achievements women have made the world over. This is something we need to enhance into the future, rather than take for granted, as much post-feminist popular culture seems to be doing these days.[8]

Military and political historians focusing on the atrocities committed during the twentieth century have kept trumpeting the relevance of their work for the entirety of the twentieth century and beyond as an important moral corrective to those atrocities.[9] I am here to question and refute the assumptions behind that masculinist approach.[10] I see little evidence in the past three decades to indicate that the innumerable histories of World War I, World War II, and the Holocaust published in the last fifty years have done much to eliminate racist and warmongering actions or even attitudes around the world. What we might want to try instead is to focus on other types of problem-solving that have developed around the world outside the mainstream mechanisms of power that propelled the two world wars. For instance, the peace movement of the twentieth century was initiated and developed by women largely outside of established political institutions and without initially having a direct say in elections. Peace activists challenged power structures from a position of vulnerability and marginality, and their impact might not look very impressive at the level of institutional politics. But that impact is quite remarkable if one examines the tools available to these activists and the less institutionalized areas of human activity reshaped by such activism.

How has the history of the peace movement been incorporated as a core component of our narratives about politics and civil society in the twentieth century? I would say poorly thus far. It may be that recent critiques of the colonial and racist undertones of some of this activism have overshadowed what women in the peace movement were actually able to accomplish. Indeed, some of these women's ideas were flawed or riddled with conflicts and shortcomings regarding race relations, economic power, and other issues, especially in post-colonial settings. Yet there are many excellent and nuanced analyses of these complex legacies, which do not side-step such questions while placing emphasis on the significant changes effected by women peace activists, from transnational networks of interest and public pressure, to legislation and public opinion.[11] The ways in which these activists defined the problems related to political, economic, and other structures and forces that generate conflict around the world are as relevant today as they were around the turn of the twentieth century, when such activities started on a transnational level.[12] Likewise, the solutions they offered, together with the more general organizational efforts that became models of peaceful collaboration (not always, but more often than the United Nations or the League of Nations, for instance), are important elements of our history that are simply insufficiently known and poorly integrated as core components of the history of the twentieth century. They are women's history, but they are also the history of humanity dealing creatively, bravely, and to some extent successfully, with the masculinist networks of power in place.

Another major area of feminist research that has not been sufficiently integrated into the mainstream history of the twentieth century is women's contributions to changing the world economy, from production and innovation to distribution consumption. This is an area in which women have played a essential role in reshaping what is made, how, where, and who has access to it in terms of economic production and capital accumulation. Yet recent global economic histories of the twentieth century, most prominently

Thomas Picketty's *Capital in the Twenty-First Century*, seem completely uninterested in this issue.[13] Thus far, even feminist critiques of this book, such as Kate Bahn's in the *Women's Review of Books*, go easy on the flawed model and narrative strategies of the French economist.[14] While Picketty's many charts and literary examples from Jane Austen and Honoré de Balzac are rife with possibilities for a gender analysis of capital accumulation and social inequality, the author fails to acknowledge, much less engage with structural gender inequality, such as property rights, access to education, and inheritance laws.[15] We can do better than Picketty, and we need to.

I have spent a good part of my twenty-five years as a professional historian examining women's lives. Having matured as a historian around the time of Joan Scott's landmark essay on gender as a useful category of analysis,[16] this approach to framing questions about the past was an integral part of my graduate education and an expectation on the part of the feminist historians who helped me hone my analytical tools.[17] Though gender analysis promised to open up important analytical vistas, over time I have become more critical of using this approach without an explicit feminist vantage point, as a fig leaf of avoiding engagement with the structural and discursive sexism embedded in the framing of most historical narratives. Simply put, a feminist perspective on women's history implicitly means dealing with wider power relation questions that pertain to how gender norms function in any time and place. By contrast, historical research on gender without an explicit feminist perspective glosses over and sometimes explicitly misrepresents the wider context, especially with regard to how political, economic, and social power are structured and function.[18] This is an issue we cannot just live with, but need to critique and redress.

From Invisibility to Marginality: twenty-five years of women's history in Romania

In the area of my expertise, modern Eastern Europe, and in particular in Romania, the country on which I have done most of my research, over the past twenty-five years important developments have taken place in the historical writing on women.[19] Before 1989, research on the history of women was sporadic, and feminist histories of women nonexistent. The tight ideological control of the Romanian Communist Party over training scholars and establishing the research agenda in the social sciences led to a lack of interest in questions about patriarchy and women's past, other than as cookie-cutter studies about class struggle with women sometimes in the mix.[20] Some of these studies provided opportunities for gendered data gathering about literacy, paid work, urbanization, and other important processes.[21] But the analyses were almost always unfailingly predictable along the Leninist agenda of the regime and devoid of serious engagement with sexism from a feminist perspective.

Post-communist historians discarded much of this research as a shameful and useless legacy, though the previous focus on political and military history retained its primacy, now with a new, more aggressive nationalist tone, especially during the first fifteen years of post-communist transition. At the same time, feminist scholars whose training was primarily in other disciplines, from literature to political science and psychology, began to introduce feminist gender analysis into their research and publication programs, as well as into graduate curricula at major universities.[22] This was the first generation of scholars to begin producing both methodologies as well as empirical studies that pointed more clearly and deliberately towards the structural and discursive patterns of gender discrimination faced by women in the present as well as the past. They are primarily responsible for the first decade of feminist publications and activism, which eventually came to encompass historical research.[23]

It was during the first decade of post-communism that a number of studies related to women's history began to appear. The most important initiative in this regard was a series entitled 'Gender Studies', which was published by Polirom, at that time a rising star among both academic and trade publishers. The series was initiated and curated by Professor Mihaela Miroiu, the founder of the first feminist studies program in Romania.[24] The volumes by Ştefania Mihăilescu were an especially important pioneering effort. They brought to public attention a wide variety of women's voices from the nineteenth and first half of the twentieth century, making visible diverse strands of feminism, nationalism, and other types of activism among Romanian women during this period.[25] Though the introductory analysis in both volumes presented a rather narrow nationalist and anti-communist reading of these sources, without much reference to any other women's historiography, the two volumes became a great starting point for teaching about and especially further research on women's movements during the modern period.[26]

During the same years, historians in search of sensational topics also started to publish more books on what might be called 'exceptional women'.[27] Though few of these volumes qualify as serious historical research on women, they at least brought more attention to women as historical agents. Unfortunately, most of these volumes did little to critique the lack of integration of women into historiography, and worse yet, reinforced the sexist assumptions about what mattered as historical evidence or what historical topics deserve attention.

Over the last decade, the breadth and depth of Romanian books focusing on women's history has grown, though one cannot speak yet of mainstream feminism in either the approach of these studies or history graduate school curricula. Initially focusing on famous (or infamous, as in the case of Elena Lupescu) women from the recent past— basically queens and courtesans—this literature has grown to encompass both a wider swath of women of prominence, from doctors to aviatrixes, as well as deeper questions about the social history of Romania with women as active agents.[28] Yet the proportion of books that make women's achievements visible while situating their lives in the larger historical context of their time in terms of gender norms is rather small. To give one example, a popular recent book tells the story of four women's lives, one of them a prominent artist, Cecilia Cuţescu-Stork.[29] Stork's life was marked by both successes and frustrations as a female artist, and she spent a great deal of her energies on feminist activism in both the arts and politics. None of these issues makes even a brief appearance in the book, which instead focuses on the relationships Stork and the other female protagonists had with various men in their lives. In short, many of these books remain in the realm of juicy scandals.

The curricula in graduate programs in history and the research proposals coming before the national agencies that provide state funding for such projects have been generally devoid of interest in women's issues and especially feminist positioning with regards to historical research questions.[30] Students interested in asking such questions have few mentors in the historical profession and very little institutional and financial support for undertaking women's history research. The few alternatives such scholars have found are to pursue graduate degrees outside of Romania or to find mentors who would support and assist them in other disciplines, such as political science or sociology.[31] This has generally meant that the ranks of practicing historians involved in training new generations have not grown significantly during this period. Some of these younger feminist scholars have found more employment opportunities in sociology, political science, or literature programs, rather than history departments and research institutes.[32] And some have decided not to return to Romania because of the lack of support for their feminist research agenda.

Still, there are more studies coming out each year with bold claims about the importance of integrating women's lives in the history of communism, the interwar period, or the late nineteenth century. Demographic history in particular has become more thoroughly gendered, and in some instances historians have presented detailed and effective arguments about power inequalities in the home and society through studies of marriage, inheritance, and divorce.[33] This field is also remarkable in terms of moving beyond ethno-centrism. Researchers in this field have made a steady effort at engaging comparatively with different ethno-religious groups, rendering their findings far more interesting and useful for women's historians interested in, for instance, marriage and property practices in Transylvania over the nineteenth century among all ethnic groups living there. These studies have also been more thoroughly integrated in the wider historiography on demography through their active engagement with the rich scholarship on related topics.

Another promising departure in the past decade has been the focus on feminism in Romania.[34] Scholars have aimed to make the historic roots of contemporary feminism more clearly visible, and at the same time have used these analyses to engage with broader questions about: the nature of the modern state; the impact of specific ideologies on shaping feminism and of feminism on shaping these ideologies in Romania; and the impact of communist rule on Romanian society. A recent book on the evolution of the communist regime focuses squarely on the ways in which the party and affiliated institutions generated new regimes of gender inequality and does so from an unapologetic feminist perspective.[35] This and a handful of other likeminded works suggest that Romanian historiography may be entering a new phase of mainstreaming women's history.[36] Women in history have become visible, though they remain marginal in broad historical narratives.

The next significant step will be to see these studies reviewed in all the relevant professional journals (including those outside Romania) as well as wider media, and their insights incorporated into the training of future historians. As such, I am hopeful that these new generations will continue to push against the conservatism of history departments in Romanian universities and that established scholars there will begin to see that it is in their best interests to engage with women's history as critical to understanding our common past. When the majority of students sitting in our classrooms is comprised of women, how can we make it more intelligible, relevant, and empowering for them to learn about the past if women do not figure centrally in our narratives?

Notes

1. There is a great deal of history about women in Romania being written outside of Romania. I am not focusing on that topic here.

2. At Indiana University, Bloomington, where I have been teaching since 1996, enrollments in history courses are down by 30% or more. Our majors are also down, though not by that large of a percentage. A relatively recent (2013) study by the American Historical Association shows similar trends nationwide, concluding that 'the discipline's share of degrees earned in 2011 declined to the lowest level in 10 years': Robert B. Townsend (2013) Data Show a Decline in History Majors, *Perspectives on History*, 51(4), https://www.historians.org/publications-and-directories/perspectives-on-history/april-2013/data-show-a-decline-in-history-majors (accessed 25 February 2016).

3. In the US there were 1.7 million women enrolled in graduate programs vis-à-vis 1.2 million men in 2012. See http://nces.ed.gov/programs/digest/d13/tables/dt13_105.20.asp (accessed 5 August 2015).

4. There are few examples more impressive than that of Zhou Quenfei, who at 44 is the world's richest woman, having risen to this level of success from very humble beginnings largely through her boundless ambition, unwavering passion for the work she does, and a relentless work ethic: David Barboza, 'How a Chinese Billionaire Built her Fortune', *New York Times*, 20 July 2015, http://www.nytimes.com/2015/08/02/business/international/how-zhou-qunfei-a-chinese-billionaire-built-her-fortune.html?_r=0 (accessed 5 August 2015).

5. The debate in the 2016 US Presidential Democratic primaries about who best represents women's interests is a great illustration of this growing fragmentation: 'Hillary's Woman Problem', *Politico*, 12 February 2016, http://www.politico.com/magazine/story/2016/02/hillary-clinton-2016-woman-problem-213621 (accessed 25 February 2016).

6. For those working on topics that take them outside the US for extended research stays, the availability of grants to pursue such projects has gone down, even as the number of people competing for them is going up. A few years ago, the State Department defunded the Fulbright Hays competition, and it was only revived after much protesting, to a fraction of its previous level of funding. For more on the state of funding for the humanities in the US, see American Academy of Arts and Sciences (2014) *The State of the Humanities: funding 2014* (Cambridge: American Academy of Arts and Sciences), http://www.humanitiesindicators.org/binaries/pdf/HI_FundingReport2014.pdf (accessed 25 February 2016).

7. This is the focus of a book I am currently writing, entitled *The Century of Women: how women reshaped the world in the twentieth century.*

8. Rosalind Gill (2007) Postfeminist Media Culture: elements of a sensibility, *European Journal of Cultural Studies*, 10(2), pp. 147–166.

9. One recent example is Richard Evans, 'Why Are We So Obsessed with the Nazis?' *The Guardian*, 6 February 2015, http://www.theguardian.com/books/2015/feb/06/why-obsessed-nazis-third-reich (accessed 7 February 2016).

10. A vigorous critique of the masculinist assumptions behind framing research in the social sciences and humanities has been ongoing for at least three decades. Some prominent examples include: Gerda Lerner (1975) Placing Women in History: definitions and challenges, *Feminist Studies* 3(1/2), pp. 5–14; Joan W. Scott (1986) Gender: a useful category of historical analysis, *The American Historical Review* 91(5), pp. 1053–1075; Denise Riley (1988) *Am I That Name? Feminism and the category of 'women' in history* (Minneapolis: University of Minnesota); Wendy Brown (1992) Finding the Man in the State, *Feminist Studies* 18(1), pp. 7–34; Kathleen Lennon & Margaret Whitford (Eds) (1994) *Knowing the Difference: feminist perspectives in epistemology* (New York: Routledge); Kathleen Canning (1994) Feminist History after the Linguistic Turn: historicizing discourse and experience, *Signs* 19(2), pp. 368–404; Mary Spongberg (2002) *Writing Women's History since the Renaissance* (Basingstoke: Palgrave); Judith Butler (2006) *Gender Trouble: feminism and the subversion of identity* (New York: Routledge).

11. Clare Midgley (1992) *Women Against Slavery: the British campaigns, 1780–1870* (London: Routledge); Vron Ware (1992) *Beyond the Pale: white women, racism and history* (London: Verso); Christine Bolt (2004) *Sisterhood Questioned: race, class and internationalism in the American and British women's movements c. 1880s–1970s* (London: Routledge); Antoinette Burton (2005) *Burdens of History: British feminism, Indian women and imperial*

culture, 1865–1915 (Bloomington: Indiana University Press); Fiona Paisley (2009) Glamour in the Pacific: cultural internationalism and race politics in the women's Pan-Pacific (Honolulu: University of Hawai'i Press).

12. Leila J. Rupp (1997) *Worlds of Women: the making of an international women's movement* (Princeton: Princeton University Press); Susan Zimmermann (2005) The Challenge of Multinational Empire for the International Women's Movement: The Habsburg monarchy and the development of feminist inter/national politics, *Journal of Women's History*, 17(2), pp. 87–117.

13. Thomas Picketty (2014) *Capital in the Twenty-First Century* (Cambridge, MA: Belknap).

14. Kate Bahn (2015) Capital Matters ... But so Does Gender, *Women's Review of Books*, 32(1), pp. 8–9.

15. For a critique of this approach see Maria Bucur, To Have and to Hold: a comparative analysis of gender regimes and property rights in the Romanian Principalities and the Habsburg Empire, 1652–1914, under review.

16. Scott, 'Gender: A Useful Category'.

17. On the impact of especially one prominent feminist historian on my approach to women's history, see Kristen Ghodsee & Maria Bucur-Deckard (2015) Sonya Michel: mentor and mensch, *Social Politics* 22(3), pp. 276–282.

18. I find Wendy Brown's 'Finding the Man in the State' (1992) still one of the clearest articulations of this systemic problem.

19. For a broader analysis of the impact of gender analysis on the historiography focusing on Eastern Europe, see Maria Bucur (2008) An Archipelago of Stories: gender history in Eastern Europe [part of the forum Revisiting Joan Scott's Gender as a Category of Analysis], *The American Historical Review*, 113(5), pp. 1375–1389.

20. Ecaterina Deliman (1977) *Femeia, personalitate politică în societatea noastră socialistă* [Woman, a political personality in our socialist society] (Bucharest: Editura politică).

21. Paraschiva Câncea (1976) *Mișcarea pentru emanciparea femeii în România: 1848–1948* [The movement for woman's emancipation in Romania: 1848–1948] (Bucharest: Editura politică).

22. The most important centers have been the Gender Theory program at the National School for Public Policy and Political Science (SNSPA) in Bucharest, which developed under the guidance of Mihaela Miroiu, a feminist philosopher, and the European Studies Program at Babeș-Bolyai University in Cluj, under the guidance of Enikő Vincze, a feminist anthropologist.

23. Bucur, 'An Archipelago of Stories'.

24. The series has published twenty-seven volumes to date, with a few (five) dedicated to historical analysis. See http://www.polirom.ro/catalog/colectii/studii-de-gen/pagina_01_dataintroducerii_DESC.html (accessed 25 February 2016).

25. Ştefania Mihăilescu (2002) *Din istoria feminismului românesc. Antologie de texte (1838–1929)* [From the history of Romanian feminism. Anthology of texts (1828–1929)] (Iași: Polirom); (2006) *Din istoria feminismului românesc. Studiu și antologie de texte (1929–1948)* [From the history of Romanian feminism. Study and anthology of texts (1929–1948)] (Iași: Polirom).

26. One serious shortcoming in terms of the selections of the material was the exclusive focus on the publications by ethnic Romanians. At that time, there was also considerable activity in this area among Hungarian, German, and Yiddish speakers, but those sources remain beyond the framework of the two collections.

27. Alina Avram (2006) *Femei celebre din România, o enciclopedie* [Famous women from Romania, an encyclopedia] (Bucharest: Editura All).

28. Adrian Cioroianu & Mihaela Simina (2015) *Maria a României. Regina care a iubit viața și patria* [Marie of Romania. The queen who loved life and her fatherland] (Bucharest: Curtea veche); George Marcu & Ilinca Rodica (2012) *Enciclopedia personalităților feminine din România* [The encyclopedia of feminine personalities in Romania] (Bucharest: Meronia).

29. Aurora Liiceanu (2010) *Patru femei, patru povești* [Four women, four stories] (Iași: Polirom).

30. The only graduate program in Romania where women's history is part of the required bibliography and coursework is the Gender Theory Master's degree led by Mihaela Miroiu at

SNSPA. In other words, a graduate program that doesn't award degrees in history. As far as funding for research is concerned, I have served as a reviewer for the primary government funding agency in Romania, as well as a potential mentor for a number of scholars who wanted to pursue a feminist project focusing on women's history at Indiana University through the Fulbright program. Not one project related to women's history was included in any of those I reviewed for the UEFISC agency over the years I served on that board. And not one of the junior scholars who applied to work on women's history through a Fulbright received a positive recommendation from the Romanian Fulbright commission.

31. Such is the case with Roxana Cheşchebec, who produced an excellent thesis on the women's movement in modern Romania at Central European University, but whose research results continue to be unknown to most historians in Romania: Roxana Cheşchebec (2005) *Feminist Ideologies and Activism in Romania (approx. 1890–1940s): nationalism and internationalism in Romanian projects for women's emancipation* (PhD thesis, Central European University).

32. See, for instance, Theodora-Eliza Văcărescu, who pursued a degree in sociology in order to get training in gender studies and also attended Central European University to get training in women's history. She is currently working in a communications and culture department as the most welcoming environment for pursuing her research and teaching interests in women's history from a feminist perspective. See http://www.fjsc.unibuc.ro/cadre-didactice/theodora-eliza-vacarescu (accessed 7 March 2016).

33. See especially the work done at Babeş-Bolyai University by the team led by Ioan Bolovan: http://hiphi.ubbcluj.ro/SDI.html (accessed 25 February 2016). Among the volumes published by this team are: Ioan Bolovan et al. (Eds) (2009) *Ciclul vieţii familiale la românii din Transilvania în a doua jumătate a sec. al XIX-lea şi începutul sec. XX* [The cycle of familial life among Romanians in the second half of the nineteenth century and the beginning of the twentieth century] (Cluj: Presa UniversitarănClujeană); Ioan Bolovan & Corneliu Pădurean (Eds) (2003) *Populaţie şi societate. Studii de demografie istorică a Transilvaniei (secolele XVIII–XX)* [Population and society. Studies of historical demography in Transylvania (eighteenth–twentieth centuries] (Cluj-Napoca: Presa Universitară Clujeană); Ioan Bolovan et al. (Eds) (2010) *În căutarea fericii: viaţa familială în spaţiul românesc în sec. XVIII–XX* [Searching for happiness. Familial life in the Romanian space in the eighteenth–twentieth centuries] (Cluj-Napoca: Presa Universitară Clujeană).

34. Alin Ciupală (2003) *Femeia în societatea românească a secolului al XIX-lea: între public şi privat* [Woman in the Romanian society of the nineteenth century: between public and private] (Bucharest: Editura Meridiane); Ghizela Cosma, Enikő Magyari-Vincze, & Ovidiu Pecican (Eds) (2002) *Prezenţe feminine: studii despre femei în România* [Feminine presences: studies about women in Romania] (Cluj: Editura Desiré); Mihaela Miroiu (2004) *Drumul către autonomie. teorii politice feministe* [The path towards autonomy: feminist political theories] (Iaşi: Polirom); Ghizela Cosma (2002) *Femeile şi politica în România. evoluţia dreptului de vot în perioada interbelică* [Women and politics in Romania: the evolution of the right to vote in the interwar period] (Cluj-Napoca: Presa Universitară Clujeană); Maria Bucur & Mihaela Miroiu (Eds) (2002) *Patriarhat şi emancipare în istoria gîndirii politice româneşti* [Patriarchy and emancipation in the history of Romanian political thought] (Iaşi: Polirom).

35. Luciana Jinga (2015) *Gen şi reprezentare în România comunistă. 1945–1989* [Gender and representation in communist Romania 1945–1989] (Iaşi: Polirom).

36. Constanţa Vintilă-Ghiţulescu (2012) *În şalvari şi cu işlic. Biserică, sexualitate, căsătorie şi divorţ în Ţara Românească a secolului al XVIII-lea* [In shalvari and with an islic: church, sexuality, marriage, and divorce in Wallachia in the eighteenth century] (Bucharest: Humanitas); Radu Pavel Gheo & Dan Lungu (Eds) (2008) *Tovarăşe de drum: experienţa feminină în communism* [Travelling fellows: the female experience under communism] (Iaşi: Polirom); Zoltán Rostás & Theodora-Eliza Văcărescu (2008) *Cealaltă jumătate a istoriei. femei povestind* [The other half of history: women telling stories] (Bucharest: Curtea Veche).

Women's History at the Cutting Edge in Japan

Rui Kohiyama

ABSTRACT

This essay explains first how women's history developed in Japan, referencing early research on the topic. Then, it will discuss the arguments about the shift from women's history to gender history, the necessity of which has been loudly insisted on since the middle of the 1990s. Third, it will explain the organizational development as observed in the establishment of the Gender History Association of Japan in which I myself participated and served as the second president from 2008 to 2010. The fourth point considered in the essay is the realignment of the Science Council of Japan to include more women and the resultant efforts on the part of practitioners of women's/gender history to change history textbooks for high school students to accommodate gendered viewpoints. Finally, the essay will discuss the task of gendering contact zones, colonialism and empire with particular attention to the issue of 'comfort women'.

For our round table in Jinan, I prepared a short essay for reading. As I have been requested to write an expanded paper for this journal, simply rewriting would not suffice. Reviewing the entire construction of the original paper, I decided to tackle the theme again from scratch and look at the cutting edge of women's history in Japan rather than answering directly all five questions raised by Prof. Chen Yen in the roundtable. In particular I will not deal with the issues surrounding gendered geography, which has not yet obtained much attention as a specific field of research among historians in Japan although I have identified several works in the field.[1]

In this essay, I will first explain briefly how women's history developed in Japan, referencing early research on the topic. Then, I will discuss the arguments about the shift from women's history to gender history, the necessity of which has been loudly insisted on since the middle of the 1990s. Third, I will explain the organizational development as observed in the establishment of the Gender History Association of Japan in which I myself participated and served as the second president from 2008 to 2010. The fourth point I wish to consider is the realignment of the Science Council of Japan to include more women and the resultant efforts on the part of practitioners of women's/gender history to change history textbooks for high school students to accommodate gendered viewpoints. Finally, I will discuss the task of gendering contact zones, colonialism and empire with particular attention to the issue of 'comfort women'.

A Brief Historiography of Women's History in Japan

According to Hiroko Nagano, a historian of the Edo period teaching at Chuo University, Tokyo, the development of women's history in Japan can be divided roughly into three periods.[2] The first is from 1930s to 1970s. The period begins with Itsue Takamure's (legendary independent historian and poet, 1894–1964) energetic work on matriarchy in ancient Japan, which was first published in 1938.[3] After World War II, as women gained the right to vote, several women's history books appeared one after another. The most popular among them was *Japanese Women's History* by Kiyoshi Inoue (1913–2001),[4] a professor emeritus at the University of Kyoto, who wrote the history from the Marxist perspective, the most influential meta-narrative among Japanese historians in those days. In the 1970s, interest in women's everyday life rose and many local study groups emerged to probe for ordinary women's past and their experiences. Representing this trend, Nobuhiko Murakami (1909–1983), an independent writer, published four volumes of *Japanese Women's History in the Meiji Period* between 1969 and 1972, in which he emphasized the importance of ordinary women and their everyday experiences in presenting women's history.[5] Murakami's work intended to criticize Inoue's Marxist narrative for its monolithic description of women's history leading toward emancipation, its narrow focus on a few emancipatory leaders such as Eiko Kageyama, and its naïve grasp of sex discrimination as part of class oppression, expecting that the former would dissolve with the victory of the laboring class over the capitalists. Murakami's criticism provoked heated discussion among historians; these debates are recorded in a book, *Documents of Contentions Concerning Women's History* edited by Yukiko Kozai.[6] Tamae Mizuta, a historian of social thought, participated in this debate and pointed out that discrimination and oppression based on sex are different from those based on class, a claim that is now taken for granted.[7]

According to Hiroko Nagano, the major characteristic of this period (1930s–1970s) is that most of the works in the field of women's history had been produced outside of academia. In other words, few historians interested in the field of women's history held faculty positions in colleges and universities in those days. The problem might have come from the conservatism of the discipline of history under the institution of Seishi (the formal history provided by the government) supported by Koza (the chair system in universities), which defined the authoritative narrative of history so as to defend the establishment. Women's history as a new field was not accepted, either in the Seishi tradition or by the Koza system, and thus, the few women historians who were most likely to write women's history could not get positions in history departments at universities. Women's history was pursued and sustained mainly at the grassroots level and by independent writers during this period. Or, when the practitioner of women's history had a professional position, the person was usually a man specializing in the history of ordinary people. *Modernity for Women*, a volume edited by the Society for the Study of Women's History in the Modern Period (1978) seems to reflect such a situation.[8] This Society's leader was Masanao Kano, a professor of history at Waseda University, who was particularly interested in ordinary people and who wrote the introduction for the book. The eleven contributors were all women except one; they came from varied backgrounds, including high school teachers, company clerks, housewives, and graduate students. A few among them later obtained teaching positions in universities. I still remember clearly that when I began to look for a topic for my dissertation and was collecting books on Japanese women's history in the latter half of 1980s, most of them were autobiographical or oral narratives of ordinary women without any scholarly apparatus such as footnotes.

In retrospect, it seems obvious that the rise of interest in women's history in the 1970s was related to the rise of the second-wave feminism in the US and its worldwide influence. According to Chizuko Ueno, a sociologist, professor emeritus at the University of Tokyo, however, few Japanese professional historians interested in women's history from early on welcomed the feminist drive.[9] Probably this is due to the fact that they were mostly men who had been sympathetic toward women as belonging to the oppressed (laboring) class or as innocent ordinary people. Not surprisingly, they were uncomfortable with radical feminists, who attacked men in general as oppressors. In spite of the apparent passion in the 1970s to excavate women's experiences, the academic leadership for the feminist movement in Japan was provided not by historians but by sociologists.

The situation began to change only in the beginning of the second period that covers the years between the 1980s and the middle of the 1990s, when women's history and women historians began to challenge the establishment and claim a voice in the academy. In this process, according to Hiroko Nagano, Haruko Wakita's contribution was most significant. From 1977 to 1979, Wakita, now a professor emeritus at the University of Shiga Prefecture, directed a large-scale project funded by the Science Council of Japan that resulted in the establishment of the Research Society for Women's History.[10] She edited the project's output as *Japanese Women's History*, which was published in five volumes in 1982, by the University of Tokyo Press, one of the most prestigious university presses in Japan.[11] She also led the publication of *Bibliography of Researches in Women's History* in two volumes (1983 and 1988), also published by the University of Tokyo Press.[12] The contributions to the five volumes came from independent women historians, women scholars who wrote women's history with academic posts in fields other than history, and male historians who stood at the center of Japanese academia. Wakita was the first awardee of the Nao Aoyama Prize for Women's History, which was established in 1986 to promote women's history in Japan.[13]

Masanao Kano, a professor emeritus at Waseda University and a leading historian of ordinary people, criticized these volumes of *Japanese Women's History* as the product of a 'cold science', unable to convey a 'sense of pain' of Japanese women who had suffered from oppression, and this criticism set off another round of controversy over the mission and methods of women's history.[14] And yet, the scholarly style and claims of objectivity seemed necessary in order to attain scholarly recognition.[15]

The 1980s saw the growth of feminist influence in academic circles, when some women's colleges and universities in Japan introduced 'women's studies' to their curriculum. Then, as it became increasingly easier for the Japanese to study abroad, a generation of young graduate students, unaware of the academic resistance in Japan, directly encountered the women's studies trend overseas. I belonged to this generation of graduate students and was first exposed to women's history as a prolific feminist field of study in the United States. After returning to Japan, I wrote a dissertation in the field of American women's history and submitted it to a Japanese university. My mentor in Japan was a renowned historian of the US and yet women's history was new to him. I believe that my dissertation was one of the first ones in Japan written in the Japanese language on the topic of US women. It was published by the University of Tokyo Press in 1992 and was awarded the Nao Aoyama Prize in the same year.[16] Meanwhile, the effort to find and locate Japanese women in history was vigorously pursued during this period and, by the beginning of the 1990s, women's history had obtained a limited recognition in Japanese historical academia.[17]

The third period in the historiography of women's history in Japan began around the middle of the 1990s and continues to this day. During this period, the necessity to shift from women's history to gender history has been the main theme in the academic field of history. The concept of 'gender' had been introduced to Japan by the beginning of the 1990s. Joan Scott's *Gender and the Politics of History* (1988) was translated and published in Japan in 1992.[18] But 'gender' only attracted serious attention in the field of history during the middle of the 1990s when Chizuko Ueno, a sociologist and theoretical leader of feminism in Japan, insisted on the importance of gendering history or shifting women's history to gender history in an article in an authoritative lecture series, *The History of Japan*, published by Iwanami Shoten, a renowned publishing house (1995).[19]

In fact, the necessity of such a shift was first asserted as early as 1984 by Hiroko Hasegawa, a professor at the University of Tokyo, although she did not use the terminology, 'gender'.[20] She had been trained in French social history and was under the influence of the *Annales* School. Her assertion was not fully accepted among Japanese historians of Japanese women's history at that time. But by the middle of the 1990s, the practitioners of women's history were ready to consider seriously the application of the concept of 'gender' in their works. Ueno suggested that as 'gender' asked how the differences between men, women and any other sexual categories were created, it would encompass men as well as other sexual categories in the study and that the marking of men as a constructed category would give equal importance to the public and the private spheres, thereby dissolving the imbalanced treatment of the latter (traditionally associated with women) as if it were a minor attachment to the former (traditionally associated with men and therefore, considered normative and universal).[21] In the 1990s as women's history was gaining a limited recognition in the discipline of history, women's historians in Japan (as elsewhere) were concerned about being 'ghettoized' by the ostensible segregation of women's history from the 'mainstream' of history as a narrative of unique but minor episodes. They welcomed the suggestion of 'gendering history' as a major tool to overcome such a walling-off. In what follows, I will elaborate on some of the important developments in the field of women's and gender history since the middle of the 1990s.

Women's History vs Gender History

Beginning in the 1990s, efforts to adopt gender history emerged in two kinds of knowledge quests: the first was about gays and lesbians, and the second was about manhood. In both fields, translations of Western scholarship appeared first: the most well-known among them were Eve Kosofsky Sedgwick, *Between Men: English literature and male homosocial desire* (1985) which appeared in translation in 2001,[22] and Thomas Kuhne (Ed.) *Manner-geschichte-Geschlechtergaschichte: Mannlichkeit im Wandel der Moderne* (1996) that appeared in translation in 1997.[23] By the early twenty-first century, publications in gendered history by Japanese scholars began to appear in print. It seems that the study of gays and lesbians preceded that on manhood and masculinities (as far as I can tell from looking at the library holdings at my university). When questioning the borderlines between the sexes and clarifying the 'construction' of men and women, gays and lesbians seemed to be the most hopeful and probable target of research as they sit just on the border. In fact, there are several books by individual Japanese authors in the field of homosexuality and homosexuals now, whereas most of the publications in the field of manhood and masculinities appear in the form of anthologies of short articles.[24] I know several Japanese graduate students who are plotting dissertations in the areas of LGBTQ or manhood and I expect to see more works in this area in the near future.

There is a definite tendency in Japan to imagine that women's history will be turned into gender history by adding studies of manhood, masculinities or homosexualities. In Japan as might be the case elsewhere, Joan Scott's methodology for analyzing how gender categories are constructed in relation to power at a certain time period has not been fully adopted by historians. This does not mean that the method is misunderstood[25] but rather suggests difficulty in applying the method, which not only requires particular sophistication and sensitivity but also is selective (in terms of texts and context) in its application.

Still, gender history that incorporates men's history and gay history is expected to contribute to the development of women's history by expanding the field of study, getting more men interested, and sounding more neutral and thus scholarly. Such developments could pave the way to becoming mainstream. Meanwhile, among some women's historians, there seems to be a deeply felt concern about this new trend. The studies of manhood, etc., are by and large focused on men, leaving women once again invisible. In Japan, despite decades of effort, women's historical experiences have just begun to be explored and we need more works focused on women, womanhood, femininities, and women's gendered power. Assuming 'neutrality' by opting for gender history rather than women's history might deprive women's history of its feminist edge or enthusiasm, which has been weak (compared to the US) from the outset as I have intimated above. When I edited with Natsuki Aruga our *Introduction to the History of Gender in the United States* (2010; published in Japanese), we had a tense discussion among editors and contributors about the title of the book: should we call it gender history rather than women's history?[26] We settled on gender history to highlight the inclusive message that 'gender' would convey, but we also worried, first, that this title might not reflect honestly the content, given that most of the chapters in the book addressed topics in women's history, and second, as the pretense of neutrality and innovation might obscure our 'old-fashioned' feminist aspirations. In the same series, historians of women's history in Britain entitled their book *Women's History in Modern Britain* (2006) while the historians of Germany called theirs *Gender in Modern Germany* (2009).[27] Clearly, there is no final consensus. I myself want to engrave women's presence in historical narratives but at the same time I hope to use the gender perspective in which women are placed in the web of power relations. In other words, I want to convey the political meaning of womanhood and politicize womanhood in my research and writing of history.

Organizational Development: women's history and gender history

Two remarkably important events in the organizational structure for women's/gender history since the turn of the century are (1) the establishment of the Gender History

Association of Japan in 2004 and (2) evidence of increased attention to women's and gender issues in general on the part of the Science Council of Japan.

The Gender History Association of Japan was established in 2004 as the first of its kind to be formally registered with the Science Council of Japan. Before this event, at least two important societies for the study of women's history had long been active in Japan—The Research Society for Women's History and the Society for Research on Women's History. The first was organized between 1977 and 1980 as Haruko Wakita pursued the large project supported by the Science Council of Japan (already mentioned above). It has long been based in the western part of Japan, especially in Kyoto. Haruko Wakita edited (with two other historians) *The Japanese Women's History* as early as 1987.[28] The other, the Society for Research on Women's History, was established in 1980. This society has been based mainly in Tokyo but it has been active in promoting local women's histories and has published *Collected Essays on Japanese Women's History* in ten volumes between 1997 and 1998 from Yoshikawa Kobunkan (an authoritative publisher for history books). Since 1990, the Society also edited four similarly titled books on Japanese women's history.[29]

The characteristics of the Gender History Association of Japan in comparison with the two women's history societies can be summarized in five points. First, as the naming suggests, this Association aims at analyzing history from a gender perspective rather than promoting women's history per se. Second, as stated above, the association has been registered with the Science Council of Japan since its beginning and formally claims the status of an academic organization. Third, the association encourages participation of not only practitioners of Japanese women's history but also those of other parts of the world. Fourth, the association promotes interdisciplinary studies of history by welcoming sociologists, anthropologists, scholars of literature, etc. Fifth, and finally, the association encourages international exchanges among scholars.

The Gender History Association has been based in Tokyo but is working to expand its membership nationwide. The current membership is a little over 300, and the association holds its annual meeting in December, followed by a symposium in the spring; the latter has usually been held outside of the Tokyo metropolitan area. The association's first president Hiroko Nagano took leadership in publishing (between 2009 and 2011) *Gender History* in eight volumes, inviting a wide variety of contributors. The titles of the eight volumes, *Economics and Consumer Society*, *Violence and War*, *Visual Representations and Music*, *Everyday Life and Welfare*, *Philosophy and Culture*, *Migration and Contact Zones*, *Power and Body*, and *Family and Education*,[30] demonstrate the range of interests among scholars of gender history in recent years.

Speaking from my experience in participating in this association and serving one term as president, one of the most attractive aspects of the association is that it facilitates exchanges among scholars of women's history specialized in different areas and nations in the world and in different time periods, who usually do not meet each other in those regular academic meetings that are organized according to traditional division of disciplines and of areas such as Japan, East Asia and the West. The eight volumes of *Gender History* mentioned above reflect these interdisciplinary and trans-regional approaches of the Gender History Association. On the other hand, this also makes it difficult to determine a common theme for organizing sessions and symposiums for the association because of the broad range of coverage it encompasses. Diversity in terms of time periods and areas often makes it difficult to set a common theme and focus for discussion. Thus, there were tendencies in the past symposiums sponsored by the association to deal more often with the modern period rather than others or with the Japanese history rather than others as a majority of members specialize either in the modern period or in Japanese history.

The establishment of the Gender History Association coincided with a reform in the Science Council of Japan in which inclusion of more women in its membership was one of the most important objectives. Between 1985 and 2000, one could find only one to three women in about two hundred members of the Science Council for each term.[31] In the seventeenth term (1997 to 2000), the Science Council established a special committee charged with addressing improvements in the environments for women scientists; the Science Council then stated that it will increase the percentage of women members to 10% over ten years. In the twentieth term (2006 to 2009), forty-two women acquired membership, about 18% of the total. In the current term (2015 to 2018), there are forty-eight women and two out of three vice-presidents are women although the president, a medical doctor, is a man.[32]

The Science Council of Japan has also set up several committees and subcommittees to evaluate women's participation in sciences in general since 2000 when the number of women members jumped from two to seven. These committees and subcommittees have met frequently and have sponsored numerous open symposiums and lectures to promote gender equality: 'Gender and Arts and Sciences in Japan', 'Scientific Research Fund and Women Scholars', 'Gender Equality in the World of Scholars', 'Sexual Harassment in the World of Arts and Sciences' in the eighteenth term (2000–2003); 'Science and Technology and Gender', 'Declining Birth Rate and Women', 'Law/Political Science and Gender', 'Human Security and Gender' in the nineteenth term (2003–2006); 'Body, Sex and Gender: Dialogue between Biology and Gender Studies', 'Future for Arts and Sciences and Society that Gender will Invite' in the twentieth term (2006–2009).[33]

More recent initiatives for gender equality in the Science Council of Japan are directly related to gender/women's history and I will discuss these in the next section.

Efforts to Integrate Gendered Historical Knowledge into Textbooks

In December 2009, the subcommittee of gender and history under the committee of history in the Science Council of Japan sponsored an open symposium, 'History Education and Gender'.[34]

In Japan after World War II, there have been several well-known instances of political and constitutional disputes over history textbooks. In the 'Ienaga Textbook Trial', the constitutionality of the textbook screening system was challenged by Saburo Ienaga (1913–2002), a professor emeritus at Tokyo University of Education. It took more than thirty years to resolve: in 1986 the Supreme Court declared that the system was constitutional.[35] More recently, a revisionist drive pursued by the right-wing conservatives such as the 'Japanese Society for History Textbook Reform' has provoked severe disputes among various parties such as historians, educators, local boards of education and politicians. The disputes over what kind of past should be transmitted to Japanese children have been widely reported in the media and the answers have affected Japan's relationship with Korea and China, both of which suffered from Japanese aggression in the modern period.[36] So, there has been much talk about history textbooks in Japan. However, discussion from a gender perspective was minimal in spite of keen attention to the question of how to write about the 'comfort women' episode in textbooks (see the next section of this article).

The 2009 symposium mentioned above was held in order to correct this neglect. There, scholars examined a wide range of historical narratives including not only textbooks but also historical novels and cartoons that might be even more influential in nurturing historical imagination among the general public. Based on the symposium, *Education of History and Gender: from textbooks to subculture* (edited by Hiroko Nagano and Toshiko Himeoka) came out in 2011; in this volume high school textbooks of Japanese and world histories are examined from the gender perspective mainly focused on women. That is, the editors and contributors examined how much of women's experiences were included or how women were described and treated in high school textbooks (part 1). It also explored in part 2 the treatment of women in history in other texts such as museum exhibitions or cartoons. The editors also made efforts to introduce comparative perspectives by including two contributions, one dealing with US school textbooks and another with museum exhibitions in Germany. Overall, the conclusion was that most of the scholarly outputs in the field of gender/women's history had not been integrated into textbooks for high school students and that women remain invisible in historical narratives, even in illustrated comics such as *Manga*, in which most of female characters were imaginary, that is, unnamed women who had never been located in history.[37]

This conclusion led the team of women's/gender historians involved to see the necessity of writing their own textbooks, to provide guidance to history teachers and others who had learned only traditional history focused on male-centered politics. In order to actually write such textbooks, they formed a 'study group for comparative gender history' and took Grants-in-Aid for Scientific Research from the Ministry of Education, Culture, Sports, Science and Technology from 2012 to 2014. The fruits of their work have just been published: *Gendered Japanese History* edited by Noriko Kurushima, Hiroko Nagano and Shimae Osa (2015) and *Gendered World History* edited by Miho Mitsunari, Toshiko Himeoka and Masako Kohama (2014).[38] The two volumes are intended to provide supplementary readings for high schools, colleges and universities and are therefore organized to complement existing history textbooks that are most commonly used in high schools.

The subtitle is, if translated literally, 'for a different reading of history', thereby expressing the passion that the editors bestowed on this project. *Gendered Japanese History* is a compact and readable guide to women's history in Japan. As for *Gendered World History*, I am a little bit disappointed as a historian on the United States because it diligently reflects the established bias of high school textbooks in treating Europe and China heavily and in carrying almost nothing for Americas even in the contemporary period. I believe, as Shiro Momoki has insisted elsewhere,[39] that world history must be constructed in an innovative way in which the established narrative divided by regions or countries be discarded, putting more focus on exchanges and contact zones.[40]

In any case, we in Japan have made vigorous efforts in recent years to make women's and gender history an integral part of historical study. However, the results are yet to be seen. *Education of History and Gender* (mentioned above) was published by Seikyu-sha (青弓社), a firm known for publishing books of philosophy and ideas: this probably indicates that women's and gender history is still considered an intellectual curiosity. Both *Gendered Japanese History* and *Gendered World History* were published by a leftist publisher, Otsuki Shoten (大月書店) known for its publication of books of the Marxist stamp. This might suggest that gendered history is still a radical project in Japan. In other words, these books that aim at integrating the narratives of women's and gender history into the major historical narratives have not yet attracted sufficient interest from the major publishers of history books, such as Yamakawa shoten (山川書店) for textbooks, Yoshikawa Kobunkan (吉川弘文館) for Japanese history or Iwanami shoten (岩波書店) and Chuo Koron sha (中央公論) for general readers.

Toward a Gendered Understanding of Contact Zones and Colonial Relations

In new critical histories of colonialism and empire, contact zones, cross-cultural encounters and racialization, gender is a key perspective in Japan just as it is in other parts of the world. I myself have mainly worked in this framework for the last ten years and have made efforts, first, to make women's presence visible in contact zones, cross-cultural encounters and colonial relationships and, second, to consider how the Japanese constructed their racial and national identity against the West as well as against the rest of Asia. In the 2000s, I participated in a project on the modern girl in East Asia, which investigated the relationships among empire, capital and gender.[41] Protestant women missionaries from the United States and their Japanese disciples, the major actors in contact zones, have always been my main subjects of research.[42]

Gender in colonial encounters has been particularly important and political in Japan because of the 'comfort women' controversy. I can find forty titles under the keyword of 'comfort women' in the holdings of my university. Most of these books were published in the 1990s and the 2000s as testimonies, records, compiled primary materials, monographs and accusations. Recent titles seem to show that efforts are being made to include 'comfort women' in the general narrative of history or at least to discuss this controversial topic within the framework of gender studies.[43]

Throughout the 1990s and until around 2005, serious controversies burst out over the issue of including in history textbooks for secondary schools any information or analysis about the wartime use of 'comfort women'. Already in 1993, Chief Cabinet Secretary Kono had publicly apologized for the Japanese military's involvement in the forced sexual coercion of these women from Korea and China and in 1995, at the fiftieth memorial of the end of the Pacific War, our Prime Minister Murayama expressed sincere regret over Japanese colonial rule and aggression in Asia. In 1993, all the history textbooks for high schools began to address the 'comfort women' episode and in 1997 all the history textbooks for middle schools began to do the same. However, a backlash followed immediately. Conservatives argued in their strained interpretation that teaching about sexual exploitation in junior high schools would be harmful to young and immature students. In 1997, the Japan Society for History Textbook Reform was organized and began its vigorous attack on the narrative of history textbooks in general and, in particular, on the insertion of this 'shameful' 'comfort women' episode in the narrative. They pointed to several cases in which testimonies by persons concerned were found to be fabricated or inaccurate and insisted—falsely—that 'comfort women' had not existed. As of now, with the surge of conservatism and nationalism in the age of globalization, none of the Japanese history textbooks for junior high schools mention 'comfort women' and the majority of those for high schools mention the episode only euphoniously without using the words, 'comfort women'.[44]

In this context, gender historians interested in contact zones or imperialism find themselves challenged not only to clarify how the system of 'comfort women' worked and how unique the system was, in comparison with other forms of sexual abuse during wartime, but also to present an understanding of how and why such a peculiar system could exist, in relation to wider social, cultural and historical backgrounds. Such scholarly efforts obviously have political significance, the possibility to repel or curtail the reactionary drive that is very strong in today's Japan.

Research and publications on the trafficking of women, gendered militarism and women's migration might provide a broader understanding of the context for the phenomenon of 'comfort women'. We already have a significant number of publications on these themes and many of these publications have been pursued in relation to the construction of manhood, men's identity and their behavior (including their sexual behavior).[45] There are also works analyzing Japanese imperialism from a gender perspective: the library search engine of my university hits twelve books under the keywords of 'empire and Japan and gender'. The catalogue of the National Diet Library lists twenty items under the same keywords.[46] The works in this field seem to be still in the rudimentary stage as many of them are collections of short articles. I expect to see more publications on such topics that will provide a multilayered understanding of the Japanese imperialism.

In sum, there have been many achievements in women's and gender history in Japan over the past two decades. Apart from abundant production in the field, monographs as well as dissertations, we have seen some important theoretical and organizational developments as well as vigorous efforts to integrate women's/gender history into the major historical narratives and to pursue gendered analysis on contact zones, imperialism and international exchanges. However, I would like to conclude by pointing out just one of the many concerns that arise as I pursue historical research in Japan, namely, the lack of efforts to build archives (to collect and preserve primary materials). In July and August this year, I had wonderful opportunities to visit with two old women in their eighties. They showed me some materials that passed down to them from their grandmother who is the target of my current research. The materials included letters from 1920s and a beautiful Christmas card from 1893 written by their mother (the daughter of my research target). Of course I got some of them photocopied but we (the old women and I) wondered together who was going to take care of these precious materials after they are gone. We do not have many local historical societies, nor do we have local libraries willing to accept artifacts left by ordinary women in Japan. My fantasy/hope is that women's universities like the one for which I work will take the lead and set up archives for women's history in the very near future.

Notes

1. 村田陽平 (2009) 『空間の男性学』 [Men's Studies on Space]京都大学出版会 ; 神谷浩夫他訳 (2002) 『ジェンダーの地理学』 [Gender and Geography]古今書院 ; ジリアン・

ローズ (吉田容子他訳) (2001)『フェミニズムと地理学』[Feminism and Geography]地人書房。Yuko Nishikawa's books on this topic include: (1998)『借家と持ち家の文学史』[History of Literature on Renting and Owning Houses]三省堂and (2004)『住まいと家族をめぐる物語』[Stories of Houses and Families]集英社新書。杉本星子・小林大祐・西川祐子 (2015)『ニュータウンの「夢」建て直します』[Rebuilding 'Dreams' of New Towns]昭和堂。

2. 長野ひろ子(2006年4月)「日本におけるジェンダー史と学術の再構築」[Gender History and Reconstruction of Arts and Sciences in Japan]『歴史評論』672, pp. 2–16頁。

3. 高群逸枝 (1938)『母系制の研究』[A Study on Matriarchy]恒星社厚生閣。

4. 井上清 (1949)『日本女性史』[Japanese Women's History]三一書房。

5. 村上信彦 (1969-1972)『明治女性史』[Women's History in the Meiji Period]全四巻、理論社。

6. 古庄ゆき子編 (1987)『資料女性史論争』[Documents of Contentions Concerning Women's History]ドメス出版。

7. 水田珠枝 (1973)『女性解放思想の歩み』[History of Thoughts on Women's Liberation]岩波書店。

8. 近代女性史研究会編 (1978)『女たちの近代』[Modernity for Women]柏書房。

9. 上野千鶴子 (1995)「歴史学とフェミニズム――「女性史」を越えて」[History and Feminism: Beyond 'Women's History']『岩波講座日本通史』別巻1、岩波書店、pp. 158–159。

10. As for this society and its history, see http://whs.html.xdomain.jp/history.html (accessed 31 March 2016).

11. 女性史総合研究会編 (1982)『日本女性史』[Japanese Women's History]全五巻　東京大学出版会。

12. 女性史総合研究会編 (1983)『日本女性史研究文献目録』東京大学出版会。同 (1988)『日本女性史研究文献目録II 1982–1986』。

13. She received the award for editing (1985)『母性を問う』[Questioning Maternity]上・下、人文書院。

14. 長野、p. 13 note 11。

15. Speaking from the current academic standard, the five volumes did not follow sufficiently the academic style in their lack of notes and bibliography.

16. 小檜山ルイ(1992)『アメリカ婦人宣教師』[American Women Missionaries]東京大学出版会。

17. As evidence, Hiroko Nagano points out that in 1990s, local histories edited and published by local governments began to absorb part of outputs by local women's historians and that the authoritative historical narrative, exemplified by *The History of Japan* [日本通史] published by Iwanami Shoten, which gave only limited space to women's history (長野, p. 15).

18. ジョーン・スコット (荻野美穂訳) (1992)『ジェンダーと歴史学』[Gender and the Politics of History]平凡社。

19. 上野。

20. 長谷川博子 (1984年5月)「女・男・子どもの関係史にむけて――女性史研究の発展的解消」[Toward the History between Women, Men and Children: overcoming the framework of women's history]『思想』719号。

21. 上野、pp. 176–178。

22. 上原早苗・亀澤美由紀訳 (2001)『男同士の絆』[Between Men]名古屋大学出版会。

23. 星野治彦訳 (1997)『男の歴史』[Mannergeschichte-Geschlechtergaschichte: Mannlichkeit im Wandel der Moderne]柏書房。

24. Examples of the books by the single author are 前川直哉 (2011)『男同士の絆』[Ties between Men]筑摩書房 ; 本合陽 (2012)『絨毯の下絵』[A Design for a Carpet] 研究社 ; 匠雅音 (2013)『ゲイの誕生』[Invention of Gay]. It seems that more works have come from the field of literature so far. Important compilations on manhood are 阿部恒久・大日方純夫・天野正子編 (2006)『「男らしさ」の現代史』[Contemporary History of 'Manliness']日本経済評論社 ; 荻野美穂編 (2009)『＜性＞の分割線』[A

Dividing Line for Sexuality]青弓社；大本喜美子・貴堂嘉之編 (2010)『ジェンダーと社会』[Gender and Society]旬報社。

25. For example, Scott's method is explained clearly in 加藤千香子「「男性史」と歴史学」['History of Men' and Historical Science]大本喜美子・貴堂嘉之編、pp. 28–37。

26. 有賀夏紀・小檜山ルイ編著 (2010)『アメリカ・ジェンダー史研究入門』[Introduction to the History of Gender in the United States]青木書店。

27. 川村貞枝・今井けい編 (2006)『イギリス近現代女性史研究入門』[Women's History in Modern Britain] 青木書店; 姫岡とし子・川越修編 (2009)『ドイツ近現代ジェンダー史入門』[Gender in Modern Germany] 青木書店。

28. See the home page of the society: http://whs.html.xdomain.jp/history.html (accessed 4 April 2016); 脇田晴子・林玲子・永原和子 (1987)『日本女性史』[Japanese Women's History]吉川弘文館。

29. See the homepage of the society: https://sites.google.com/a/sogojoseishi.com/zong-he-nue-xing-shi-xue-hui/ (accessed 4 April 2016); 総合女性史研究会編 (1997–1998)『日本女性史論集』[Collections of Articles on Japanese Women's History]全10巻、吉川弘文館。同 (1992)『日本女性の歴史　性、愛、家族』[Japanese Women's History: Sex, Love and Family]角川書店。同 (1993)『日本女性の歴史　女のはたらき』[Japanese Women's History: Women's Work]角川書店。同 (2000)『資料にみる日本女性のあゆみ』[Records of Japanese Women's History]吉川弘文館。同 (2010)『時代を生きた女性たち　新・日本女性通史』[Women in History: a new history of Japanese women]朝日新聞出版. Noriyo Hayakawa is one of the early leaders of this group and reported many of the works in Noriyo Hayakawa (1991) The Development of Women's History in Japan, in Karen Offen, Ruth Roach Pierson & Jane Rendall (Eds) *Writing Women's History: international perspectives* (Bloomington: Indiana University Press), pp. 171–179.

30. The series was published by Akashi Shoten. For details, see http://www.akashi.co.jp/search/s2913.html (accessed 4 April 2016).

31. Only about 200 people are members of the Science Council, with has about 2000 cooperative members.

32. 長野ひろ子 (2007)「日本学術会議の再編とジェンダー枠の動向について」[Reforms in the Science Council of Japan and Gender Quota]『女性史学』17、pp. 52–59; 日本学術会議会員一覧 http://www.scj.go.jp/ja/scj/member/ (accessed 4 April 2016).

33. 長野、2007、pp. 54–57。

34. 長野ひろ子・姫岡とし子編著 (2011)『歴史教育とジェンダー』[Education of History and Gender]青弓社、p. 11。

35. 教科書検定訴訟を支援する全国連絡会 (1998)『家永教科書裁判のすべて』[Ienaga Textbook Trials]民衆社。

36. 小熊英二・上野陽子 (2003)『＜癒し＞のナショナリズム』[Therapeutic Nationalism]慶應義塾大学出版会。「つくる会のあゆみ」[History of the Society] http://www.tsukurukai.com/aboutus/ayumi.html (accessed on 20 April 2016).

37. 長野ひろ子・姫岡とし子編著。

38. 久留島典子・長志珠江・長野ひろ子編著 (2015)『歴史を読み替える　ジェンダーから見た日本史』[Gendered Japanese History]大月書店；三成美保・小浜正子・姫岡とし子編著 (2014)『歴史を読み替える　ジェンダーから見た世界史』[Gendered World History]大月書店。

39. 長野ひろ子・姫岡とし子編著、第11章。

40. In Japan, few positions are allocated to historians of the US and the Americas in history departments in universities. They are usually in the departments of political science, international relations, liberal arts, literature, etc. The Japanese generally think that the US does not have history. However, second only to those of Japanese women's history, practitioners of US women's history are the major force in the Gender History Association.

41. This project based at Ochanomizu Women's University was pursued in collaboration with the team working on the 'Modern Girl around the World' then at the University of Washington. The outcome of the project was published as 伊藤るり・坂元ひろ子・タニ・E・

バーロウ編著 (2010)『モダンガールと植民地的近代』[Modern Girls and Colonial Modernity]岩波書店in which I wrote a chapter on Hani Motoko.

42. Since I wrote (1992)『アメリカ婦人宣教師』[Women Missionaries from the US]東京大学出版会, I have written many articles on the topic and many of them try to clarify the nature of the U.S. expansion to Asia.

43. https://opac.library.twcu.ac.jp/opac/opac_search/?lang=0&amode=2&appname=&version=&kywd=従軍慰安婦&x=27&y=14 (accessed 17 April 2016). Searching the National Diet Library catalogue, you will find 201 books under the keywords of comfort women and history.

44. 安丸良夫 (2009年3月)「「従軍慰安婦」問題と歴史認識」[The Problem of 'Comfort Women' and the Interpretation of History]『学術の動向』、pp. 76–78。新しい歴史をつくる会ホームページhttp://www.tsukurukai.com/index.html (accessed 17 April 2016).

45. For example, the National Diet Library catalogue shows 335 books under the keywords of women and migration and 161 books under the keyword of trafficking (人身取引).

46. https://opac.library.twcu.ac.jp/opac/opac_search/?lang=0&amode=2&appname=Netscape&version=5&cmode=0&smode=0&kywd=日本%E3%80%80帝国%E3%80%80ジェンダー; https://ndlopac.ndl.go.jp/F/GPRJXK1Q21PU88LMGA4QGK1DF21N34U17EETTUA4MY66N4ETX5-19993?func=find-b&request=日本%E3%80%80帝国%E3%80%80ジェンダー&find_code=WRD&adjacent=N&filter_code_4=WSL&filter_request_4=&x=34&y=11 (both accessed 18 April 2016).

Women's and Gender Studies of the Russian Past: two contemporary trends

Natalia Pushkareva and Maria Zolotukhina

ABSTRACT
The paper addresses the pressing question of why, in Russia, gender studies in history still have to prove their worth in the Russian academic world — and in the general public; why they operate in two discourses, and how common ground can be found between these. The first discourse is that of traditional gender roles which tends to legitimize the role of a woman as important but complementary with regard to the role of a man. The second discourse casts serious doubt on the naturalness or the essentialist predicament of the mutual complementarity of gender roles. The adherents to such a methodological perspective imply a feminist reflection both in posing their questions and choosing their approach to empirical data.

Women's and gender history is definitely an integral part of a transnational development in academic humanities research - Women's and Gender Studies - that originated about forty years ago. Although intellectual inquiry in this field of study in Russia has been continuous and consistent ever since *women's history* emerged as a continuation of a more than two-hundred-year-long interest in *women's issues* in anthropology and history,[1] gender studies in history still have to prove their worth in the Russian academic world.

Back in the mid-1970s, when one of us (Natalia Pushkareva) became interested in the topic of *women in history*, nobody in Russia wanted to follow this path; it seemed extraordinarily difficult to demonstrate the significance of the topic for analytical approaches in the humanities in general and for thematic schemes of our particular subject in our own country. In the meantime, the 1970s and 1980s in Western Europe and the United States were an era in which there was almost exponential growth in the number of scholars interested in seeking answers to the question of whether there was a specifically *female* history.

Like our 'professional sisters' in Europe and North America, Russian pioneers in women's history topics encountered a lack of understanding in academy; we were criticized and could find no support. The creators of the *Gender and History* journal (which celebrated its 25th anniversary in 2015) complained about the difficulties of translating this new knowledge into the common language of historical narratives. However, believing that they were in the vanguard of the new trend and being certain it had a future, female researchers from Western Europe, the US, etc. wasted little time in uniting their efforts. For each of the female adepts and followers of the new academic field, 'history of women' also meant 'history *for* women' - a means to explain social injustice and a search for ways to overcome it. They quickly formed a circle of like-minded female scholars, created laboratories, projects, and organized conferences in their respective countries. A number of European and American colleagues viewed their goal as achieving equal inclusion of women's and gender history in the realm of methodological reflection, by which we understand testing new approaches to empirical data and historical sources.

One could not even have dreamt about that in Russia!

Up until the early 1990s Russian historical studies had been hemmed in by strict instructions to view any social process from the standpoint of Marxist and Leninist theory. Marriage between Marxism and Feminism, as you may remember, was unlucky.[2] The classics that had worked within this theoretical paradigm had not been particularly generous to women. Possibly (and gender theory hints precisely at that) the causes of such negligence were to be found in the authors' own life stories. Karl Marx was not really interested in his wife's needs, and indifferent to those of his daughters. Friedrich Engels, who had two female partners but never married, was childless. V. I. Lenin developed but one passionate love and also had no children. It did not seem to occur to them to reflect on women being special, having their own particular forms of logic, female-specific language, their own public and group interests, or forms of self-expression. For them the women's movement was not more than a social ferment meant to accelerate the social process - or, in their case, revolution.[3]

By the early 1990s, when the collapse of the USSR was approaching, along with the collapse of the theoretical grounding of Soviet historical methods, historians from many European and other western countries had come to the conclusion that it would be wise to coordinate internationally the efforts of those who shared the conviction of the importance of women's history. The creation of the International Federation for Research in Women's History (IFRWH) and its entry into the International Committee of Historical Sciences was confirmed in 1987. In 1990 at the 17th International Congress of Historical Sciences in Madrid; one of us (Natalia Pushkareva) represented the field of Russian women's history. She had recently authored the book *Women of Ancient Russia*, which was published in 1989 during a wave of interest in women's history in Russia; its sales of over 100,000 copies couldn't quench the Russian public's thirst for the history of everyday life that included women![4]

Around the same time as the international congress in Madrid, a collective of mostly European historians, headed by French historians Georges Duby and Michelle Perrot, published the Italian version of their immense 'History of Women in the West from Antiquity to the 20th Century'.[5] These five volumes provided a synthesis of studies on many topics concerning the history of women, the results of the preceding twenty years of research in Europe and North America. More than seventy scholars of different ethnic backgrounds representing a range of countries (mainly female scholars from France, although there were eleven men among the authors, also representing several countries) presented new themes to explore and new research topics that had originated thanks to the emergence of this prolific trend in the branches of science that explore the past. Among those topics (that were outlined in the book and were later researched in greater depth and more actively) were female labor (both paid and unpaid, i.e. work performed in the family), the history of motherhood and various forms of termination of pregnancy, the history of everyday life as the history of practices in the context of the emotions of people who had lived in the past, the history of private life and changing notions of friendship, love, happiness, family conflicts and family joys (and not simply the history of fertility and marriage rates and forms of lineage — the way it had been researched before by historical demographers), the history of women's rights and lack thereof, the women's movement and the evolution of feminism.

Some critics of this publication from the United States took notice of the absence (or, rather, insufficiency) of topics related to the history of sexual culture, as well as the peculiar avoidance of such aspects as the interaction of cultures, migration, and the effects of colonialism. By that time these topics had already attracted considerable attention in the United States. Nothing, however, was said about the East European side of women's history; the case of Russia was almost forgotten and women's history in Russia was only presented in the last volume of this edition and covered the twentieth century. That short chapter was written by a French sovietologist, Francoise Navailh, as at that time there were no distinguished experts writing on these issues in Russia. Prior to the Internet and the forging of closer relationships between Russian and Western scholars, information about new Western texts was effectively unavailable in the USSR. Researchers in Russia had addressed women's issues only by talking about the 'resolution of the women's question' in the course of the Bolshevik Revolution, by which they meant the right of women to work the same as men.

The publication of these five volumes allowed 'women's history' to cross the first threshold on its way to legitimacy in Western Europe: the new field of research could no longer be ignored. Women had found their own history. This women's Pentateuch would soon be translated into many European languages, as well as Chinese and Japanese. Russia kept silent (the translation of this edition was delayed by a long period - thirty years; the last two volumes appeared in 2015). Among the Slavic countries Poland had become the first to advocate for women's history: in the early 1930s—at an earlier international congress of historical sciences in Warsaw, it was Polish scholar Lucia Charewiczowa who proposed the study of 'women's history' for its own sake.[6]

In various countries in Eastern Europe, the publication of these five volumes provoked the investigation of national 'women's histories'.[7] In their subsequent publications women's history was being reconstructed with the additions of new topics for consideration; these now encompassed notions and ideas about femininity and masculinity in different eras that had been forgotten, as well as the topic of regime change and the politics of sexuality, the status of female intellectuals and writers, and the access of all women to civil rights. Blank spots of Russian and universal history were soon filled in.

The most heated debates, however, were caused by questions of how to move forward and how to further develop the field. Should it ideologically serve feminism? Russian historians gave a negative answer to this question — except for some 'laboratories of gender studies' in universities in provincial cities. Some scholars in France did not think that this new history should necessarily be of a 'feminist' kind. Many of the French and especially British scholars (and this is particularly noticeable in the style that pervaded 'History of Women in the West') believed that while women's and gender history is *naturally fueled* by the women's movement and feminism, it seemed to them that it was necessary to study the social past of women in many aspects, taking into consideration both the discourse of the venerable universal history (that feminists labeled as patriarchal) and of feminism, the history of the struggle for women's rights over the course of recorded history, the examination of individuals and groups of women of historical significance, and the effect that historical events had had on women. Women's history became a spearhead for historical revisionism, seeking to challenge or expand the traditional historical consensus. Some historians insisted that, compared to class, social and group hierarchies were more important than gender ones (as non-antagonistic differences and conflicts between the sexes). It would suffice to mention the work of Sheila Rowbotham — a distinguished British scholar of neo-Marxist views.[8]

Another reason why no common ground could be found among the Russian scholars of women's history lay in the fact that there was no agreement as to whether to accept the concept 'gender' in the Russian language, much less the concept of gender in academic field of history. Over two decades the concept of gender had made its triumphant victory in many fields in the Western humanities, initially in psychology and sociology. But not all women's historians were so sure that the term is really needed — as an addition. It is important to note that in 2010 (in Amsterdam) the delegates of the IFRWH voted against replacing the word 'women's' with 'gender' in the name of their organization. They refused to consider writing women's history as a *past stage* of historiography's development.

While arguing for the independent significance of women's history, some members of the IFRWH criticized gender studies for its somewhat abstract nature among historical fields. They claimed that gender history was an attempt at mimicry to appear academically respectable, calling it a euphemization of women's issues and the women's cause. Ultimately such an approach could have led to an erasing of patriarchal structures and the central task (posed by feminists) to look for mutual complementarity between the sexes (genders) everywhere but also to examine power relations and hierarchies between them.

Female historical scholars continued to argue about what was to be understood by gender history — simply the *social history of the relations between genders*, the history of gender asymmetry, disproportions and discriminations. Or should gender history be a *part of cultural history*, the history of mentalities (inspired by the linguistic turn)? Should one attempt to reconstruct not as much the past (the question being whether it is at all possible to do so — to dig that far and that deep) but to prioritize reflections of the past in historical sources? Perhaps, one has to specify the task of gender history as examining the changing notions about the female and male, masculinity and femininity, the history of the transformation of cultural knowledge about gender differences?

Constructivist, anti-essentialist discourse ('one is not born, but rather becomes a woman', as Simone de Beauvoir reminded us), an interest in the ways in which individuals resisted imposed social standards as well as an interest in identity crises at critical turning points in history provided common ground for the two ways of understanding gender history in Europe and the United States. Both these directions in the development of women's and gender history actively called for the revision of prior accounts of historical events and phenomena from the standpoint of how the factor of sex and gender (those of the participants and creators of the narratives) had affected them. At the turn of the twenty-first century the new social realities resulting from rapid globalization have raised the issue of intersectionality with regards to how power and gender relate to class, ethnic groups or race.

The desire to understand what effect major recognized historical events have had on women, to review historical phenomena from the perspective of gender (e.g., did women have a Renaissance, or did The Great French Revolution liberate women)[9] became one more uniting factor both for the female adherents of treating gender history as a social history of one gender being oppressed by another and for those women scholars who stand by the intensified research in the field of the social psychology of gender and the history of mentalities. Such studies helped promote peace between those who viewed history as a guide to action (feminists) and those who saw history as the science that helps to reflect upon the world and oneself.[10]

Historical bias was changing the look of cultural history itself by allowing the presentation of social change as a continuous and unlimited intersectionality — an intersection and mutual influence of opinions and a struggle between concepts. Using an analysis of the seeming inescapable reproduction of gender contradictions and asymmetry in the past, political scientists developed a clearer sense of the complexities and difficulties modern democracies face.[11]

The interest in the history of private life that had not been adequately described in the past and was once viewed as secondary in importance became a fashionable research topic in the 1970s and 1980s.[12] By the late 1990s this interest shifted towards analyzing the history of the growth of women's rights (as well as how it was recorded in documents), the examination of individual and groups of women of historical significance, the history of how women were drawn into the public sphere, how they became involved in management, foreign policy, diplomacy, science and male-dominated professions or occupations, how gender power relations in the twentieth century had been reorganized in the face of rapid social change in totalitarian regimes (Stalin's Russia, Hitler's Germany, Mao's China).[13] The concept of *agency* (the capacity to act as an engaged subject) formulated by American historians and previously unused by their European counterparts suddenly occupied a significant place in studies of women's history.[14] Reflections on the history and consequences of the masculinization of women from the beginning of the Renaissance and Modern Age to the present turned into a collective work (three volumes) of the history of virility.[15] Both female adherents of the pragmatic use of history to justify feminist campaigns and cultural anthropologists who have developed the concept of gender over the last fifteen to twenty years began to look at biographical history in a new way. Research of individual life strategies is becoming a preferred path for studying social realities of the present and the past.[16] Autobiographies, autoginographies,[17] ego-documents have been completely rehabilitated; previously much less significance had been ascribed to them. A new level of trust in personal archives made the analysis of the anthropological element of any faceless social process a key pillar of European and American academic pursuits, encouraging researchers everywhere to listen to and hear individual voices, voices that at times did not form one chorus.[18]

Together with the interest in the intimate sphere, the history of male and female sexuality that had long been 'off limits' in the curriculum of western liberal arts courses was rehabilitated as well. The background for this process was third-wave feminism, which recognized shortcomings of the second wave and distinguished itself around issues of sexuality, challenging female heterosexuality and celebrating sexuality as a means of female empowerment. Since 1997 the *International Journal of Sexuality and Gender Studies* (a print journal, but now offered online) has been publishing articles where one can discover new aspects of well-known themes, such as the stances of Christianity and Islam with regard to the sexual life of men and women, the issue of individual freedom and forced heterosexuality, the history of sexology as a science. Even wars are now being studied from the standpoint of the history of sexuality[19] (including issues of marital fidelity among conscripted soldiers, prostitution in time of war, the problem of rape by armies during military conflict).[20]

Since the turn of the twenty-first century, the comparison of female everyday practices in foraging, housework, childrearing, sexual relations and emotional life on different continents, regions and countries has become a new concern (previously handled exclusively by ethnographers) and has provided new common ground for those who write women's and gender history. Among issues debated in the last fifteen years are the questions of how cultural transfer and globalization affect gender relations, the gender consequences of political, ideological and confessional trends. Migration in general, gender politics and immigration, gender differences in the rates and forms of naturalization have become compelling problems in the 2010s.[21] It now seemed obvious that there are so many difficulties in finding solutions for these issues that there was no room for the polarization of activists (feminists) and intellectuals, who tend to view the history of women and femininity as first and foremost the history of ideas. For some researchers it became evident that this history could be reconstructed, without being ideologically engaged (in this case from a feminist standpoint).[22]

This brief overview sheds some light on the evolution of women's and gender history over the past twenty-five years of its development in Europe and the United States. In Russia it took a rather different turn, one closely related to political developments during the post-Soviet period.

It is not accidental that this topic was at the center of discussion of our roundtable at the 22nd International Congress of Historical Sciences in China (August 2015). Using both discourses of women's and gender history in Western historical science as a background, the first related to feminism, its past and present and social history and the second associated with a linguistic and cultural (linguocultural, in the vocabulary of the Russian historiographical tradition) turn towards researching the past as the history of emotions and reflections, it seems important to define the place that Russian historians and their achievements occupy in studying, women, gender orders and asymmetries in the past and the present.

Russian women's history emerged as a field of investigation in the 1980s and experienced a period of tremendous attention during the 1990s, when the publication boom occurred. During those 'the gender 1990s'[23] (which in the history of Russian politics are now typically referred to as 'the wild 1990s'), these academic efforts were supported by grants from Western foundations, such as the Open Society Foundation, the MacArthur Foundation, IREX, and the Fulbright program, and attracted a huge number of young intellectuals.[24] It is quite obvious that women and gender studies in Russian academia of the 1990s found themselves literally in the position of Danae: the intellectual thought of the West appeared to them in the form of a golden rain of financial grants. Thanks to these grants, dozens of works from Western languages were translated into Russian, including the first three volumes of the distinguished five-volume *A History of Women in the West* (the last two volumes were only published in 2015).[25]

Ten or twelve years afterward, this publication boom collapsed. Today the question of recognition for women's history and women's issues is posed less by an adversarial (hostile) environment of the traditional androcentric historical science, than by a mounting public indifference accompanied by the assertion that its time has already passed, along with the period when there were plenty of Western grants for its development. There are a quite a few skeptics who accuse Russian specialists in the field of women's studies of having failed to reach an agreement (over the course of some twenty-five years) as to what precisely constitutes the focus of their work, or to determine the message that informs their research efforts.[26] There are also two types of discourse in contemporary Russia that more or less confront each other even as they claim to be marked as gender discourses in Russian historiography (just as in the historiography of other post-Soviet states, notably Ukraine and Belarus).

The *first* discourse, as we indicated earlier, is one of support for traditional gender roles. Fundamentally, it legitimizes the role of a woman as important as but complementary to the role of a man.[27] Olga A. Voronina, a Soviet/Russian philosopher has called this discourse 'the false theory of gender'[28] and Alla V. Kirilina, a linguist, asserts that we are in fact dealing with a return to the old prefeminist narrative about the subject.[29] It was precisely this old approach that informed the renaming of numerous centers, laboratories, and departments in Russia's humanities research institutions. Those which used to study the sociology of sex differences (ethnology of sex differences, sociology and ethnology of the family, the history of family and demographics) are now called centers, chairs, departments and laboratories of women and gender studies. Among those who, in our opinion, are experienced professional contributors to women's history but now tend to distance themselves from the feminist rhetoric and ideology are numerous professors.[30] These are all scholars with Doctoral degrees (according to the Russian Federation system which requires academics to defend two theses - first, a Candidate (PhD) and then, the next level up, a Doctorate) who are professors and often have their own academic schools of thought. Their students (both male and female), not to mention themselves, some of whom were once students of gender programs or courses have become independent researchers (again, men and women) but remain impervious to feminist ideology. In an academic sense they were raised and socialized in the spirit of traditionalism. Even such widely-renowned professors as Olga Khasbulatova (Ivanovo), without the works of whom it would be impossible to imagine studying the women's liberal movement in nineteenth-century Russia,[31] or Lorina Repina who in fact had introduced the very term *gender* into our historiography (she is now the head of the series 'Adam and Eve: The Almanac of Women's History' and is present in this Congress in China)[32] are unlikely to call themselves earnest feminists when they are giving a lecture or a speech.

The *second* discourse casts serious doubt on the naturalness or the 'essentialist' predicament of the mutual complementarity of gender roles in the past and in the present. It is important to underscore the fact that the adherents of such a methodological perspective share a different approach to the collection of empirical data, since the very questions that they pose imply a different type of feminist reflection. We see ourselves among this less numerous group and dare to hope that our ranks are bound to grow.[33] These are the truly renowned gender historians, often the authors of books and editors of collective works written from novel points of view.

Many of these anti-essentialist historians are younger than those of the first generation who produced the first type of women's history narratives (O. Khasbulatova, L. Repina). They witnessed the process of introducing the concept of gender to Russia at a time when their own life experiences were open to its better perception. This is why their gender studies of the past are based on the sources of the particular regions they come from. Special attention needs to be drawn to the fact that the authors listed above are not only younger than the 'traditionalists', but they also represent academia in different parts of Russia (i.e. from different regions of Russia which, in fact, gave rise to the first gender centers as nurseries of free thought).[34] This is why in the current decade the route that we have chosen (via annual academic conferences held by the Russian Association for Research in Women's History — set up at Natalia Pushkareva's initiative in 2002 — RARWH (see *www.rarwh.ru*) — is the only possible form of developing women's studies (in different fields). RARWH is the only organization in the entire Russian academic community that succeeds in bringing together three to four hundred applicants (usually more than a hundred of them attend personally) representing fifty-two cities of Russia - from Kaliningrad in the West to Vladivostok in the East. Financial matters are always resolved together with the university which provides the opportunity and the premises for carrying out conferences. In 2016 the site for the conference is Smolensk, close to the border with Belarus; in 2017 the tenth conference will take place in the Russian North, at Arkhangelsk at the White Sea and will address the 'power of the weak' - the issues of women's leadership.

Still, the various approaches to the interpretation of the contents of gender studies have become so greatly intertwined that one and the same academic center or institute may be home - at least as far as the historical sciences in Russia are concerned — to the followers (both female and male) of differing ideas and approaches. And in our view this is just fine. The above-mentioned conferences are informal political events, made possible by the existence of a dissenting web-like community, which can be nothing else at this point. At least we strongly believe that our Russian association of women historians (which has more than four hundred members from more than two dozen universities) and our conferences represent a truly new phenomenon and are not politically ineffective (formal and stable) post-Communist institutions.

The history of how the proponents of women's history in Russia have combined their efforts with those who do gender research in the sciences about the past is a history of how an integrating element could be found for the researchers (mostly women and only a few men) with different (and sometimes conflicting) ideas and attitudes. In this history one may find the beginning of new ventures that are capable of updating modern social theories, social, political and cultural anthropology, the history of everyday practices and gender history. Reflecting on this, a good friend and colleague Irina Zherebkina, the founder of the Ukrainian school of gender studies (1998–2011), views the development of a somewhat utopian and yet rather pragmatic notion of a 'democracy as a hereafter': as the principal task for all our Academies of sciences. She talks about democracy in the future which she ingeniously calls 'post-terrorist, post-totalitarian, tolerant',[35] in other words providing opportunities to raise new, unusual topics for research, bringing together efforts of a variety of approaches, including the older ones.

The second effect of the web-like (as opposed to hierarchical) perception of the two discourses (the first effect, as noted above, is mutual tolerance) may in fact become the principal one from a methodological standpoint. The concept implied is the one about the erasure of the distinction between Western and non-Western intellectual strategies in the practices of the social sciences and arts.

What are we to offer to the Western social theorists to whom we looked with hope, without criticism or doubt, back in the 1990s, simply wishing to repeat after them? Can we (in fact, will we be able in the future) to come up with our own methods, ideas, interpretations and understandings? Russian studies of women's issues that have emerged within the framework of traditionalist discourse have contributed a great deal, so that the conditions for the dissemination of the principal ideas of feminist epistemology and their further development are in place. We all are focusing now on micro-politics and we challenge the second wave's paradigm as to what is, or is not, good for women, and tend to employ post-structuralist understandings of gender and sexuality.

We will be frank with you: gender studies remain marginalized in Russian ethnology and history. What appears to be equally puzzling if not disturbing is the fact that, generally speaking, gender 'literacy' remains in a nascent form and, in particular, it has not had any noticeable effect on the secondary education curriculum or on the overall understanding of gender-related concepts by the broader public, where explicitly anti-feminist statements are becoming increasingly frequent. In fact, the very word feminism is often used as a curse.

The more descriptive 'women's history' is clearly more successful with Russian readers than is gender history, as is attested by substantial sales of the book on the worlds of Russian women by V. V. Ponomareva and L. B. Khoroshilova.[36]

The coexistence of these two discourses (which we refer to as 'essentialist'[37] and 'feminist') continues to separate the community of researchers and creates competition between research centers, not to mention a strong divergence between 'theory' and 'practice' — the research that takes place in the centers along with contemporary political activism. Today's new Russian ideologues increase financial support to NGOs (including those with academic and educational purposes) to support the study of conventional forms of social processes (in particular, the family with a traditional division of roles) and to weaken the penetration of Western ideas into the Russian women's movement and women's academic research (including historical research), and to make unacceptable Western 'permissive' attitudes towards sexual minorities, gay marriage, small families and reduced fertility as well as feminism itself.[38] This is viewed as a way of strengthening the position of neopatriarchy while invoking the 'spiritual bondage' of Russian culture.

It is not only possible but also necessary to overcome the division of these two discourses in academia and different centers of women and gender studies. One must be heard and understood not just by those who represent your own academic group but by others as well. We have to meet at conferences and develop dialogues between feminist historians and those who work within the framework of what some call the 'false theory of gender'. We have to become more tolerant and find new ways to exchange opinions.

The transformation of the 'other's' concept into 'your own' (including the transformation of the 'other's' feminism in its Russian version) must take the form of an individual interiorization of some of its concepts. Mastering the theories themselves via their cultural appropriation is not a loss or a defect in itself. Agreeing to disagree, tolerance for different points of view, and a willingness to listen and understand the logic of an argument, and to entertain the evidence on which it rests, are the basis for future interaction between those who are currently confrontational and irreconcilable.

In today's Russian society (including the academic community), there is little or no acceptance or tolerance of the actions by contemporary so-called feminist groups such as Femen and Pussy Riot. This is one of the reasons why female historians in the Russian academic world, writing the history of women and gender, find themselves with a serious academic mission. By telling the stories of the earlier Russian women's movement, we are trying to convince our contemporaries that feminism is not strictly a 'Western thing' and that, in fact, it is deeply rooted in the country's past, together with a long tradition of women's social and political activism.[39] Therefore, the only path forward for all of us, the historians, is that of collaborative work, combining our efforts instead of remaining separate, using our daily intellectual interaction, mundane at times and yet so necessary in its everyday routine, to explain our views and attitudes and share our historical research by speaking a language that will reach a broader audience. The multifaceted history of women — using the examples from the past to inform the present — may help to demonstrate that, both in Russia and beyond Russia, feminism is multifaceted and that, over time, many varieties of feminism have existed.

We find it difficult not to be concerned with the fact that, in Russia, the critical feminist potential of gender theory has been neutralized in its political form whereas the public discourse seems to be shifting, unnoticeably but persistently, to concern itself exclusively with the so-called 'male issues'. This is why it is of utmost importance for us to build upon the results of the more active interaction of the 1990s between the Russian and Western academic circles by taking into consideration new challenges and concerns. We have to embody true feminist solidarity while supporting one another's academic efforts. Russia is continuing to undergo changes and gender theory provides us all with an important tool to ensure that these changes are favorable to women.

Notes

1. Natalia L. Pushkareva (2002) *Russian Women: past and present: history of investigation of women's issues in Russian and foreign sciences. 1800–2000. Some data for bibliography* (Moscow: Ladomir) [Russkaya zhenshchina: istorija I sovremennost. Istoriya izuchenija zhenskoj temy v russkoj i zarubezhnoj nauke. 1800–2000. Materialy k bibliografii/Наталья Л. Пушкарева. Русская женщина: история и современность. История изучения 'женской темы' русской и зарубежной наукой. 1800–2000: Материалы к библиографии. Москва: Ладомир]. In the notes, the Russian titles are given in Cyrillic and in transliterated form, along with an English translation. For place of publication, St Petersburg is shown as StP and Moscow as M.
2. Natalia L. Pushkareva (2002) Women's Issue in Marxist Theory (why has the marriage between Marxism and feminism failed?), *Woman in Russian Society* Zhenskij vopros v teorii marxizma (pochemu brak marxizma s feminizmom okazzalsja neschstlivym Zhenschina v rossijskom obschestve/Пушкарева Н.Л. Женский вопрос в теории марксизма (почему брак марксизма с феминизмом оказался несчастливым?) // Женщина в российском обществе], 1, pp. 2–14.
3. Vladimir Lenin (1958) On the Tasks of Women's Workers' Movement in the Soviet Republic [O zadachah zhenskogo rabochego dvizhenija v Sovetskoj respublike / О задачах женского рабочего движения в Советской республике], in Vladimir Lenin, *Complete Set of Works* [*Polnoe sobranie sochinenij*/Ленин В.И. Полн. Собр. Соч] (Moscow, Politizdat), vol 39, p.

200; Mary Evans (1987) Engels: materialism and morality, in J. Sayers, M. Evans & N. Redclift (Eds) (1987) *Engels Revisited: new feminist essays* (London: Tavistock).

4. Natalia L. Pushkareva (1989) *Women of Ancient Russia* [Zhenschiny Drevmej Rusi] (Moscow: Mysl); Anna V. Belova, Igor V. Groshev & Pavel P. Scherbinin (2014) The Role of an Individual in Creating 'Women's History' in Russian Historiography [A Rol lichnosti v sozdanii napravlenija 'zhenskoj istorii' v otechestvennoj istoriografii], *Herald of Tambov University. History Series* [Vestnik Tambovskogo universiteta, serija istorii], 10 (138), pp. 171-176. [Женщины Древней Руси. М.: Мысль; Белова А.В., Грошев И.В., Щербинин П.П. (2014) Роль личности в создании направления «женской истории» в отечественной историографии // Вестник Тамбовского университета. Серия История. 10(138). с. 171–176.]

5. Pauline Schmitt Pantel (Ed.) (1994). *History of Women in the West, Volume I: From Ancient Goddesses to Christian Saints* (Cambridge, MA: Harvard University Press). Translated by Arthur Goldhammer. Series edited by Georgers Duby and Michelle Perrot; Christiane Klapisch-Zuber (Ed.) (1994). *History of Women in the West, Volume II: Silences of the Middle Ages* (Cambridge, MA: Harvard University Press). Translated by Arthur Goldhammer. Series edited edited by Georgers Duby and Michelle Perrot; Natalie Zemon Davis & Arlette Farge (Eds) (1995) *History of Women in the West, Volume III: Renaissance and the Enlightment Paradoxes* (Cambridge, MA: Harvard University Press). Translated by Arthur Goldhammer; Genevieve Fraisse (Ed.) (1993). *History of Women in the West. Volume IV: Emerging Feminism from Revolution to World War* (Cambridge, MA: Harvard University Press). Translated by Arthur Goldhammer; Francoise Thebaud (Ed.) (1996). *History of Women in the West, Volume V: Toward a Cultural Identity in the Twentieth Century* (Cambridge, MA: Harvard University Press). Translated by Arthur Goldhammer.

6. Lucia Charewiczowa (1933) Est-il fondé d'écrire une histoire spéciale de la femme?, in La Pologne au 7e Congrès International des sciences historiques, 1, Warsaw, pp. 309–313; Charewiczowa, Luja (1938) Kobieta w dawnej Polsce: do okresu rozbiorow. Lwow: Panstwowe Wydawnictwo Ksiazek Szkolych; "Drukarnia Polska" Boleslawa Wystoucha.

7. Maria Bucur (2008) An Archepelago of Stories: gender history in Eastern Europe, *American Historical Review*, 113 (5), pp. 1375–1389; Andrea Petö & Judith Szapor (2007) The State of Women's and Gender History in Eastern Europe: the case of Hungary, *Journal of Women's History*, 19 (1), pp. 160–166.

8. Sheila Rowbotham (1992) *Hidden from History: 300 years of women's oppression and the fight against it* (London: Pluto Press, first published 1973); Sheila Rowbotham (1997) *A Century of Women: the history of women in Britain and the United States* (London: Viking).

9. Joan Kelly (1984) Did Women have a Renaissance?, in *Women, History & Theory: the essays of Joan Kelly* (Chicago: The University of Chicago Press), pp. 19–50; Françoise Thébaud (2007) Writing Women's and Gender History in France: a national narrative?, *Journal of Women's History*, 19 (1), pp. 167–172.

10. Юкина Ирина Игоревна. Русский феминизм как вызов современности. СПб.: Алетейя, 2007. —544 с. Yukina Irina Igorevna Russkiy feminism kak vyzov sovremennost (Saint Petersbourg: Aleteya, 2007). Irina I Yukina (2007) *Russian Feminism as a Challenge for Modernity* (Sant Petersbourg: Aleteya).

11. Русские женщины в лабиринте равноправия (Очерки политической теории и истории). — М.: РИК Русанова, 1998; Aivazova S.G. Russkiye zhenschiny v labirinte ravnopravia [Айвазова С.Г.Русские женщины в лабиринте равноправия]; Svetlana G. Aivazova (1998) *Russian Women in the Labyrinth of Equality (Essays on political theory and history)* (Moscow: RIK Rusanova); Айвазова С. Г. Российские выборы: гендерное прочтение. М.: Консорциум женских неправительственных объединений; Институт социологии РАН, 2008; Ayvazova Svetlana Gregor'yevna Rossiyskiye vybory: gednernoye prochtenye, M Konsortsium nepravitel'stvennykh ob'yedineniy: Institut sotsiologii RAN; Svetlana G. Aivazova (2008) *Looking at the Russian Elections through the Prism of Gender* (M. Consortium of women NGOs. Institute of Sociology. RAS)

12. Philippe Ariès & Georges Duby (Eds) (1992–1998) *A History of Private Life, 5 volumes* (Cambridge, MA: Harvard University Press).

13. Beth Holmgren (1993) *Women's Works in Stalin's Time: on Lidiia Chukovskaia and Nadezhda Mandelstam* (Bloomington: Indiana University Press); Elizabeth A. Wood (1997) *The Baba and the Comrade: gender and politics in Revolutionary Russia* (Bloomington: Indiana University Press); Renate Bridenthal, Atina Grossmann & Marion Kaplan (1984) *When Biology Became Destiny: women in Weimar and Nazi Germany* (New York: New Feminist Library, Monthly Review Press); Gail Hershatter & Wang Zheng (2008) Chinese History: a useful category of gender analysis, *American Historical Review*, 113 (5), pp. 1404–1421; Gail Hershatter (2007) *Women in China's Long Twentieth Century* (Berkeley: University of California Press); Ермаков Александр Михайлович. 'Школа немецкой нации': женская Служба труда в нацистской Германии. Ярославль: Изд–во Яросл. Гос.-ПедУн–та, 2006 Yermakov Aleksandr Mikhaylovich . 'shkola nemetskoy natsii': zhenskaya Sluzhba truda v natsistskoy Germanii; Yaroslavl': Izd - vo Yarosl . Gos.PedUn - ta , 2006; Alexander M. Yermakov (2006) 'The school of German nation': women's labour service in the Nazi Germany. (Yaroslavl: Isdatel'stvo Yarosl. Gos. Ped. Un-ta); Ермаков А. М. Союз немецких девушек в нацистской Германии. Ярославль: Изд–во ЯГПУ, 2007; Yermakov A. M. Soyuz nemetskikh devushek v natsistskoy Germanii . Yaroslavl' : Izd - vo YAGPU, 2007; Alexander M. Yermakov (2007) The Union of German young women in the Nazi Germany (Yaroslavl: Isdatel'stvo Yarosl. Gos. Ped. Un-ta); *Дампилон, Надежда Баировна.* Динамика роли женщины в условиях модернизации китайского общества. Улан-Удэ: Бурятский гос. университет, 2011; Dampilon, Nadezhda Bairovna . Dinamika roli zhenshchiny v usloviyakh modernizatsii kitayskogo obshchestva. Ulan–Ude: Buryatskiy gos. universitet, 2011; Nadezhda B. Dampilon (2011) *The Dynamics of Women's Role in the Chinese Society going through Modernization* (Ulan–Ude: Buryatscky Gos. Universitet).

14. Бессмертный Юрий Львович. Жизнь и смерть в средние века. Очерки демографической истории Франции. Москва: Наука, 1991; Bessmertnyy Yuriy L'vovich, Zhizn' i smert' v sredniye veka. Ocherki demograficheskoy istorii Frantsii (Moskva: Nauka); Yuri L. Bessmertny (1991) *Life and Death in the Middle Ages: essays on demographic history of France* (Moscow: Nauka); Варьяш Ольга Игоревна. Пиренейские тетради: право, общество, власть и человек в средние века. М.:Наука, 2006; Var'yash Ol'ga Igorevna. Pireneyskiye tetradi: pravo , obshchestvo , vlast' i chelovek v sredniye veka (Moscow: Nauka, 2006); Olga I. Variash (2006) *The Pyrenees notes: law, society, power and individual in the Middle Ages* (M: Nauka) Ястребицкая Алла Львовна (отв. ред.) Культура и общество в Средние века и раннее Новое время. М.: ИНИОН, 1998; Yastrebitskaya Alla L'vovna (otv. Red.) Kul'tura i obshchestvo v Sredniye veka i ranneye Novoye vremya (Moscow: INION); Alla L. Yastrebitskaya (Ed.) (1998) *Culture and Society in the Middle Ages and Early Modern Times* (Moscow: INION); Пушкарева Наталья Львовна. Женщины России и Европы на пороге Нового времени (Moscow: ИЭА РАН); Pushkareva Natal'ya L'vovna . Zhenshchiny Rossii i Yevropy na poroge Novogo vremeni (Moscow: IEA RAN); Natalia L. Pushkareva. (1996) *Women of Russia and Europe on the Threshold of Modern Times* (Moscow: IEA RAN).

15. Alain Corbin, *Jean*-Jacques Courtine & Georges Vigarello (2011) in Georges Vigarello (Ed.) *Histoire de la virilité* (T. I. L'invention de la virilité. De l'Antiquité aux Lumières; Alain Corbin (Ed)T. II Le triomphe de la virilité. Le XIXe siècle; Jean-Jacques Courtine (Ed.) T. III La Virilité en crise? *XXe–XXIe siècle* (Paris: Edicion du Soleil).

16. Wilhelm Schroeder (1979) *Kollektive Biografien in den historischen Socialforschungen. Lebenslauf und Gesellschaft* (Stuttgart: Stuttgart Klett-Cotta); Cristel Eckart, Ursula Jaerisch & Helgard Kramer (1979) *Frauenarbeit in Familie und Fabrik. Eine Untersuchung von Bedingungen und Barrieren der Interessenwahrnehmung von Industriearbeiterinnen* (Frankfurt am Main: Campus Verlag); Judith Shapiro (1981) Anthropology and the Study of Gender, in Elizabeth Langland & Walter Gove (Eds) *A Feminist Perspective in the Academy* (Shapiro: University of Chicago Press) pp. 110–115. Jutta Lauth (1993) Gleichwertig, andersartig, nachrangig. Variationen zum Geschlechterkonflikt aus ethnologischer Sicht, in Anette Kreis-Schink,

Brigitte Liebig & Kathrin Schafroth (Eds) *Feministische Perspektiven in der Wissenschaft* (Zurich: Verl. der Fachvereine) pp. 53–55.

17. Domna Stanton (1987) Autogynography: is the subject different? In Domna C. Stanton (Ed.) *The Female Autograph: theory and practice of autobiography from the tenth to the twentieth century* (Chicago: University of Chicago Press), p. 4.

18. Пушкарева Наталья Львовна. У истоков женской автобиографии в России // Филологические науки. № 3. 2000. С. 62–70; Pushkareva Natal'ya L'vovna. U istokov zhenskoy avtobiografii v Rossii // Filologicheskiye nauki. № 3. 2000. S. 62–70; Natalia L. Pushkareva (2000) The origins of female autobiographies in Russia, in *Philologicheskiye nauki* (3) pp. 62–70; Савкина Ирина Леонардовна. Пишу себя. Автодокументальные женские тексты в русской литературе первой половины XIX века. Tampiere. University of Tampere. 2001; Savkina Irina Leonardovna. Pishu sebya. Avtodokumental'nyye zhenskiye teksty v russkoy literature pervoy poloviny XIX veka. Tampiere. Universitet Tampere. 2001; Irina L. Savkina (2001) *I Am Writing Myself: autobiographical female texts in Russian literature of the first half of the nineteenth century* (Tampiere: University of Tampere); Самофалова Елена Александровна. Жанровые признаки семейной хроники в женской мемуарно–автобиографической прозе второй половины XIX века. Курск: Курский государственный педагогический университет, 2015; Samofalova Yelena Aleksandrovna. Zhanrovyye priznaki semeynoy khroniki v zhenskoy memuarno - avtobiograficheskoy proze vtoroy poloviny XIX veka (Kursk: Kurskiy gosudarstvennyy pedagogicheskiy universitet); Yelena A. Samofalova (2015) *Genre Characteristics of Family Chronicle in Female Memoires and Autobiographical Prose in the Second Half of the Nineteenth Century* (Kursk: Kurskii gosudarstvenny pedagogichesky universitet).

19. Кон Игорь Семенович (1997) *Клубничка на березке: Сексуальная культура в России* (М.: ОГИ); Kon Igor' Semenovich Klubnichka na berezke: Seksual'naya kul'tura v Rossii. M .: OGI , 1997; Igor S. Kon (1997) *Strawberry on a Birch-tree: sexual culture in Russia* (M: OGI) or Igor S. Kon (1995) *The Sexual Revolution in Russia: from the age of the Czars to Today* (New York: Free Press).

20. E.g. James Jones (2001) Acceptable Homosexual Heterosexuality: Hanns Heinz Ewers's Fundvogel and National Socialist Ideology, *International Journal of Sexuality and Gender Studies*, 6 (4), pp. 319–327; Мухина Зинара Зиевна, Пушкарева Наталья Львовна. Женщина и женское в традиционной русской сексуальной культуре (до и после великих реформ XIX века) // Вестник Пермского университета. Серия: История. 2012. Выпуск № 3 (20). С. 43–55; Mukhina Zinara Ziyevna, Pushkareva Natal'ya L'vovna . Zhenshchina i zhenskoye v traditsionnoy russkoy seksual'noy kul'ture (do i posle velikikh reform XIX veka) // Vestnik Permskogo universiteta. Seriya: Istoriya. 2012. No. 3 Vypusk (20). S. 43–55; Zinara Z.Mukhina & Natalia L.Pushkareva (2012) Women and Female in Traditional Russian *Secular* Culture (before and after the Great reforms of the *nineteenth* century) *Vestnik Permskogo Universiteta. History* 3 (20), pp. 43–55; Щербинин Павел Женщина и война в поэзии и повседневности Первой мировой войны 1914–1918 гг. Тамбов: Изд–во ТГУ, 2001; Shcherbinin Pavel Zhenshchinana i voyna v poezii i povsednevnosti Pervoy mirovoy voyny 1914–1918 gg. Tambov : Izd - vo TGU, 2001; Pavel P. Scherbinin (2001) *Women and War in Poetry and Everyday Life of the First World War of 1914–1918* (Tambov: Isdatel'stvo TGU); Щербинин Павел Петрович. Военный фактор в повседневной жизни русской женщины в XVIII–начале XX в. Тамбов: Изд–во «Юлис», 2004; *Pavel Petrovich* Shcherbinin (2004) Voyennyy faktor v povsednevnoy zhizni russkoy zhenshchiny v XVIII– XX v nachale (Tambov : Izd — vo 'Yulis'); Pavel. P. Scherbinin (2004) *Military Factor in the Everyday Life of Russian Women of seventeenth–early twentieth centuries* (Tambov: Julis); Дубина Вера Сергеевна Болезненная тема второй мировой войны: память о сексуальном насилии по обе стороны фронта // Вестник Российского государственного гуманитарного университета. 2011. № 17 . С. 47–54; Dubina Vera Sergeyevna Boleznennaya tema vtoroy mirovoy voyny : pamyat' o seksual'nom nasilii po obe storony fronta // Vestnik Rossiyskogo gosudarstvennogo gumanitarnogo universiteta. 2011. № 17 . S. 47–54; *Vera S. Dubina (2011) A Painful Theme for World War II: memory*

of sexual violence along both sides, Vestnik Rossiiskogo Gosudarstvennogo Gumanitarnogo Universiteta, *17, pp. 47–54.*

21. S. Cenads (2003) *Women Asylum Seekers in the UK: a gender perspective: some facts and figures* (London: Refugee Women's Resource Project 'Asylum Aid'); Lauren Engle (2004) *The World in Motion: short essays on migration and gender* (Geneva: International Organization for Migration).

22. Никонов Александр. Конец феминизма. Чем женщина отличается от человека. М. НЦ ЭНАС., 2005. Aleksandr Nikonov. Konetz feminizma. Chem zhenschina otlichaetsya ot cheloveka. (M. NTS ENAS, 2005). Aleksandr Nikonov (2005) *The end of feminism. How is a woman different from a human being* (Moscow: NTS ENAS).

23. Irina Zherebkina (2003) *The Gender 90's, or There Is No Phallos* (St Petersburg: Alleteya) Жеребкина, И.А. Гендерные 90–е, или Фаллоса не существует. СПб.: Алетейя, 2003.

24. Natalya L. Pushkareva (2014) Gendering Russian Historiography (Women's History in Russia: Status and Perspectives), in Marianna Muravyeva & Natalya Novikova (Eds) *Women's History in Russia: (re)establishing the field* (Cambridge, MA: Cambridge Scholars), pp. 2–16.

25. Georges Duby & Michelle Perrot (Eds) *A History of Women in the West,* translated in Russian (2009) (Natalya Pushkareva - Translation Editor) История женщин на Западе. В 5–ти томах. Т. 1 / Под общ. Ред. Ж.Дюби, М.Перро / Пер. с англ. Отв. редактор перевода Н.Л.Пушкарева. СПб.: Алетейя, 2005–2015

26. See, for example, Nikonov Op.cit, Alexander Genis Pyrrova pobeda feminizma Alexander Genis The Pyrrhe??? Victory of feminism; Antonov Социология семьи Alexander Nikonov; Никонов Александр. Конец феминизма. Чем женщина отличаесяот человека. Alexander Nikonov (2005) The eEnd of feminism. How is a woman different from a human being. Nikonov Aleksandr . Konets feminizma .Chem zhenshchina otlichayetsya ot cheloveka. Yekaterna Gadal Feminism or the Strategy of France's Doom = Yekaterna Gadal, http://katehon.com/ru/article/feminizm-ili-strategiya-gibeli-francii (accessed 16 January 2017). Feminism ili strategiya gibeli Frantsii = Екатерина Гадаль. Феминизм или стратегия гибели Франции, http://www.apn.ru/publications/print21045.htm; Oleg Novoselov The Truth about Feminism and Women's Fascism = Oleg Novoselov. Pravda o feminizme I zhenskov fashizme. = Олег Новоселовю правда о феминизме и женском фашизме http://nfor.org/stati/dom-i-semja/pravda-o-feminizme-i-zhenskom-fashizme.html (accessed 16 January 2017); S. A. Stroyev The Real Goal of Feminism =S.A. Stroyev. Istinnaja tsel' feminizma = С.Ф.Строев. Истинная цпль феминизма http://www.contrtv.ru/common/3430/ (accessed 16 January 2017); V. I. Krasikov (2006) You are not born a woman, you become one (2006) Exteme. *Interdisciplinary philosophical study of causes, forms and patterns of extremist mentality* Vodoloey. Moscow.= Zhenschinoy ne rozhdajutsya, eju stanovyatsya. *Mezhdistsiplinarnoye filosofskoye issledovaniye prichin, form y patternov extremistskogo soznaniya.* Vodoley Moskva = В.И.Красиков. (2006) Женщиной не рождаются, ей становятся. Междисциплинарное философское исследование причин, форм и паттернов экстремистского сознанияю Водолей. Москва. Also: Igor Kulagin. Feminism does not have a female face = Igor Kulagin. U feminiz,a ne zhenskoye litso = Игорь Кулагин. У феминизма не женское лицоhttp://menalmanah.narod.ru/rnet/face.html.

27. On the one hand at the time following more than seventy years of declared (proclaimed) equality of men and women there can be no mentioning of the male role viewed as superior and the female role as inferior in any official documents, including legislation. However, the traditional narrative finds many ways of presenting itself via media, pop culture, in the church-related sphere, and, of course, in part of academia; it underscores the deeply rooted belief that the traditional upbringing of women is the only 'right' one - oriented towards family, a wife' s role as her husband's helper (not as an autonomous person with clear ambitions and goals of her own). Such patterns and styles of upbringing emphasize the ability to remain calm and reserved and self-possessed, to comply, and to accept another's leadership and superiority. For instance, the book by V. Ponomareva and L . Khoroshilova (published three times - with a sophisticated page layout and numerous illustrations) fails

to address such issues as family violence against women or female sexuality (except for some of the related themes - such as single parenting by women) or female leadership while the very title claims a universalistic approach - the *World of Russian Women*. In general, one can say that broad discussions of such issues, which imply an existing wide spectrum of opinions, are not welcomed by the society as a whole. Since 2008 the symptoms or signs of neopatriarchy are quite obvious. This does not involve the letter of the law itself but has to do more with the practices and the public discourse, e.g. condemning abortion, refusing to discuss juvenile justice and family violence (e.g. the recent initiative on Facebook to share personal accounts of sexual abuse −−'I am not afraid to speak up'−−provoked major discussion with openly antifeminist rhetoric), intolerance towards gay parenting and gay issues in general, reducing women's destiny to traditional wife/mother roles.

28. Olga A. Voronina (1980) The Ideology of the Feminist Movement, in *USA: economics, politics, ideology*, no. 9, p. 38–49 = Olga Voronina (1980) Ideologiia feministskogo dvizheniya, in *SSHA: ekonomika, politika, ideologiia*, no. 9, pp. 38–49

29. Alla V. Kirilina [Алла В.Кирилина] (1999) Gender: the linguistic aspects [Gender: lingvisticheskie aspekty/ Гендер: лингвистические аспекты] (Moscow: Institut sociologii RAN), p. 54; Пономарева В.В., Хорошилова Л.Б. Мир русской женщины: воспитание, образование, судьба. XVIII—начало XX века (М: ООО «ТИД «Русское слово— РС», 2009; V. V. Ponomareva and L. B. Khoroshilova (2009) Mir russkoy zhenshchiny: vospitaniye, obrazovaniye, sud'ba . XVIII - nachalo XX veka (M: ООО « TID « Russkoye slovo - RS'; V. V. Ponomareva & L. B. Khoroshilova (2009) *The World of Russian Women: upbringing, education, fate (life-course) in the eighteenth–early twentieth century* (M :TID Russkoye slovo - RS). It was precisely due to the fact that this book had been written from an essentialist perspective that it was republished three times!

30. Tatyana B Kotlova (2003) *Russian Woman in a Provincial Town at the Turn of the nineteenth to twentieth century, 1890-1914* [Rossijskaya zhenshchina v provincial'nom gorode na rubezhe XIX–XX vv. 1890-1914/Российская женщина в провинциальном городе на рубеже XIX–XX вв. 1890–1914] (Ivanovo: IvGU); Scherbinin, *The Military Factor*; Rima N. Suleimanova (2011) *Women in Social and Political Life of Bashkiria in the Twentieth Century* [ZHenshchiny v obshchestvenno–politicheskoj zhizni Bashkirii HKH veka/ Женщины в общественно–политической жизни Башкирии XX века] (Yekaterinburg: UGU); Madina A. Tukueva (2006) *Gender as a Sociocultural Construct of the Adyg Society* [*Gender kak sociokul'turnyj konstrukt adygskogo obshchestva*/Гендер как социокультурный конструкт адыгского общества] (Nalchikm: KBGU); Valentina A. Veremenko (2007) *Families of the Nobility and State Policy in Russia* [*Dvoryanskaya sem'ya i gosudarstvennaya politika Rossii*/Дворянская семья и государственная политика России] (Spb: Dmitry Bulanin); Zinara Z. Mukhina (2015) *The Transformation of Women's Status in Russian Peasant Families of mid 19th-early 20th Centuries* [*Transformaciya statusa zhenshchiny v russkoj krest'yanskoj sem'e serediny XIX--nachala XXveka*/ Трансформация статуса женщины в русской крестьянской семье середины XIX--начала XX века].

31. Olga A. Khasbulatova (1994) Experience and Tradition of Women's Movement in Russia (1860-1917) (Ivanovo: Yunona) = Olga A. Hasbulatova (1994). Opyt i tradicii zhenskogo dvizheniya v Rossii (1860-1917 gg.) (Ivanovo: Yunona); Olga A. Khasbulatova (2001) State policy and women's movement in Russia (1900-2000) (Ivanovo, Yunona) = O. A. Hasbulatova Gosudarstvennaya politika i zhenskoe dvizhenie v Rossii (1900-2000 gg.) Ivanovo: Yunona; Ольга А.Хасбулатова (1994). Опыт и традиции женского движения в России (1860-1917 гг.). Иваново: Юнона), Ольга А. Хасбулатова (2001). Государственная политика и женское движение в России (1900-2000 гг.) (Иваново: Юнона)

32. Repina has been elected to the incoming Board/Bureau of the CISH (for 2015-2020). See Lorina P. Repina (2002) Women and Men in History: new perspectives on the historical past. Essays. A reader (M, Rossiiskaya politicheskaya enthiklopedia) = Repina L.P. ZHenshchiny i muzhchiny v istorii. Novaya kartina istoricheskogo proshlogo. Ocherki. Hrestomatiya. M.: Rossijskaya politicheskaya ehnciklopediya, 2002; Репина Л.П. Женщины и

мужчины в истории. Новая картина исторического прошлого. Очерки. Хрестоматия. М.: Российская политическая энциклопедия, 2002.

33. Anna V. Belova (2010) *The Four Ages of a Woman* [*Chetyre vozrasata zhenschiny*/ Четыре возраста женщины] (SPb: Aleteya); Natalya A. Mitsjuk (2013) *Women of the Russian Province of the Nineteenth to Early Twentieth Century: upbringing, education, social and cultural mileu and everyday life (based on materials of Smolensk guberniya)* [*Zhenschiny rossijskoj provincii XIX–XX veka: vospitanie, obrazovanie, sociokulturnoe prostransvo I povsednevnaja zhizn (na materialah Smolenskoj gubernii)*/ Мицюк Женщины российской провинции XIX – начала XX в.: воспитание, образование, социокультурное пространство и повседневная жизнь (на материалах Смоленской губернии)] (Smolensk: Svitok); Natalya A. Mitsjuk (2015) *The Birth of a Mother: subculture of motherhood in the upper class of industrial Russia* (Smolensk: SGT) = Natalia A. Mitsjuk (2015). Rozhdenie materi. Subkultura materinstva v vysshih slojah obschestva industrialnoj Rossii. (Smolensk: SGT); Мицюк Н.А. (2015) Рождение матери. Субкультура материнства в высших слоях общества индустриальной России. (Смоленск: СГТ)/; Marianna G. Muravoyva & Natalya L.Pushkaryova (Eds) (2012) *Violence in the History of Russian Everyday Life (XI–XXI Centuries)* (SPB, HSE) = M. G. Muravieva & N. L. Pushkareva N.L. (Eds) (2012) Bytovoe nasilie v istorii rossijskoj povsednevnosti (XI–XXI vv.) Sankt-Petersburg: VShE = Марианна Г.Муравьева, Наталья Л. Пушкарева (ред.) (2012) Бытовое насилие в истории российской повседневности (XI—XXI вв.) (СПб.: ВШЭ). Elena Gapova, Andrea Peto & Almira Usmanova (Eds.) (2002) *Gender Stories of Eastern Europe*. Minsk = Yelena Gapova, Andrea Peto and Al'mira Usmanova (2002) Gendernye istorii Vostochnoy Yevropy.Minsk. - Елена Гапова, Альмира Усманова и Андреа Пето (2002) Гендерные истории Восточной Европыю Минск; Maria V. Zolotukhina (1992) The Concept of Independence in Soviet and American families, in Phylis Lan Lin et al . (Eds) *Families: East and west* (Indianapolis: University of Indianapolis Press); Maria V. Zolotukhina, Maria V. Kotovskaya & Natalya V. Shalyguina (1993) *Envy Me, I Am A Woman!* [*Zavidujte, ja zhenschina*/ Завидуйте, я--женщина!] (Moscow: IEA); Maria V. Zolotukhina, Maria V. Kotovskaya & Natalya V. Shalyguina (1995) Social Functions of Gender in a Changing World in Russia, in Phylis Lan Lin & Weh-hui Tsai (Eds) *Marriage and the Family: a global perspective* (Indianapolis: University of Indianapolis Press).

34. Included here were centers in Petrozavodsk (Karelia), Murmansk (Kola Peninsula), Samara and Saratov (Volga region), Tver and Tambov (Central Russia), Rostov-on-Don (Southern Federal District (okrug) of Russia, Arkhangelsk (Russian North), where NGOs emerged in the first place. However in early 2000s due to the overall conservative turn in Russian politics, they reduced their activities and then terminated them altogether. The strongest ones were declared 'foreign agents' and were destroyed during the time that the NGOs which had been receiving Western grants for their development, were being attacked.

35. Irina A. Zherebkina (2000) 'Read *my wish…* ': *postmodernism, psychoanalisys. Feminism* ['*Prochti moe zhelanie…* ' *postmodernizm. psihoanaliz. feminism*/Прочти моё желание …' Постмодернизм. Психоанализ. Феминизм] (Moscow: Ideya-Press), p. 26.

36. See note 30 above.

37. In our view, advocates of the essentialist approach do not accept feminist theory as a methodological basis for research. Yet they view women's issues as special. They may incorporate a comparativist or holistic approach or aggregate more and more sources. In other words their grasp of facts is quite impressive and yet their interpretation (or lack thereof) is obvious. There needs to be a particular place for them in the current historiography.

38. Linda Racioppi & Katherine O'Sullivan (1997) *Women's Activism in Contemporary Russia* (Philadelphia: Temple University Press), pp. 47–50; Suvi Salmenniemi (2008)`Democratization and Gender in Contemporary Russia (London: Routledge), p. 264.

39. Western researchers have long been interested in Russian women's history, and in particular, the history of women's liberation efforts under the tsars, during the Russian Revolution, and in the USSR. But none of those early (1970s) works in English were translated into Russian until much later. For example, the landmark contribution of Richard Stites did not appear in

Russian until 2004. See Richard Stites (2004) Женское освободительное движение b России: Феминизм, нигилизм и большевизм (*Zhenskoe osvoboditel'noe dvizhenie v Rossii: feminizm, nigilizm i bol'shevism, 1860–1930/The Women's Liberation Movement in Russia: feminism, nihilism, and bolshevism* (Princeton: Princeton University Press, 1978, new edn 1991)] (Moscow: ROSSPEN). Another landmark work on this topic appeared first in German: Bianka Pietrow-Ennker (1999) *Russlands 'neue Menschen': Die Entwicklung der Frauenbewegung von den Anfängen bis zur Oktoberrevolution* (Frankfurt: Campus Verlag), was translated into Russian and published in 2005: 'НоВЫе ДЮДИ' России Развитие женскогодвижения от истоков ло Октябрьской революции (Moscow: RGGU).

Two other English-language authors have also been translated into Russian: Eve Levin and Laura Engelstein. See Eve Levin (1989) *Sex and Society in the World of the Orthodox Slavs: 900–1700* (Ithaca: Cornell University Press) translated as: Е. Левина (1999) *Секс и общество в мире православных славян 900–1700* ['А се грехи злые, смертные ... ' Любовь, эротика и сексуальная этика в доиндустриальной России (X - первая половина XIX в.)] М.Ладомир; Laura Engelstein (1992) *The Key to Happiness* (Ithaca: Cornell University Press) translated as: Лора Энгельштейн (1996) *Ключи счастья. Секс и поиски путей обновления России на рубеже XIX - XX веков* (Москва: Терра); (2003) *Castration and the Heavenly Kingdom: a Russian folktale* (Ithaca: Cornell University Press) translated as: Л. Энгельштейн (2002) *Скопцы и Царство Небесное: Скопческий путь к искуплению.* Авториз. Пер. С английского В.Михайлова при участии Е.Филипповой и Е.Левинтовой (М. НЛО).

Funding

This research was supported by a grant from Russian Scientific Fund for the Humanities [grant number 16-01-00136] and Russian Academy of Sciences Fundamental Research Program 'Russian Identity and Historical Memory'.

'A Glass Half Full'? Women's history in the UK

June Purvis

ABSTRACT

This article offers an overview of the development of women's history in the UK over the last twenty years or so. It is noted that over this period women's history has expanded massively, an expansion that has cut across national boundaries and drawn in scholars from other disciplines than History. Eight themes in women's history are identified as being prominent during this time—a focus on the modern period (post 1780), a strong empirical bent, a questioning of the dominance of a separate spheres discourse, a 'spatial turn', an interest in life stories and biographies, an interest in the women's suffrage movement, a 'religious turn' and a 'transnational turn'. Lastly, consideration is given to the influence of the digital revolution on the development and direction of women's history.

In 1995 I published an edited book titled *Women's History Britain, 1850–1945: an introduction.*[1] In my own chapter in this book I drew upon the work of many scholars as I outlined the development of women's history in the UK, from a concern with 'women worthies' in the nineteenth century, often a political or religious figure of some importance, to the more diverse field that it had become by 1995.[2] This textbook sold well and has now been complemented by others in the field.[3] Since 1995 there have been few attempts to assess the state of the field of women's history in the UK, particularly over the last twenty years or so, which is why I particularly welcome this Roundtable session.[4] Although the bulk of the research referred to in this article about British women's history has been written by women historians living in the UK it is important to remember, as shown here, that scholars overseas—especially from the USA, Australia and Canada—have made important contributions to the field.[5]

This Roundtable has been organised by Chen Yen and Karen Offen who have asked the participants to consider five questions—what have been the achievements of women's and gender history over the past two decades? To what extent has it succeeded in making women's history an integral part of historical study than an optional specialist area? What impact has the study of manhood, masculinities and men's gendered power had on our understanding of women's lives? What is the relationship between gender studies and new critical histories of colonialism and empire, contact zones, cross-cultural encounters and racialisation? How is new work on cultural geography and spatial categories impacting on our historical understanding of bodily difference?[6] I shall attempt to answer these questions through a consideration of several key themes which I consider to have been central to the advance of women's history in the UK. However, before I do so I would like to say something about the growth of the field before 1995.

It is important to remember that the development of the writing of women's history in the UK has been inextricably linked to contemporary feminist politics.[7] The organised women's movement of the late nineteenth century and early twentieth inspired a number of women to research their foremothers in the past.[8] But as the women's movement fragmented after the First World War these early studies were rarely consulted. However, the advent of the so-called 'Second Wave' of feminism in the late 1960s sparked off renewed interest in finding women in History which had mainly been written by men and about men's activities in war, politics, administration and business. Women were usually excluded or, when made visible, belittled in some way or portrayed in sex-stereotypical roles, such as wives, mothers, daughters and mistresses. Generalisations about humanity in the past had not been either 'objective' or 'inclusive', but based on a male view of the world.

Restoring women to history and finding their voices therefore involved questioning the gender politics that shaped the writing of the male-centred past. It meant not just making women visible but questioning the way they had been represented, portraying them as actors in the making of history in their own right, not simply as passive beings whose lives were determined. Thus the growth of women's history from the 1970s in the UK was closely intertwined with the politics of the Women's Liberation Movement and especially with socialist feminist historians who wanted to write a 'history from below', researching the lives of working-class women, such as poorly paid home workers, domestic servants, single mothers, factory hands and political activists.

Sheila Rowbotham's 1973 text *Hidden from History: 300 years of women's oppression and the fight against it* is usually regarded as the taking off point for women's history in the UK. Written from a socialist feminist perspective, it emphasised that women's struggle against oppression was allied with the class struggle against capitalist exploitation, that gender and class divisions were closely intertwined.[9] A particularly influential book in this genre was *One Hand Tied Behind Us: the rise of the women's suffrage movement*, written by Jill Liddington and Jill Norris. It gave an account of the involvement of working-class women in radical suffragist politics in early twentieth-century Lancashire, emphasising that the only significant form of struggle was class exploitation and that working-class women did not march with the supposedly 'middle-class' suffragettes of the Women's Social and Political Union (WSPU), founded by Emmeline Pankhurst in 1903 to campaign for the parliamentary vote for women.[10]

Although socialist feminism was the dominant voice at this time, shaping and influencing the growth of women's history it was not the only feminist voice making an impact. In the 1980s, liberal feminists, such as Olive Banks, Jane Rendall and Carol Dyhouse shifted the parameters in a different direction as they published on middle-class women's lives in the feminist movement and in the family.[11] Radical feminist writers, such as Sheila Jeffreys and Dale Spender, also made important contributions, discussing issues such as the politics of sexuality and exposing men's control over knowledge, a control that effectively erased women's creative intellectual thought from the historical record.[12] Some of these writers, such as Banks and Spender, were located in academic fields other than History.[13] Yet despite the differing emphases of these feminist researchers, perhaps one book in particular epitomised the feminist approach in the 1980s, namely the *Sexual*

Dynamics of History, edited by the London Feminist History Group. The various contributors to this volume argued that while it was men's power that shaped women's experiences, women were not helpless victims but persons who individually and collectively found ways to challenge that power and to survive.[14] All this discussion and debate was, of course, not isolated from what was going on in the women's movement elsewhere, particularly in North America, where women's history courses were being established in universities. There was a vibrant cross-fertilisation of ideas and exchange of knowledge, which continues to the present day.

By the 1980s, however, it was evident in the UK that not all women's history was necessarily *feminist* women's history. Although women's history takes women as its subject matter it could be written without feminist sympathies, without a feminist analysis, without a women-centred approach.[15] Nonetheless, the links between women's history and feminism have been strong.[16] However, during the 1980s in the UK, the women's movement began to fragment. In particular, black and lesbian feminists raised key questions about racism and 'compulsory heterosexuality', pointing out how their experiences had been marginalised. At the same time that these debates were being aired, Women's Studies was becoming a major growth area in higher education. In some universities, such as the Open University, women's history became an integral part of the Women's Studies curriculum, and was not taught in its History department. In others, as at Essex University, it was mainly located in Sociology where Leonore Davidoff, who has made an incalculable contribution to the development of gender history, was appointed to a lectureship in 1975.

But gradually, as Women's Studies became more theoretical, often being re-named 'Gender Studies' to accompany new work on masculinities, women's history in the UK became primarily located in History departments, and there it remains today. It is now rarely taught on Women's or Gender Studies Courses and has lost some of its feminist edge.[17] This is a regrettable loss. As the American medievalist Judith Bennett argues, studying women in the past offers a unique and critical contribution to the feminist struggle today, a study that illuminates continuity as well as change.[18] She highlights in particular how 'patriarchy'—which usually refers to male domination and to the systematic and individual power relationships whereby men dominate women—was readily talked about by historians of women in the 1970s and 1980s but in the twenty-first century is 'barely whispered'.[19]

It is undoubtedly the case that over the last two decades in the UK women's history has become less feminist in this hard-hitting sense, less concerned with the sexual dynamics of power between women and men. But we must remind ourselves that the writing of a women-centred women's history cannot be contained by just one mould. Not all historians of women wish to make the sexual dynamics of power a central feature of their analysis. The late Bridget Hill, for example, argued that the belief in 'the supremacy of patriarchy over all other factors in women's history … promises to be an arid study', since it might alienate the male allies that have been won since the 1960s. 'As women', she insisted, 'we will never achieve real equality and the enrichment that quality could bring relationships without carrying men with us'.[20] This diversity of approaches to the writing of women's history has enabled the massive expansion of the field over the last two decades, an expansion that has cut across national boundaries and drawn in scholars from disciplines other than History—researchers in film and media, in literary studies, in cultural studies, in human geography, in colonial and postcolonial history as well as scholars located outside the UK. So what broad themes might we identify as characterising women's history in the UK over the last two decades?

First and foremost, women's history in the UK has mainly focused on the modern period, from about 1780 and second, it has always had a strong empirical focus. Thus in addition to the sources already quoted there are, for example, many studies of women's work, singleness, the family, motherhood and of old age, as well as research into the gendered dimensions of industrialisation and of social class formations.[21] Not unexpectedly, it is in studies of love and birth control that we see clearly how the study of manhood, masculinities and men's gendered power has had a profound impact upon our understanding of heterosexual women's lives. This aspect of daily existence has, of course, been long recognised by women themselves in the past. As Mrs M. B. Cooke expressed it in 1923, five years after certain categories of women over the age of thirty had been granted the parliamentary vote: 'What does it avail a woman that she has the franchise if she cannot call her body her own, and is at the mercy of her husband's desires and wishes.'[22]

Undoubtedly the strong empirical emphasis in women's history in the UK partly accounts for the fact that there is much less discussion in our country than in the USA about the field itself, about the very notions of 'women's history' and 'gender history'.[23] Perhaps too this absence also partly reflects the much smaller number of scholars in the UK researching women's varied pasts, compared with their North American counter-parts. Nonetheless, women's history and gender history are closely related and co-exist, sharing many common concerns, despite some earlier heated discussions. For example, in 1999, Penelope Corfield implied that gender history was superior to women's history when she argued that women's history was 'broadening *fruitfully* into gender history' and 'enriching historical studies' (my emphasis), a claim that Amanda Weatherill and I keenly disputed. Amanda and I suggested instead that gender history was a 'malestream incorporation strategy' that decentred the study of women as women; such an argument, we felt, was especially relevant in the bleak academic climate of the late 1990s when academic women felt obliged to suppress their feminist politics in order to gain respectability and access to permanent institutional positions.[24] My scepticism towards gender history has mellowed over the intervening years since women's and gender history have ended up complementing each other more than detracting from each other. I agree with Karen Offen's position paper 'Women's History at the Cutting Edge: a joint paper in two voices' that 'gender history' is not superior to women's history, that there is really no choice between 'women' and 'gender' since both are closely intertwined. As she remarks, the analysis of gender relations has given us the opportunity to revisit and rethink male-centred 'master narratives', such as the rise of capitalism in England and Europe, the 'gender' of nation-states and of notions of citizenship.[25] And we can see this revisiting and rethinking in the profusion of articles found in journals such as *Women's History Review*, *Gender and History* and *History Workshop Journal*, all located in the UK as well as in the many textbooks commonly used on core undergraduate History courses.

For example, if we look at undergraduate courses in Themes in Modern British History and particularly Themes in Modern European Western History, we find a plethora of text-books in these areas so that in this twenty-first century it would now be unthinkable for such courses not to have some lectures and seminars on women's/gender history, even if they are not fully integrated throughout.[26] The list of books below, to which must be added the innumerable articles published in the journals named above, is impressive. That has been one of the great achievements of the past two decades, something we should celebrate. In addition to core undergraduate courses in History, most universities in Britain now also offer options and special subjects in women's/gender history – perhaps on women's history Britain 1850–1945,[27] Victorian women,[28] the history of women's education and intellectual culture,[29] sexuality,[30] crime,[31] the First or Second World War,[32] media in the twentieth century,[33] gender, culture and society c.1920–1980,[34] or women's activism.[35] What is offered depends heavily on the particular interests of the lecturer and the students. But it is noteworthy that the parameters of women's history have expanded in innumerable ways to now include genteel and elite women as well as right-wing women, including women who identified as fascists.[36]

Third, over the last two decades or so some accepted 'truths' in women's history have also been questioned. For example, the dominance of a 'separate spheres' discourse, articulated by Catherine Hall and the late Leonore Davidoff in their highly influential 1987 book *Family Fortunes: men and women of the English middle class 1780–1850*, has been challenged by amongst others Amanda Vickery, Kathryn Gleadle and Sarah Richardson. Whereas Hall and Davidoff focused on the limitations that separate spheres discourse placed on women located within the private sphere of the home, Vickery asserts that in the course of the late eighteenth and early nineteenth centuries the activities of genteel women did not diminish but greatly expanded. Similarly, Gleadle and Richardson are sensitive to the nuances, contradictions and tensions within separate spheres discourse, arguing that it did not imply denial of female political identity but rather informed women's political expression and agency.[37]

Thus consideration of spatial categories, one of the questions we were asked by Chen Yen and Karen Offen to address, has been central to the development of women's history and is not a new phenomenon.[38] Nonetheless, the advent of cultural geography since the 1980s, with its emphasis upon the relationships between space, place and the construction of identity has impacted on History, especially in the fields of urban, architectural and political history. Women's history in the UK over the last two decades has not been immune to this changing landscape and has experienced, some would claim, a 'spatial turn'.[39] Timothy Jones, for example, in exploring the resistance of the Church of England to calls for the ordination of women as priests from 1910 to 1930, adopted an analysis that explored the opposition of the male hierarchy to the 'placement' of women's bodies within the gendered spaces of the pulpit and chancel.[40]

A fifth theme that is evident in the expansion of women's history in the UK over the last two decades is the interest in life stories, personal narratives, oral histories and biographies. Indeed, Barbara Caine, who was born in South Africa and migrated to Australia, suggests that the turn to 'biography' is part of the move away from structuralist approaches and explanations, such as Marxism, that has been evident in the social sciences over the past three or four decades. 'As questions about the importance of gender, race and class and about experience and representation have come to the fore', she points out, 'so too has the recognition that the detailed analysis of individual or collective lives offers one of the best ways to explore them'.[41] Certainly biographies of well-known feminists have proliferated in the UK over the last two decades, although they are mainly of white, middle-class women.[42]

A sixth theme we may identify in women's history in the UK over the last twenty years is the enduring interest in the women's suffrage movements of the nineteenth and twentieth centuries, articles about which appear regularly in *Women's History Review* in addition to a new wave of books on the topic.[43] This is not surprising, given the interest of present-day feminists to find out about their foremothers in the past plus readily accessible sources in The Women's Library, now housed at the London School of Economics. In particular, since the showing from October 2015 of the feature film *Suffragette*, directed by Sarah Gavron with script by Abi Morgan, more and more young women are developing an interest in the Edwardian suffragette movement, and claiming the title 'feminist', a process that is greatly aided by social media campaigns.[44] Indeed, the very word 'suffragette' regularly pops up in public discourse, as a symbol for women's activism in the present.

Over the last two decades, research in the British women's suffrage campaigns has challenged many of the earlier assumptions in a constantly evolving, vibrant field. Thus the claim by Jill Liddington and Jill Norris in their influential 1978 text, *One Hand Tied Behind Us: the rise of the women's suffrage movement*, that few working-class socialist women joined the Women's Social and Political (WSPU), the most militant suffrage society in Edwardian Britain, has been keenly disputed. June Hannam and Karen Hunt, Krista Cowman and myself all contend that working-class socialist women were active WSPU members, especially in the regions.[45]

If women's suffrage has been a constant theme in women's history in the UK in the late twentieth and early twenty-first centuries, other emerging trends can also be identified over this period. Thus we come to our seventh theme, a 'religious turn'. As Sue Morgan and Jacqueline de Vries point out, a resurgence in religion and spirituality 'would have been unimaginable in British feminist history circles thirty years ago'.[46] As noted earlier, women's history in the UK has never been isolated from wider debates in the field, particularly in North America, and we can see that influence here, in cross-cultural contacts. Thus the 1998 book edited by North American academics, Beverly Mayne Kienzle and Pamela J. Walker, titled *Women Preachers and Prophets through Two Millennia of Christianity* included three essays that focused particularly on Britain—Quaker women preachers in the eighteenth-century, the ministry of women in the Salvation Army and preaching and prophecy in the women's suffrage movement.[47] Further the study by the Anglo-Canadian scholar Joy Dixon on how theosophy—regarded as an ancient religion of the East—became a crucial part of the feminist movement in late Victorian and Edwardian England, received very favourable reviews.[48] Here in the UK, Sandra Holton's fine study of Quaker women's kinship networks created by the marriage in 1839 of Elizabeth Priestman and the future radical Quaker statesman, John Bright, included not just an analysis of female participation in the women's rights movement but also women's involvement in civil society and radical politics. More recently, the innovative research by Anne Summers into the networks and relationships between Christian and Jewish women in Britain from 1880 to 1940 examines, amongst other aspects, religious organisations which initiated the first interfaith campaigning movement in British history. This pioneering research makes an important contribution not just to the 'religious turn' in women's history but also to the history of multiculturalism.[49]

The links between the East and the West, so evident in Joy Dixon's study, the relationship between women's studies and the new critical histories of colonialism and empire, contact zones, cross-cultural encounters and racialisation has been particularly pronounced in North American scholarship. And some of this scholarship—such as Moira Ferguson's study of British women writers and colonial slavery and Antoinette Burton's text on British feminists, Indian women and imperial culture—has much to say about Britain.[50] A small but growing number of researchers in women's history in the UK, such as Clare Midgley, Barbara Bush, Sumita Mukherjee and Caroline Bressey are exploring these issues.[51] Thus we come to our eighth theme in women's history in the UK over the last two decades, namely the 'transnational turn', strongly evident in the work of histories of colonialisation and empire and in the studies of women's transnational activism.[52] Transnational and global histories pose the greatest challenges to the writing of women's history in the UK. How can we write a global women's history, a history that keeps women's voices and experiences central to the analysis? What are the biases of our Western paradigms? What kinds of frameworks and methodology should be used?

Last but not least, we cannot ignore in this twenty-first century the influence of the digital revolution on the development and direction of women's history.[53] Traditionally we researchers in women's history have seen 'the archive' as a paper archive, a place we love to explore hoping we might find a long lost letter or a document that might provide an answer to a problematic issue. But this is no longer the case. More and more archives are being put online, such as the *Sisterhood and After Project*, involving life history interviews with sixty female activists in Britain from the 1960s to the 1980s, held at the British Library.[54] This widening of access to sources in British women's history must be welcomed. It can only lead to the growth of interest in our subject.

Overall, as this brief survey reveals, over the last two decades or so women's history in the UK has been very much at the cutting edge of historical enquiry. However, as one would expect, the developments remain uneven. In particular, the voices of black, Asian and ethnic minority women are very much under-represented amongst our undergraduates, lecturing staff and researchers. While the necessary data is not always available, one source notes that in 2014 there were only four black academic historians of African/Caribbean heritage, two of whom were women, and only six black history PhD students (the gender was not specified).[55] This is a matter of deep concern, and not the only one.

The expansion of women's history is losing momentum, especially during this age of austerity when there is roughly an equal gender balance amongst school and university students but more than 60% of academic History staff in UK universities are male and only 20.8% of History professors female.[56] Senior staff who helped to develop the field of women's history are retiring and not always being replaced. Fewer undergraduates want to study for a PhD when university tuition fees in England of £9,250 per year (and likely to rise), plus living expenses, leave too many with heavy debts at a time when there is contraction rather than expansion in the academic job market. Amongst academic staff, being awarded government monies or winning research council grants is becoming increasingly competitive, encouraging perhaps a move towards researching the 'local'. The result of the Referendum held on 23 June 2016, that the UK should leave the European Union, has added to the uncertainty over research funding and the hiring of young talent from around the world. Further, a research assessment exercise, undertaken every six years or so, assesses not just the quality of publications of those submitted but also, and in particular, whether academics have engaged in 'impact' with non-academic audiences. The pressures on academics in this macho work culture, which shows no interest in a reasonable work/life balance is difficult, especially for women academics with small children and/or other dependents. The *Gender Equality and Historians in UK Higher Education Report*, published by the Royal Historical Society in 2015, identifies a range of continuing barriers to gender equality, both formal and informal, in the historical profession, but it remains to be seen whether these barriers can be, or will be, eliminated.[57] The implications of all these changes in higher education for women's history in the UK have yet to be played out.

However, such pessimistic circumstances must be tempered by a number of positive factors. In the UK, the Women's History Network (WHN), founded in 1991, is still going strong and has attained a paying membership of about 400, the highest number since its inception. The WHN Book Prize, awarded each year for a first single-authored monograph in women's or gender history that is written in an accessible style, is very competitive. The introduction of two £1000 Small Grant Schemes, awarded for facilitating a one-day conference on women's history organised by teaching, research staff or postgraduates in universities or other institutions of higher education in the UK, or by staff in further education colleges, museums or heritage sites in collaboration with any one such institution, should prove popular. The WHN Community History Prize, initially sponsored by The History Press, attracted an impressive twenty-three entries in 2015, all of high quality. The award of such a Prize reveals the WHN's commitment to public engagement, as well as support for the diversity of women's and gender history's many forms. There is an active Women's History Scotland and an energetic Women's History Association of Ireland.[58] *Women's History Review*, of which I am the Editor, is attracting an abundance of submissions, so that we now publish six issues a year, usually with seven articles per issue.

Further, History has become a part of popular culture in the UK. While many of the programmes on our TV screens are about men's histories, especially at this time when we are commemorating the centenary of the First World War, there are some spaces for TV and YouTube programmes about women's lives.[59] And there are also some spaces in popular History magazines, such as *History Today* and *BBC History Magazine* for articles on women's history as well as *Women's History*, the journal of the Women's History Network, devoted solely to the field.[60] There is a renewed interest in feminism amongst young women in particular, partly fuelled by the social media success of the 'Everyday Sexism' project, developed by Laura Bates.[61] All indications are that women's history in the UK is here to stay and that it will continue to be reconceptualised and reformulated as it is communicated in more diverse forms than we could ever have imagined in the 1970s.

Notes

1. June Purvis (Ed.) (1995) *Women's History Britain, 1850–1945* (London: UCL Press).
2. June Purvis, From 'Women Worthies' to Poststructuralism? Debate and controversy in women's history in Britain, in Purvis, *Women's History Britain*, pp. 1–22. For other overviews of women's history in the UK see especially Jane Rendall, 'Uneven Developments': women's history, feminist history and gender history in Great Britain, in Karen Offen, Ruth Roach

Pierson & Jane Rendall (Eds) (1991) *Writing Women's History: international perspectives* (Houndmills: Macmillan), pp. 45–57; June Hannam, Women, History and Protest, in Diane Richardson & Victoria Robinson (Eds) (1993) *Introducing Women's Studies* (Houndmills: Macmillan), pp. 303–323; Jane Rendall, 'Women's History in Britain, Past, Present and Future: gendered boundaries?' *Women's History Magazine*, February 2002, pp. 4–11; Sue Morgan (2006) Introduction: Writing Feminist History: theoretical debates and critical practices, in Morgan (Ed.) *The Feminist History Reader* (London: Routledge), pp. 1–48; Kathryn Gleadle (2013) The Imagined Communities of Women's History: current debates and emerging themes, a rhizomatic approach, *Women's History Review*, 22 (4), pp. 524–540. For an overview of women's history worldwide see especially Karen Offen, History of Women, in Bonnie G. Smith (Ed.) (2008) *Women in World History* Vol. 2 (Oxford: Oxford University Press), pp. 463–471, and for the USA Susan Pedersen (2000) The Future of Feminist History, *American Historical Association*, 38, pp. 20–25; Joan Scott (2004) Feminism's History, *Journal of Women's History*, 16 (2), pp. 10–29; Afsaneh Najmabadi (2004) From Supplementarity to Parasitism? *Journal of Women's History*, 16 (2), pp. 30–35; Evelynn M. Hammonds (2004) Power and Politics in Feminism's History--and Future, *Journal of Women's History*, 16 (2), pp. 36–39. For Australia see particularly Joy Damousi (2014) Does Feminist History Have a Future? *Australian Feminist Studies*, 29 (80), pp. 189–203

Inevitably in a survey essay such as this, due to limitations of space, I have had to be selective in the references cited. My views on the topic of women's history in the UK reflect my own location as a white, middle-class woman academic who has taught in higher education in the UK for many years and would identify as a 'feminist'. My own research has mainly focused on the education of girls and women in nineteenth-century England and now especially on the suffragette movement in Edwardian Britain, including biographies of the two main suffragette leaders, Emmeline and Christabel Pankhurst. See the journals *Women's History Review* and *Gender and History* in particular, for many articles published about women's history in the UK.

3. See, for example, Susan Kingsley Kent (1999) *Gender and Power in Britain, 1640–1990* (London: Routledge); Sue Bruley (1999) *Women in Britain Since 1900* (Houndsmills: Macmillan); Ina Zweiniger-Bargielowska (Ed.) (2001) *Women in Twentieth-Century Britain* (Harlow: Pearson); Susie Steinbach (2004) *Women in England 1760–1914* (London: Weidenfeld and Nicholson); Sheila Rowbotham (1997) *A Century of Women: the history of women in Britain and the United States* (London: Viking); Hannah Barker & Elaine Challus (Eds) (2005) *Women's History: Britain, 1700–1850* (London: Routledge) and Alison Twells (Ed.) (2007) *British Women's History: a documentary history from the Enlightenment to World War I* (London and New York: Tauris). An earlier influential text was Jane Lewis (1984) *Women in England 1870–1950* (Brighton: Wheatsheaf Books).

4. Two key exceptions to this general claim are Morgan, Introduction; Sue Morgan (2009) Theorising Feminist History: a thirty-year retrospective, *Women's History* Review, 18 (3), pp. 381–407; Gleadle, 'The Imagined Communities'.

5. There are also historians in the UK who do not research women's history in the UK but have made important contributions to the history of women in other countries. See, for example, Linda Edmondson (1984) *Feminism in Russia, 1900–1917* (Stanford: Stanford University Press); Barbara Bush (1990) *Slave Women in Caribbean Society 1650–1838* (London: James Curry); Linda Edmondson (Ed.) (1992) *Women and Society in Russia and the Soviet Union* (Cambridge: Cambridge University Press); Lynn Abrams & Elizabeth Harvey (Eds) (1996) *Gender Relations in German History: power, agency and experience from the sixteenth to the twentieth century* (London: UCL Press); Jane McDermid & Anna Hillyar (1998) *Women and Work in Russia, 1880–1930: a study in continuity through change* (Harlow: Longman); Jay Kleinberg (1999) *Women in the United States, 1833–1945* (Houndmills: Palgrave MacMillan); Hanna Diamond (1999) *Women and the Second World War in France, 1939–48* (Harlow: Longman); Anna Hillyar & Jane McDermid (2000) *Revolutionary Women in Russia, 1870–1917* (Manchester: Manchester University Press); Sian Reynolds (2004) *France Between The Wars* (London: Routledge); Padma Anagol (2005) *The Emergence*

of Feminism in India, 1850–1920 (Aldershot: Ashgate); Lyndal Roper (2006) *Witch Craze: women and evil in Baroque Germany* (New Haven: Yale University Press); Christina de Bellaigue (2007) *Educating Women: schooling and identity in England and France 1800–1867* (Oxford: Oxford University Press); Perry Willson (2009) *Women in Twentieth-Century Italy* (Houndmills: Palgrave Macmillan); Katharina Rowold (2010) *The Educated Woman: minds, bodies, and women's higher education in Britain, Germany, and Spain, 1865–1914* (London: Routledge); Henrice Altink (2011) *Destined For A Life of Service: defining African Jamaican womanhood, 1865–1938* (Manchester: Manchester University Press); Rebecca Fraser (2012) *Gender, Race and Family in Nineteenth Century America: from northern woman to plantation mistress* (Houndmills: Palgrave MacMillan); Sian Reynolds (2012) *Marriage & Revolution: Monsieur & Madame Roland* (Oxford: Oxford University Press); Helen Boak (2013) *Women in the Weimar Republic* (Manchester: Manchester University Press); Maude Bracke (2014) *Women and the Re-Invention of the Political: feminism in Italy, 1968–1983* (London: Routledge); Simone Laqua-O'Donnell (2014) *Women and the Counter-Reformation in Early Modern Munster* (Oxford: Oxford University Press); Natalya Vince (2015) *Our Fighting Sisters: nation, memory and gender in Algeria, 1954–2012* (Manchester: Manchester University Press), and Megha Humar (2016) *Communalism and Sexual Violence in India: the politics of gender, ethnicity and conflict* (London: Tauris).

6. Chen Yen & Karen Offen (2017) Women's History at the Cutting Edge, *Women's History Review*, this Special Issue.

7. Hannam, 'Women, History and Protest', p. 303.

8. See, for example, Josephine E. Butler (Ed.) (1869) *Woman's Work and Woman's Culture: a series of essays* (London: MacMillan); Emily Pfeiffer (1888) *Women and Work: an essay treating on the relation to health and physical development of the higher education of girls, and the intellectual or more systematised effort of women* (London: Trubner); Charlotte Carmichael Stopes (1894) *British Freewomen, Their Historical Privilege* (London: Swan Sonneschein); Georgina Hill (1896) *Women in English Life from Medieval to Modern Times* Two Volumes (London: Richard Bentley); Barbara Hutchins (1915) Women in Modern Industry (London: G. Bell); Alice Clark (1919) *Working Life of Women in the Seventeenth Century* (London: Routledge); Eva Shaw McLaren (Ed.) (1919) *A History of the Scottish Women's Hospitals* (London: Hodder & Stoughton); Ivy Pinchbeck (1930) *Women Workers and the Industrial Revolution 1750–1850* (London: Routledge).

9. Sheila Rowbotham (1973) *Hidden From History: 300 years of women's oppression and the fight against it* (London: Pluto Press).

10. Jill Liddington & Jill Norris (1978) *One Hand Tied Behind Us: the rise of the women's movement* (London: Virago).

11. Olive Banks (1981) *Faces of Feminism: a study of feminism as a social movement* (Oxford: Martin Robertson); Jane Rendall (1985) *The Origins of Modern Feminism: women in Britain, France and the United States 1780–1860* (Houndmills: Macmillan); Carol Dyhouse (1989) *Feminism and the Family in England 1880–1939* (Oxford: Blackwell).

12. Dale Spender (1982) *Women of Ideas and What Men Have Done To Them* (London: Routledge); Sheila Jeffreys (1985) *The Spinster and Her Enemies: feminism and sexuality 1880–1930* (London: Pandora Press).

13. Olive Banks was a Professor of Sociology at the University of Leicester. Dale Spender, an Australian, was for some time involved in teacher training at the Institute of Education, the University of London before becoming Editor of *Women's Studies International Forum* and a full-time writer.

14. London Feminist History Group (1983) *The Sexual Dynamics of History: men's power, women's resistance* (London: Pluto Press).

15. For example, Elizabeth Roberts (1984) *A Woman's Place: an oral history of working-class women 1890–1940* (Oxford: Basil Blackwell), pp. 1–2 seeks to distance herself from any claim that the book is a 'feminist history' although she believes it to be 'a contribution to that literature' . David Mitchell (1977) *Queen Christabel: a biography of Christabel Pankhurst* (London: MacDonald and Jane's) is a decidedly anti-feminist text.

16. Judith Bennett (1989) Feminism and history, *Gender and History*, 1 (3), p. 253.

17. Gabriele Griffin (2009) The 'ins' and 'outs' of Women's/Gender Studies: a response to reports of its demise in 2008, *Women's History Review*, 18 (3), pp. 485–496, suggests that, taking a broadly European view, Women's/Gender Studies courses have now been 'mainstreamed' into undergraduate curricula and continue to attract research funding and significant numbers of postgraduate students. It is interesting to note that Oxford University seems to buck the trend in that its Women's Studies postgraduate course does include women's history. Thus in the advertisement for the MSt in Women's Studies it is stated that five departments within the Humanities Division contribute option choices and supervision expertise––the Faculties of English, History, Classics, Philosophy and Modern Languages. The programme does not 'normally involve' departments within the Social Sciences Division.

18. Judith M. Bennett (2006) *History Matters: patriarchy and the challenge of feminism* (Philadelphia, Pennsylvania: Philadelphia University Press).

19. Bennett, *History Matters*, pp. 21–22. For the debate in the UK in the 1970s and 1980s about 'patriarchy' see, for example, Sheila Rowbotham, The Trouble with Patriarchy, reprinted in R. Samuel (Ed.) (1981) *People's History and Socialist Theory* (London: Routledge), pp. 364–369, first published in *New Statesman*, December 1981; Sally Alexander & Barbara Taylor (1981) In Defence of 'Patriarchy', in Samuel, *People's History and Socialist Theory*, pp. 370–373. For a brilliant text that successfully combines patriarchy with a class analysis see Barbara Taylor's 1983 study of the tensions between socialism and feminism in early nineteenth-century England, *Eve and the New Jerusalem: socialism and feminism in the nineteenth century* (London: Virago).

20. Bridget Hill (1993) Women's History: a study in change, continuity or standing still? *Women's History Review*, 2 (1), pp. 5–22.

21. See, for example, Leonore Davidoff & Catherine Hall (1987) *Family Fortunes: men and women of the English middle class, 1780–1850* (London: Hutchinson); Jane Rendall (1990) *Women in an Industrializing Society: England 1750–1880* (Oxford: Blackwell); Judy Lown (1990) *Women and Industrialization: gender at work in nineteenth-century England* (Cambridge: Polity Press); Eleanor Gordon & Esther Breitenbach (Eds) (1990) *The World is Ill Divided: women's work in Scotland in the nineteenth and early twentieth centuries* (Edinburgh: Edinburgh University Press); Sonya O. Rose (1992) *Limited Livelihoods: gender and class in nineteenth-century England* (London: Routledge); Esther Breitenbach & Eleanor Gordon (Eds) (1992) *Out of Bounds: women in Scottish society 1800–1945* (Edinburgh: Edinburgh University Press); Ellen Ross (1993) *Love & Toil: motherhood in Outcast London 1870–1918* (Oxford: Oxford University Press); Sally Alexander (1994) *Becoming a Woman and Other Essays in 19th and 20th Century Feminist History* (London: Virago); Leonore Davidoff (1995) *Worlds Between: historical perspectives on gender and class* (Cambridge: Polity Press); Deborah Valenze (1995) *The First Industrial Woman* (Oxford: Oxford University Press); Anna Clark (1995) *The Struggle for the Breeches: gender and the making of the British working class* (London: Rivers Oram); Gerry Holloway (1995) *Women and Work in Britain since 1840* (London: Routledge); Pamela Sharpe (Ed.) (1998) *Women's Work: the English experience 1650–1914* (London: Arnold); Deborah Simonton (1998) *A History of European Women's Work: 1700 to the present* (London: Routledge); Ellen Jordan (1999) *The Women's Movement and Women's Employment in Nineteenth Century Britain* (London: Routledge); Leonore Davidoff, Megan Doolittle, Janet Fink & Katherine Holden (1999) *The Family Story: blood, contract and intimacy, 1830–1960* (London: Longman); Katrina Honeyman, (2000) *Women, Gender and Industrialisation in England, 1700–1870* (Houndmills: Macmillan); Claire Langhamer (2000) *Women's Leisure in England, 1920–1960* (Manchester: Manchester University Press); Eleanor Gordon & Gwyneth Nair (2003) *Public Lives: women, family and society in Victorian Britain* (New Haven: Yale University Press); Selina Todd (2005) *Young Women, Work, and Family in England 1918–1950* (Oxford: Oxford University Press); Pat Thane (2005) *The Long History of Old Age* (London: Thames and Hudson); Lynn Abrams (2005) *Myth and Materiality in a Woman's World: Shetland 1800–2000* (Manchester: Manchester University Press); Tanya

Evans (2005) *'Unfortunate objects': lone mothers in eighteenth-century London* (Houndmills: Palgrave Macmillan); Hannah Barker (2006) *The Business of Women: female enterprise and urban development in Northern England, 1760–1830* (Oxford: Oxford University Press); Katherine Holden (2007) *The Shadow of Marriage: singleness in England, 1914–60* (Manchester: Manchester University Press); Katie Roiphe (2007) *Uncommon Arrangements: seven portraits of married life in London literary circles 1910–1939* (London: Virago);Virginia Nicholson (2007) *Singled Out: how two million women survived without men after the First World War* (London: Viking); Ginger S. Frost (2008) *Living in Sin: cohabiting as husband and wife in nineteenth-century England* (Manchester: Manchester University Press); Anne Lawrence, Josephine Maltby & Janette Rutterford (Eds) (2009) *Women and Their Money 1700-1950 : essays on women and finance* (London: Routledge); Claire G. Jones (2009) *Femininity, Mathematics and Science, 1880–1914* (Houndmills: Palgrave Macmillan); Lucy Delap (2011) *Knowing Their Place: domestic service in twentieth-century Britain* (Oxford: Oxford University Press); Pat Thane & Tanya Evans (2012) *Sinners? Scroungers? Saints?: unmarried motherhood in twentieth-century Britain* (Oxford: Oxford University Press); Lucy Lethbridge (2013) *Servants: a downstairs view of twentieth-century Britain* (London: Bloomsbury); Katherine Holden (2013) *Nanny Knows Best: the history of the British nanny* (Stroud: The History Press); Helen McCarthy (2014) *Women of the World: the rise of the female diplomat* (London: Bloomsbury); Barbara Caine (Ed.) (2015) *Letters Between Mothers and Daughters*, Special Issue of *Women's History Review* 24 (4); Julie-Marie Strange (2015) *Fatherhood and the British Working Class, 1865–1914* (Cambridge: Cambridge University Press); Laura King (2015) *Family Men: fatherhood and masculinity in Britain, 1914–1960* (Oxford: Oxford University Press) ; Gillian Sutherland (2015) *In Search of the New Woman: middle-class women and work in Britain 1870–1914* (Cambridge: Cambridge University Press).

22. Quoted in preface to Clare Debenham (2014) *Birth Control and the Rights of Women: post-suffrage feminism in the early twentieth century* (London: Tauris). See also Hera Cook (2004) *The Long Sexual Revolution: English women, sex and contraception 1800–1975* (Oxford: Oxford University Press); Kate Fisher (2006) *Birth Control, Sex, & Marriage in Britain 1918–1960* (Oxford: Oxford University Press); Simon Szreter & Kate Fisher (2010) *Sex before the Sexual Revolution: intimate life in England 1918–1963* (Cambridge: Cambridge University Press); Stephen Brooke (2011) *Sexual Politics: sexuality, family planning, and the British Left from the 1880s to the present day* (Oxford: Oxford University Press); Claire Langhamer (2013) *The English in Love: the intimate story of an emotional revolution* (Oxford: Oxford University Press); Alana Harris & Timothy Willem Jones (Eds) (2015) *Love and Romance in Britain, 1918–1970* (Houndmills: Palgrave Macmillan), and relevant articles in Raffaella Sarti (Ed.) (2015) *Men at Home: domesticities, authority, emotions and work*, Special Issue of *Gender & History*, 27 (3).

23. Compare, for example, the content of the American based *Journal of Women's History* with that of the UK based *Women's History Review* and *Gender and History*.

24. Penelope J. Corfield (1997) History and the Challenge of Gender History, *Rethinking History*, 1 (3), pp. 241–258 and June Purvis & Amanda Weatherill (1999), Playing the Gender History Game: a reply to Penelope J. Corfield, *Rethinking History*, 3 (3), pp. 333–338.

25. Yan & Offen, 'Women's History at the Cutting Edge'.

26. In regard to Britain, see for example, Paul Johnson (Ed.) (1994) *20th Century Britain: economic, social and cultural change* (London: Harlow) which has two chapters by Pat Thane titled 'The Social, Economic and Political Status Of Women' and 'Women Since 1945' and Martin Pugh (Ed.) (1997, reprinted 1998, 2000) *A Companion to Modern European History 1871–1945* (Oxford: Basil Blackwell) which has a chapter by Pugh 'The Rise of European Feminism'. In regard to text books specifically on women's/gender issues in Britain and Modern Western Europe the list is long but see, for example, Renate Bridenthal & Claudia Koonz (Eds) (1977) *Becoming Visible: women in European History* (Boston: Houghton Mifflin), third edn (1998) edited by Renate Bridenthal, Susan Mosher Stuard & Merry E. Wiesner; Susan Groag Bell & Karen M. Offen (Eds) (1983) *Women, the Family, and*

Freedom: the debate in documents 1750–1950 2 Vols (Stanford: Stanford University Press); Martha Vicinus (1985) *Independent Women: work and community for single women 1850–1920* (London: Virago); Bonnie S. Anderson & Judith P. Zinsser (1988) *A History of Their Own: women in Europe from prehistory to the present* 2 Vols (London: Penguin); Maria Luddy (Ed.) (1995) *Women in Ireland, 1800–1918: a documentary history* (Cork: Cork University Press); Laura L. Frader & Sonya O. Rose (Eds) (1996) *Gender and Class in Modern Europe* (Ithaca: Cornell University Press); Rowbotham, *A Century of Women*; Robert Shoemaker & Mary Vincent (Eds) (1998) *Gender and History in Western Europe* (London: Arnold); Bruley, *Women in Britain Since 1900*; Kingsley Kent, *Gender and Power in Britain*; Barbara Caine & Glenda Sluga (2000) *Gendering European History* (London: Leicester University Press); Karen Offen (2000) *European Feminisms 1700–1950* (Stanford: Stanford University Press); Zweiniger-Bargierlowska, *Women in Twentieth-Century Britain*; Lynn Abrams (2002) *The Making of Modern Woman* (London: Longman); Fiona Montgomery & Christine Collette (Eds) (2002) *The European Women's History Reader* (London: Routledge); Gisela Bock (2002) *Women in European History* (Oxford: Blackwell); Steinbach, *Women in England*; Deborah Simonton (Ed.) (2006) *The Routledge History of Women in Europe Since 1700* (London: Routledge); Sue Morgan (Ed.) (2006) *The Feminist History Reader* (London: Routledge); Fiona Montgomery (Ed.) (2006) *Women's Rights: struggles and feminism in Britain c. 1770–1970* (Manchester: Manchester University Press); Twells, *British Women's History*; Sheila Rowbotham (2010) *Dreamers of a New Day: women who invented the twentieth century* (London: Verso); Deborah Simonton (2011) *Women in European Culture and Society: gender, skill and identity from 1700* (London: Routledge).

27. See note 3 above for relevant texts plus a number of other books cited throughout, including Todd, *Young Women, Work, and Family*; Holden, *The Shadow of Marriage*; Evans and Thane, *Sinners? Scroungers? Saints?* and Anne Summers (2017) *Christian and Jewish Women in Britain, 1880–1940* (Houndmills: Palgrave Macmillan).

28. The list of publications is extensive but in addition to relevant texts cited earlier, especially in note 21, see for example, Mary Poovey (1989) *Uneven Developments: the ideological work of gender in Mid-Victorian England* (London: Virago); Mary Lyndon Shanley (1989) *Feminism, Marriage, and the Law in Victorian England, 1850–1895* (Princeton: Princeton University Press); Judith R. Walkowitz (1992) *City of Dreadful Delight: narratives of sexual danger in Late-Victorian London* (London: Virago); A. James Hammerton (1992) *Cruelty and Companionship: conflict in nineteenth-century married life* (London: Routledge); Erika Diane Rappaport (2000) *Shopping for Pleasure: women in the making of London's West End* (Princeton: Princeton University Press); Kathryn Gleadle (Ed.) (2001) *British Women in the Nineteenth Century* (Houndmills: Palgrave); Kathryn Gleadle (Ed.) (2002) *Radical Writing on Women, 1800–1850: an anthology* (Houndmills: Palgrave Macmillan); Gordon & Nair, *Public Lives*; Simon Morgan (2007) *A Victorian Woman's Place: public culture in the nineteenth century* (London: Tauris); Kelly Boyd & Rhona McWilliam (Eds) (2007) *The Victorian Studies Reader* (London: Routledge); Kathryn Gleadle (2009) *Borderline Citizens: women, gender, and political culture in Britain 1815–1867* (Oxford: Oxford University Press); Ben Griffin (2012) *The Politics of Gender in Victorian Britain: masculinity, political culture and the struggle for women's rights* (Cambridge: Cambridge University Press); Sarah Richardson (2013) *The Political Worlds of Women: gender and politics in nineteenth-century Britain* (London: Routledge).

29. See, for example, Carol Dyhouse (1981) *Girls Growing Up in Late Victorian and Edwardian England* (London: Routledge); Sylvia Harcstark Myers (1990) *The Bluestocking Circle: women, friendship, and the life of the mind in eighteenth-century England* (Oxford: Oxford University Press); June Purvis (1991) *A History of Women's Education in England* (Buckingham: Open University Press); Kate Flint (1993) *The Woman Reader 1837–1914* (Oxford: Oxford University Press); Carol Dyhouse (1995) *No Distinction of Sex? Women in British Universities 1870–1939* (London: UCL Press); Dina M. Copelman (1996) *London's Women Teachers: gender, class and feminism 1870–1930* (London: Routledge); Alison Oram (1996) *Women Teachers and Feminist Politics 1900–39* (Manchester: Manchester University

Press); Jane Martin (1999) *Women and the Politics of Schooling in Victorian and Edwardian England* (Leicester: Leicester University Press); Jane Martin & Joyce Goodman (2004) *Women and Education, 1800–1980* (Houndmills: Palgrave Macmillan); Stephanie Spencer (2005) *Girls and Career Choice in the 1950s* (Houndmills: Palgrave Macmillan); Sarah Knott & Barbara Taylor (Eds) (2005) *Women, Gender and Enlightment* (Houndmills: Palgrave Macmillan); Mary Spongberg, Barbara Caine & Ann Curthoys (Eds) (2005) *Companion to Women's Historical Writing* (Houndmills: Palgrave Macmillan); Carol Dyhouse (2006) *Students: a gendered history* (London: Routledge); de Bellaigue, *Educating Women*; Rowold, *The Educated Woman*.

30. See, for example, Margaret Jackson (1994) *The 'Real' Facts of Life: feminism and the politics of sexuality c1850–1940* (London: Taylor and Francis); Lucy Bland (1995) *Banishing the Beast: English feminism and sexual morality 1885–1914* (London: Penguin); Lesley A. Hall (2000) *Sex, Gender and Social Change in Britain Since 1880* (Houndmills: Macmillan); Paula Bartley (2000) *Prostitution: prevention and reform in England, 1860–1914* (London: Routledge); Alison Oram & Annmarie Turnbull (Eds) (2001) *The Lesbian History Sourcebook: love and sex between women in Britain from 1780–1970* (London: Routledge); Lesley Hall (Ed.) (2005) *Outspoken Women: an anthology of women's writing on sex, 1870–1969* (London: Routledge); Rebecca Jennings (2007) *A Lesbian History of Britain: love and sex between women since 1500* (Oxford: Greenwood); Alison Oram (2007) *Her Husband Was A Woman: women's gender-crossing in modern British popular culture* (London: Routledge), Lucy Bland (2013) *Modern Women on Trial: sexual transgression in the age of the flapper* (Manchester: Manchester University Press); Rebecca Jennings (2013) *Tomboys and Bachelor Girls: a lesbian history of post-war Britain 1945–71* (Manchester: Manchester University Press); Laura Doan (2013) *Disturbing Practices: history, sexuality, and women's experiences of modern war* (Chicago: University of Chicago Press); Jennifer Redmond, Sonja Tiernan, Sandra McAvoy & Mary McAuliffe (Eds) (2015) *Sexual Political in Modern Ireland* (Dublin: Irish Academic Press); Angharad Eyre, Jane Mackelworth & Elsa Richardson (Eds) (2016) *Love, Desire and Melancholy: inspired by Constance Maynard*, Special Issue of *Women's History Review*, 25 (1).

31. See, for example, Shani D'Cruze (1998) *Crimes of Outrage: sex, violence and Victorian working women* (London: UCL Press); Margaret L. Arnot & Cordelie Usborne (Eds) (1999) *Gender and Crime in Modern Europe* (London: UCL Press); Louise A. Jackson (2000) *Child Sexual Abuse in Victorian England* (London: Routledge); Shani D'Cruze (Ed.) (2000) *Everyday Violence in Britain, 1850–1950: gender and class* (Harlow: Pearson); Mark Jackson (Ed.) (2002) *Infanticide: historical perspectives on child murder and concealment, 1550–2000* (Aldershot: Ashgate); Louise Jackson (2006) *Women Police: gender, welfare and surveillance in the twentieth century* (Manchester: Manchester University Press); Joanna Bourke (2007) *Rape: a history from 1860 to the present* (London: Virago); Anne Logan (2008) *Feminism and Criminal Justice: a historical perspective* (Houndmills: Palgrave Macmillan); Eleanor Gordon & Gwyneth Nair (2009) *Murder and Morality in Victorian Britain* (Manchester: Manchester University Press); Shani D'Cruze & Louise Jackson (2009) *Women, Crime and Justice in England Since 1660* (Houndmills: Palgrave Macmillan).

32. See, for example, Gail Braybon & Penny Summerfield (1987) *Out of the Cage: women's experiences in two world wars* (London: Pandora Press); Susan Kingsley Kent (1993) *Making Peace: the reconstruction of gender in interwar Britain* (Princeton: Princeton University Press); Angela Woollacott (1994) *On Her Their Lives Depend: munitions workers in the Great War* (Berkeley: University of California Press); Christine Gledhill & Gillian Swanson (Eds) (1996) *Nationalising Femininity: culture, sexuality and British cinema in the Second World War* (Manchester: Manchester University Press); Penny Summerfield (1998) *Reconstructing Women's Wartime Lives: discourse and subjectivity in oral histories of the Second World War* (Manchester: Manchester University Press); Susan R. Grayzel (1999) *Women's Identities at War: gender, motherhood, and politics in Britain and France during the First World War* (Chapel Hill: University of North Carolina Press); Susan R. Grayzel (2002) *Women and the First World War* (Harlow: Pearson); Nicoletta F. Gullace (2002) *'The*

Blood of Our Sons': men, women, and the renegotiation of British citizenship during the Great War (Houndmills: Palgrave Macmillan); James Hinton (2002) *Women, Social Leadership, and the Second World War: continuities of class* (Oxford: Oxford University Press); Sonya O. Rose (2003) *Which People's War? National identity and citizenship in wartime Britain 1939–1945* (Oxford: Oxford University Press); Lyn Smith (2005) *Forgotten Voices of the Holocaust: true stories of survival-- from men, women and children who were there* (London: Ebury); Lucy Noakes (2006) *Women in the British Army: war and the gentle sex, 1907–1948* (London: Routledge); Penny Summerfield & Corinna Peniston-Bird (2007) *Contesting Home Defence: men, women and the Home Guard in the Second World War* (Manchester: Manchester University Press); Jo Vellacott (2007) *Pacifists, Patriots and the Vote: the erosion of democratic suffragism in Britain during the First World War* (Houndmills: Palgrave Macmillan); Juliette Pattinson (2007) *Behind Enemy Lines: gender, passing and the Special Operations Executive in the Second World War* (Manchester: Manchester University Press); Alison S. Fell & Ingrid Sharp (Eds) (2007) *The Women's Movement in Wartime: international perspectives, 1914–19* (Houndmills: Palgrave Macmillan); Christine E. Hallett (2009) *Containing Trauma: nursing work in the First World War* (Manchester: Manchester University Press); Lucy Noakes and Juliette Pattison (Eds) (2013) *British Cultural Memory and the Second World War* (London: Bloomsbury); Lindsey German (2013) *How a Century of War Changed the Lives of Women* (London: Pluto Press); Alison S. Fell & Christine E. Hallett (Eds) (2013) *First World War Nursing: new perspectives* (London: Routledge); Maggie Andrews & Janis Lomas (Eds) (2014) *The Home Front in Britain: images, myths and forgotten experiences since 1914* (Houndmills: Palgrave Macmillan); Jane Brooks & Christine Hallett (Eds) (2015) *One Hundred Years of Wartime Nursing Practices, 1854–1953* (Manchester: Manchester University Press); Julie V. Gottlieb (2015) *'Guilty Women', Policy and Appeasement in Inter-War Britain* (Houndmills: Palgrave Macmillan); Sarah Helm (2015) *If This Is A Woman: inside Ravensbruck Hitler's concentration camp for women* (London: Little, Brown); Christine Hallett (2016) *Nurse Writers of the Great War* (Manchester: Manchester University Press); Angela K. Smith (2016) *British Women of the Eastern Front: war, writing and experience in Serbia and Russia, 1914–20* (Manchester: Manchester University Press); Corinna Peniston-Bird & Emma Vickers (2016) (Eds) *Gender and the Second World War: lessons of war* (Houndmills: Palgrave Macmillan), and Zoe Waxman (2016) *Women in the Holocaust : a feminist history* (Oxford: Oxford University Press).

33. See, for example, Penny Tinkler (1995) *Constructing Girlhood: popular magazines for girls growing up in England, 1920–1950* (London: Taylor & Francis); Margaret Beetham (1996) *A Magazine of Her Own? Domesticity and desire in the women's magazine, 1800–1914* (London: Routledge); Adrian Bingham (2004) *Gender, Modernity, and the Popular Press in Inter-War Britain* (Oxford: Oxford University Press); Michelle Elizabeth Tusan (2005) *Women Making News: gender and journalism in modern Britain* (Urbana and Chicago: University of Illinois Press); Maria DiCenzo with Lucy Delap & Leila Ryan (2011) *Feminist Media History: suffrage, periodicals and the public sphere* (Houndmills: Palgrave Macmillan); Maggie Andrews (2012) *Domesticating the Airwaves: broadcasting, domesticity and femininity* (London: Continuum); Maggie Andrews & Sally McNamara (Eds) (2014) *Women and the Media: feminism and femininity in Britain, 1900 to the present* (London: Routledge); Catriona Clear (2015) *Women's Voices in Ireland: women's magazines in the 1950s and 60s* (London: Bloomsbury); Laurel Forster (2015) *Magazine Movements: women's culture, feminisms and media form* (London: Bloomsbury); Kate Murphy (2016) *Behind the Wireless: a history of early women at the BBC* (Houndmills: Palgrave Macmillan).

34. A number of the texts listed previously would be relevant here including Bland, *Modern Women on Trial* but see also Wendy Webster (1998) *Imagining Home: gender, race and national identity, 1945–64* (London: Routledge); Carol Dyhouse (2010) *Glamour: women, history, feminism* (London: Zed Books); David Gutzke (2013) *Women Drinking Out in Britain Since the Early Twentieth Century* (Manchester: Manchester University Press). For a definition of 'material culture' and references to this see note 39.

35. In addition to relevant texts listed in note 26 see Jill Liddington (1989) *The Long Road to Greenham: feminism and anti-militarism in Britain since 1820* (London: Virago); Sybil Oldfield (1989) *Women Against the Iron Fist: alternatives to militarism 1900–1989* (Oxford: Blackwell); Jane Lewis (1991) *Women and Social Action in Victorian and Edwardian England* (Aldershot: Edward Elgar); Martin Pugh (1992) *Women and the Women's Movement in Britain 1914–1959* (Houndmills: Macmillan); Barbara Caine (1992) *Victorian Feminists* (Oxford: Oxford University Press); Olive Banks (1993) *The Politics of British Feminism, 1918–1970* (Aldershot: Edward Elgar); Pamela M. Graves (1994) *Labour Women: women in British working-class politics 1918–1939* (Cambridge; Cambridge University Press); Sasha Roseneil (1995) *Disarming Patriarchy: feminism and political action at Greenham* (Buckingham: Open University Press); Kathryn Gleadle (1995) *The Early Feminists: radical Unitarians and the emergence of the women's rights movement, 1831–51* (Houndmills: Macmillan); Barbara Caine (1997) *English Feminism 1780–1980* (Oxford: Oxford University Press); G. E. Maguire (1998) *Conservative Women: a history of women and the Conservative Party, 1874–1997* (Houndmills: Macmillan); Helen Rogers (2000) *Women and the People: authority, authorship and the radical tradition in nineteenth-century England* (Aldershot: Ashgate); Amanda Vickery (Ed.) (2001) *Women, Privilege and Power: British politics, 1750 to the present* (Stanford: Stanford University Press); June Hannam & Karen Hunt (2002) *Socialist Women Britain, 1880s to 1920s* (London: Routledge); Heloise Brown (2003) *'The Truest Form of Patriotism': pacifist feminism in Britain, 1870–1902* (Manchester: Manchester University Press); Krista Cowman (2004) *'Mrs Brown is a Man and a Brother!': women in Merseyside's political organisations 1890–1920* (Liverpool: Liverpool University Press); Tusan, *Gender and Journalism*; Lucy Delap (2007) *The Feminist Avant-Garde: transatlantic encounters of the early twentieth century* (Cambridge: Cambridge University Press); Clare Midgley (2007) *Feminism and Empire: women activists in Imperial Britain, 1790–1865* (London: Routledge); Megan Smitley (2009) *The Feminine Public Sphere: middle-class women and civic life in Scotland, c. 1870–1914* (Manchester: Manchester University Press); Annmarie Hughes (2010) *Gender and Political Identities in Scotland, 1919–1939* (Edinburgh: Edinburgh University Press); Ursula Masson (2010) *For Women, for Wales and for Liberalism* (Cardiff: University of Wales Press); Ingrid Sharp & Matthew Stibbe (Eds) (2011) *Aftermaths of War: women's movements and female activists, 1918–1923* (Lieden: Brill); Catrionia Beaumont (2013) *Housewives and Citizens: domesticity and the women's movement in England, 1928–64* (Manchester: Manchester University Press); Krista Cowman (2013) *Women in British Politics, c. 1689–1979* (Houndmills: Palgrave Macmillan); Julie V. Gottlieb & Richard Toye (Eds.) (2013) *The Aftermath of Suffrage: women, gender, and politics in Britain, 1918–1945* (Houndmills: Palgrave Macmillan); Julie V. Gottlieb (Ed.) (2014) 'Feminism and Feminists After Suffrage', Special Issue of *Women's History Review*, 23 (3); Francisca de Haan, Margaret Allen, June Purvis & Krassimira Daskalova (Eds) (2013) *Women's activism: global perspectives from the 1890s to the present* (London: Routledge); Laura Schwartz (2013) *Infidel Feminism: secularism, religion and women's emancipation, England 1830–1914* (Manchester: Manchester University Press).

36. See, for example, Amanda Vickery (1998) *The Gentleman's Daughter: women's lives in Georgian England* (New Haven: London: Yale University Press); Julia Bush (2000) *Edwardian Ladies and Imperial Power* (Leicester: Leicester University Press); Elaine Chalus (2005) *Elite Women in English Political Life c.1754–1790* (Oxford: Oxford University Press); Gleadle, *Borderline Citizens*; Richardson, *The Political Worlds of Women*; Martin Durham (Ed.) (1998) *Women and Fascism* (London: Routledge); Julie V. Gottlieb (2000) *Feminine Fascism: women in Britain's fascist movement, 1923–1945* (London: Tauris).

37. Vickery, *The Gentleman's Daughter*; Gleadle, *Borderline Citizens*; Richardson, *The Political Worlds of Women*.

38. Yen & Offen, 'Women's History at the Cutting Edge', in this Special Issue.

39. Kathryne Beebe, Angela Davis & Kathryn Gleadle (2011) Introduction to their edited *Space, Place and Gendered Identities: feminist history and the spatial turn*, Special Issue of *Women's History Review*, 21 (4), p. 524. Jane Hamlett & Leonie Hannan (Eds) (2016) *Gender and*

Material Culture in Britain Since 1600 (Houndmills: Palgrave Macmillan), pp. 5–7 make a similar point, noting that influenced by cultural geography, many historians have begun to study 'space' and 'place' and particularly 'material culture' which is defined as objects or physical structures that had a particular use or meaning, or set of values attached to them, such as the material cultures of home. Text in this field include John Styles & Amanda Vickery (Eds) (2006) *Gender, Taste and Material Culture in Britain and North America, 1700–1830* (New Haven and London: Yale University Press); Karen Harvey (Ed.) (2009) *History and Material Culture: a student's guide to approaching alternative sources* (London: Routledge); Dianne Lawrence (2012) *Genteel Women: empire and domestic material culture, 1840–1910* (Manchester: Manchester University Press); Karen Harvey (2012) *The Little Republic: masculinity and domestic authority in eighteenth-century Britain* (Oxford: Oxford University Press); Jane Hamlett (2015) *At Home in the Institution: material life in asylums, lodging houses and schools in Victorian and Edwardian England* (Houndmills: Palgrave Macmillan).

40. Timothy Willem Jones (2011) 'Unduly conscious of her sex': priesthood, female bodies, and sacred space in the Church of England, *Women's History Review*, 21 (4), pp. 639–655.

41. Barbara Caine (2010) *Biography and History* (Houndmills: Palgrave Macmillan), p. 3.

42. The list is extensive but see, for example, David Rubinstein (1991) *A Different World for Women: the life of Millicent Garrett Fawcett* (Hemel Hempstead: Harvester Wheatsheaf); Paul Berry & Mark Bostridge (1995) *Vera Brittain: a life* (London: Chatto & Windus); Angela V. John (1995) *Elizabeth Robins: staging a life, 1862–1952* (London: Routledge); Maxine Berg (1996) *A Woman in History Eileen Power, 1889–1940* (Cambridge: Cambridge University Press); Delia Jarrett-Macauley (1998) *The Life of Una Marson 1905–65* (Manchester: Manchester University Press); Marion Shaw (1999) *The Clear Stream: a life of Winifred Holtby* (London: Virago); Jane Jordan (2001) *Josephine Butler* (London: John Murray); Martin Pugh (2001) *The Pankhursts* (London: Allen Lane); Margaretta Jolly (Ed.) (2001) *Encyclopedia of Life Writing: autobiographical and biographical forms* (London: Fitzroy Dearborn); Paula Bartley (2002) *Emmeline Pankhurst* (London: Routledge); June Purvis (2002) *Emmeline Pankhurst: a biography* (London: Routledge); Barbara Taylor (2003) *Mary Wollstonecraft and the Feminist Imagination* (Cambridge: Cambridge University Press); Shirley Harrison (2003) *Sylvia Pankhurst: a crusading life 1882–1960* (London: Aurum Press); Susan Pedersen (2004) *Eleanor Rathbone and the Politics of Conscience* (New Haven: Yale University Press); Deborah McDonald (2004) *Clara Collett 1860–1948: an educated working woman* (London: Woburn); Lyndall Gordon (2005) *Mary Wollstonecraft: a new genus* (London: Little, Brown); Barbara Caine (2005) *Bombay to Bloomsbury: a biography of the Strachey family* (Oxford: Oxford University Press); Jane Jordan (2005) *Kitty O'Shea: an Irish affair* (Stroud: Sutton); Sybil Oldfield (2006) *Doers of the Word: British women humanitarians 1900–1950* (London: Continuum); Elizabeth Evan, Sue Innes & Sian Reynolds (Eds) Rose Pipes Co-ordinating Editor (2006) *The Biographical Dictionary of Scottish Women: from the earliest times to 2004* (Edinburgh: Edinburgh University Press); Maureen Wright (2011) *Elizabeth Wolstenholme Elmy and the Victorian Feminist Movement: the biography of an insurgent woman* (Manchester: Manchester University Press); Lesley A. Hall (2011) *The Life and Times of Stella Browne: feminist and free spirit* (London: Tauris); Sonja Tiernan (2012) *Eva Gore-Booth: an image of such politics* (Manchester: Manchester University Press); Lorna Gibb (2013) *West's World: the extraordinary life of Dame Rebecca West* (London: MacMillan); Angela V. John (2013) *Turning the Tide: the life of Lady Rhondda* (Cardigan: Parthian); Caroline Bressey (2013) *Empire, Race and the Politics of Anti-Caste* (London: Bloomsbury); Katherine Connelly (2013) *Sylvia Pankhurst: suffragette, socialist and scourge of empire* (London: Pluto Press); Rachel Holmes (2014) *Eleanor Marx: a life* (London: Bloomsbury); Paula Bartley (2014) *Ellen Wilkinson: from red suffragist to Government Minister* (London: Pluto Press); Matt Perry (2014) *'Red Ellen' Wilkinson: her ideas, movements and world* (Manchester: Manchester University Press); Lyndsey Jenkins (2015) *Lady Constance Lytton: aristocrat, suffragette, martyr* (London: Biteback); Anita Anand (2015) *Sophia: princess, suffragette, revolutionary* (London: Bloomsbury); Laura Beers

(2016) *Red Ellen: the life of Ellen Wilkinson, socialist, feminist, internationalist* (Cambridge, MA: Harvard University Press).

43. The list is again extensive, but see especially David Rubinstein (1986) *Before the Suffragettes: women's emancipation in the 1890s* (Brighton: Harvester); Sandra Stanley Holton (1986) *Feminism and Democracy: women's suffrage and reform politics in Britain 1900–1918* (Cambridge: Cambridge University Press); Leah Leneman (1991) *A Guid Cause: the women's suffrage movement in Scotland* (Aberdeen: Aberdeen University Press); Glenda Norquay (Ed.) (1995) *Voices and Votes: a literary anthology of the women's suffrage campaign* (Manchester: Manchester University Press); Sandra Stanley Holton (1996) *Suffrage Days: stories from the women's suffrage movement* (London: Routledge); Caine, *English Feminism*; Maroula Joannou & June Purvis (Eds) (1998) *The Women's Suffrage Movement: new feminist perspectives* (Manchester: Manchester University Press); Elizabeth Crawford (1999) *The Women's Suffrage Movement: a reference guide 1866–1928* (London: UCL Press); Martin Pugh (2000) *The March of the Women: a revisionist analysis of the campaign for women's suffrage, 1866–1914* (Oxford: Oxford University Press); Catherine Hall, Keith McClelland & Jane Rendall (2000) *Defining the Victorian Nation: class, race, gender and the British Reform Act of 1867* (Cambridge: Cambridge University Press); June Purvis & Sandra Stanley Holton (Eds) (2000) *Votes for Women* (London: Routledge); Ian Christopher Fletcher, Laura E. Nym Mayhall & Philippa Levine (Eds) (2000) *Women's Suffrage in the British Empire: citizenship, nation and race* (London: Routledge); Fran Abrams (2003) *Freedom's Cause: lives of the suffragettes* (London: Profile Books); Angela K. Smith (2005) *Suffrage Discourse in Britain during the First World War* (Aldershot: Ashgate); Jill Liddington (2006) *Rebel Girls: their fight for the vote* (London: Virago); Elizabeth Crawford (2006) *The Women's Suffrage Movement in Britain and Ireland* (London: Routledge); Paula Bartley (2007, third edn) *Votes for Women* (London: Hodder Murray); Mitzi Auchterlonie (2007) *Conservative Suffragists: the women's vote and the Tory party* (London: Tauris); Louise Ryan & Margaret Ward (Eds) (2007) *Irish Women and the Vote: becoming citizens* (Dublin: Irish Academic Press); Julia Bush (2007) *Women against the Vote: female anti-suffragism in Britain* (Oxford: Oxford University Press); Krista Cowman (2007) *Women of the Right Spirit: paid organisers of the Women's Social and Political Union (WSPU) 1904–18* (Manchester: Manchester University Press); Griffin, *The Politics of Gender in Victorian Britain*; Jill Liddington (2014) *Vanishing for the Vote: suffrage, citizenship and the battle for the census* (Manchester: Manchester University Press).

44. See Sarah Gavron (2015) The Making of the Feature Film *Suffragette, Women's History Review*, 24 (6), pp. 985–995.

45. Hannam & Hunt, *Socialist Women*; Cowman, *Mrs Brown*; Purvis, *Emmeline Pankhurst*.

46. Sue Morgan & Jacqueline de Vries (2010), Introduction, in Morgan & de Vries (Eds) *Women, Gender and Religious Culture in Britain, 1800–1940* (London: Routledge) , pp. 1–2.

47. Phyllis Mack, In a Female Voice: preaching and politics in eighteenth-century British Quakerism; Pamela J. Walker, A Chaste and Fervid Eloquence: Catherine Booth and the Ministry of women in the Salvation Army; Jacqueline R. deVries, Transforming the Pulpit: preaching and prophecy in the British women's suffrage movement, all in Beverley Mayne Kienzle & Pamela J. Walker (Eds) (1998) *Women Preachers and Prophets through Two Millennia of Christianity* (Berkley: University of California Press) pp. 248–263, 288–302, 318–333, respectively.

48. Joy Dixon (2001) *Divine Feminine: theosophy and feminism in England* (Baltimore: John Hopkins University Press).

49. Sandra Stanley Holton (2007) *Quaker Women: personal life, memory and radicalism in the lives of women friends, 1780–1930* (London: Routledge) and Summers, *Christian and Jewish Women in Britain*. For other relevant studies on religion see Joanna de Groot & Sue Morgan (Eds) (2000) *Sex, Gender and the Sacred: reconfiguring religion in gender history* (Oxford: John Wiley & Sons).

50. Moira Ferguson (1992) *Subject to Others: British women writers and colonial slavery, 1670–1834* (London: Routledge); Antoinette Burton (1994) *Burdens of History: British feminists,*

Indian women, and imperial culture, 1865–1915 (Chapel Hill and London: University of North Carolina Press). See also Fletcher, Mayhall & Levine, *Women's Suffrage*; Antoinette Burton (2015) *The Trouble with Empire: challenges to modern British imperialism* (Oxford: Oxford University Press).

51. Although the focus in women's history has been on gender, there has always been a recognition that gender also is not enough to explain the complex histories of women's lives which is why some scholars today prefer to use the word 'intersectionality', a term more commonly used by those working in sociology and gender/cultural studies. Although intersectionality has now become a 'buzz' term it is also an important theoretical concept for the multiple forms of simultaneous domination experienced by women and men in the past and how these influence historians' reconstructions. Myra Marx Ferree (2006) Globalization and Feminism: opportunities and obstacles for activism in the global area, in Myra Marx Ferree & Aili Mari Tripp (Eds) (2006) *Global Feminism: transnational women's activism, organizing, and human rights* (New York: New York University Press), p. 10 states that 'intersectionality means that privilege and oppression, and movements to defend and combat these relations, are not in fact singular. No one has a gender but not a race, a nationality but not a gender, an education but not an age. The location of people and groups within relations of production, reproduction, and representation (relations that are organized worldwide in terms of gender inequality) is inherently multiple.' Linda Gordon (2016) 'Intersectionality', Socialist Feminism and Contemporary Activism: musings by a second-wave socialist feminist, *Gender and History*, 28 (2), pp. 340–357 notes that the basic concept that multiple forms of domination interact and even fuse into new forms has a long history in Left feminism and anti-racist, anti-nationalist and anti-colonial discourse, and that 'intersectionality' is used today by many activist groups.

52. See, for example, Bush, *Slave Women in Caribbean Society*; Clare Midgley (1992) *Women against Slavery: the British campaigns 1780–1870* (London: Routledge); Clare Midgley (Ed.) (1998) *Gender and Imperialism* (Manchester: Manchester University Press); Barbara Bush (1999) *Imperialism, Race and Resistance: Africa and Britain, 1919–1945* (London: Routledge); Catherine Hall & Sonya O. Rose (Eds) (2006) *At Home with the Empire: metropolitan culture and imperial world* (Cambridge: Cambridge University Press); Midgley, *Feminism and Empire*; Rehana Ahmed & Sumita Mukherjee (Eds) (2011) *South Asian Resistances in Britain, 1858–1947* (London: Continuum); Bressey, *Empire, Race and the Politics of Anti-Caste*; de Haan, Allen, Purvis & Daskalova (Eds.) *Women's Activism: global perspectives*; Marie Sandall (2015) *The Rise of Women's Transnational Activism: identity and sisterhood between the World Wars* (London: Tauris); Clare Midgley, Alison Twells & Julie Carter (Eds) (2016) *Women in Transnational History* (London: Routledge); Barbara Bush & June Purvis (Eds) (2016) *Connecting Women's Histories: the local and the global*, Special Issue of *Women's History Review*, 25 (4). A fascinating book in this category is Linda Colley (2007) *The Ordeal of Elizabeth Marsh: a woman in world history* (London: Harper Press). Elizabeth Marsh (1735–1785) was conceived in Jamaica by a ship's carpenter working for the British navy and a widowed woman described as English but possibly of mixed race. She travelled *in utero* from Kingston to England, the first of many oceanic journeys outlined in this transnational biography. Colley teaches British history at Princeton in the USA.

53. See Paula Hamilton & Mary Spongberg (Eds) (forthcoming) *Feminist Histories and the Digital Revolution*, Special Issue of *Women's History Review*.

54. Sisterhood and After: the Women's Liberation Oral History Project, British Library Sound Archive. The Women's Liberation Movement in Britain, including its relationship to men, appears to be a growing field of research interest. See, for example, Eve Setch (2002) The Face of Metropolitan Feminism: the London Women's Liberation Movement, 1969–1979, *Twentieth Century British History*, 13 (2), pp. 171–190; Jeska Rees (2010) A Look Back at Anger: the Women's Liberation Movement in 1978, *Women's History Review*, 19 (3), pp. 337–356; Margaretta Jolly & Sasha Roseneil (Eds) (2012) *Researching Women's Movements: FEMCIT and Sisterhood and After* Special Issue of *Women's Studies International Forum*, 35 (3); Sarah Browne (2014) *The Women's Liberation Movement in Scotland*

(Manchester: Manchester University Press); Lucy Delap (2016) Feminist Bookshops, Reading Cultures and the Women's Liberation Movement in Great Britain, c.1974–2000, *History Workshop Journal*, 81 (Spring), pp. 171–196; Laurel Forster & Sue Bruley (Eds) (2016) *Historicising the Women's Liberation Movement in the Western World, c1960–1990* Special Issue of *Women's History Review*, 25 (5).

55. Hakin Adi & Shantelle George, Letter to the Editor of the *Times Higher Education Supplement*, 30 October 2014; Hakim Adi email to me, 14 August 2015. Baroness Amos, appointed in 2015 as the Head of the School of Oriental and African Studies, University of London, is the first black woman to lead a UK university, Baroness Amos: 'I was taken aback when I found out I was the first black female head of a university', *The Observer*, 19 July 2015.

56. Royal Historical Society Report (January 2015) *Gender Equality and Historians in UK Higher Education*, p. 3. Here are only 18 black women with UK professorships: *The Times Higher Education Supplement*, 18 August 2016.

57. Royal Historical Society Report, *Gender Equality*, p. 3.

58. Women's History Scotland was founded as the Scottish Women's History Network in 1995 and became Women's History Scotland in 2004. The Women's History Association of Ireland, which encompasses scholars form the Republic of Ireland and from Northern Ireland, was founded in 1989.

59. See, for example, the series titled *Shopgirls: the true story of life behind the counter* which traced the history of Britain's shopworkers and consumer cultures from 1860 to the present and was presented on BBC TV in 2014 by Professor Pamela Cox, Department of Sociology, University of Essex; the series *Suffragettes Forever! The story of women and power* which explored, in three programmes the struggle for women's political rights in Britain, a battle fought over many centuries before the foundation of the suffragette movement in Edwardian Britain, presented in 2015 on BBC TV by Professor Amanda Vickery, Department of History, Queen Mary, University of London; *Sophia: suffragette princess*, the story of Sophia Duleep Singh, born into Indian royalty, presented on BBC TV in 2015 by her biographer Anita Anand (see note 42), and *Fallen Women*, a short moving film by Lily Ford about the unmarried mothers who had their babies taken in by London's Foundling Hospital in the nineteenth century: https://youtube.com/watch?v=04T3nG55 ysA (accessed 24 December 2016).

60. *Women's History: the journal of the Women's History Network* is usually about forty to fifty pages long. The Summer 2016 Issue was a Special Issue on *Pregnancy*. For articles on women's history in *BBC History Magazine* see, for example, Lucy Noakes, 'Our Excess Girls', *BBC History Magazine*, March 2012, pp. 25–27; June Purvis, 'Anti-Suffragette Postcards', *BBC History Magazine*, August 2012, pp. 36–40; June Purvis, 'Emily Davison: the suffragette martyr', *BBC History Magazine*, June 2013, pp. 46–49; Nicola Tallis, 'Why did Lady Jane Grey have to die? ', *BBC History Magazine*, November 2016, pp. 25–28; Victoria Leslie, 'Fallen Women', *History Today*, January 2017, pp. 35–38, and Michael Jones, 'Margaret Beaufort: mother of the Tudors, *BBC History Magazine*, January 2007, pp. 50–55.

61. See http://everydaysexism.com

Acknowledgements

Thanks to all the participants for their comments on a first version of this paper when presented at the Roundtable 'Women's History at the Cutting Edge', organised by the International Federation for Research in Women's History at the 22nd International Congress of Historical Sciences, Jinan, China, 23–29 August 2015. Thanks also to the referees and especially Karen Offen and Sue Morgan for many helpful suggestions. However, any errors or omissions remain my own.

Women's History in Many Places: reflections on plurality, diversity and polyversality

Joanna de Groot

ABSTRACT

This piece addresses the key questions posed by Chen Yan and Karen Offen in their joint position paper on the current state of women's history and its place at the cutting edge of historical practice. Having made the case that women's and gender history has had a significant and multi-level impact (empirical, conceptual, methodological and theoretical) on that practice, my article observes that acknowledgement of this is still very limited among those not centrally involved in the field. It notes the tensions between the aspiration both to identify and pursue women's and gender history as discrete fields of scholarly endeavour and the aspiration for women and gender to be treated as topics/categories which should be constitutive of all historical inquiry. It goes on to consider the relationship of women's history to gender history, to post-colonial and cross-cultural scholarship, and to recent work in spatial histories. It argues that in the first case the two approaches are mutually reinforcing, and that in the other two cases women's and gender history has been at the leading edge of these developing fields and is uniquely positioned to make innovative contributions there. The capacity of women's and gender history to continue as a leading edge area of historical practice will be grounded in its ongoing commitment to reflexivity about problems and limitations in the field, and to sustaining its key insights into the links between the personal and the structural, the global and the local, and the material and the cultural.

My contribution to the discussion opened up by Karen Offen and Chen Yan draws on my own experience as a historian of women, genders, feminisms and sexualities with particular interests in the Middle East, especially Iran, since c.1750, and in histories of empire since c.1700. It also draws on my involvement with comparative history, with interdisciplinary women's studies, and with the study of the concepts, methods and theories that sustain historical practice, which has taken me beyond the chronological and geographical confines of my other work. My experience is shaped by my membership of a generation who developed as historians in the UK through the 'history from below' revival of social history in the 1960s and 1970s, the 'cultural turn' of the 1980s and 1990s, and the more recent postcolonial turn.[1] This piece responds to the questions addressed in the main position paper, with particular reference to cross-cultural, trans-national, and post-colonial themes and approaches. It refers to work published or translated into English, but is fully appreciative of important work on the history of women and gender which has appeared in various languages from the work of Chinese, Japanese and Turkish scholars, to histories of women and gender in Europe and Latin America written in indigenous languages.

This analysis of the achievements of women's history over recent decades identifies three crucial and demonstrable levels of impact. At the *substantive level* existing scholarly practice has been modified by the recuperation of ignored or marginalized ideas and information regarding women and gender for use in historical research and writing. The study of ancient slavery or modern labour movements, like accounts of religious practice or monarchical governance, has been transformed by work based on evidence about the distinctive roles and perceptions of women, men, families, and sexualities.[2] At the *conceptual level* such information has led to a rethinking of terms regularly used by historians to depict and comment on past societies. Notions of 'work', 'politics', 'nation', 'family' and 'religion', to name just a few concepts regularly used in historical writing, acquire changed meanings once that evidence is taken into account.[3] At the *level of general analysis* the 'big stories' of, say, the making of western European Christianity, conversion in nineteenth-century Africa, or nineteenth- and twentieth-century 'industrialisations' and modern politics are also transformed once due attention is given to the gendered character of production, governance, or culture.[4] Moreover, from an early stage in its development, work in women's history has challenged the underpinning structures and intellectual tools of modern historical practice, including basic assumptions about periodisation and organising concepts, and continues to do so. The arguments of Kelly on notions of a 'Renaissance', and Walby on patriarchy, or of Clark on the history of Christianity and Anagol on Indian history illustrate the challenges and contributions.

Beyond these three levels, the work of scholars aware of women and gender in a range of disciplines has generated concepts and theoretical insights with potential to transform the whole field of historical practice. These include analyses of patriarchies and sexualities as conceptual categories useful to historians as well as socio-political structures which have shaped human existence in different times and cultures, the conceptualisation of men as gendered subjects, and the development of queer and postcolonial theory. Deconstructive strategies for approaching material from various periods and places, alongside woman-centred critiques of categories like 'experience' challenge many of the assumptions behind conventional social and political history.[5] Like Karen Offen, I do not regard the development of 'gender' as a category or question for historical analysis as diminishing the need for, and relevance of, the question or category 'women.' Rather, I would suggest that (1) women's history has provided the conceptual and empirical stimulus for the relational approach from which gender theory has emerged, and (2) since that emergence the two ideas have had a fruitful if fraught relationship. It is important to note here how Anglophone historians of women have *initiated* important theoretical and conceptual developments in social and cultural theory rather than just responding to, or adapting, existing thinking. Bradford's studies of gender, race, and capitalism in South Africa, or Sinha's development of the notion of 'imperial social formation', like Najmabadi's work on modernity and hetero-normativity in Iran, exemplify innovative conceptual/theoretical work on the past solidly grounded in women's and gender history.[6]

It can thus be argued that the achievements of women's history range from the production of important studies of specific situations in the past, to the enhancement of historians' conceptual and methodological toolkits, and the creation of new analytical and theoretical frameworks.

Turning to the second question, I would suggest that what has *not* been achieved is the mainstreaming of either the empirical or the conceptual and methodological contributions made by women's history to historical scholarship over the last few decades. It is certainly possible to identify the impact of work in women's history through citations of that work, and through more frequent reference to women as part of the past which historians investigate. It is less easy to argue that the mindset or practices of historians in general have been significantly modified, or that women's history has a normal or guaranteed place in history curricula, or in general and survey texts on the history of particular periods, places or themes. Returning to the three levels used earlier to evaluate the impact of women's history, practitioners have been willing to acknowledge the recuperative work of women's history but have proven far more resistant to the conceptual and analytical implications of that work for *all* historical narratives and interpretations. Insofar as it is recognised, women's history is most often treated as an acceptable specific specialist field or interest for those historians who choose to pursue it, rather than as a *constitutive element within historical practice* which ought to inform *any* investigation or interpretation of the past. Insofar as that is not the case, it is more likely that women's role in any past society will get some degree of rather unspecific recognition from those who identify as 'social historians', and from some cultural historians. Mainstream economic histories are still unlikely to incorporate analyses of the care and maintenance work done mainly by women in families and households in their approaches to the history of work and production, commerce and consumption.

Much historical scholarship dealing with government, 'high politics', or political movements, has not found it necessary even to consider the forms and perceptions of women's inclusion or exclusion from these areas, let alone foreground it. Indeed, one eminent historian of modern Iran, himself the author of insightful analyses of the social bases of political change there, reacted publicly and angrily to suggestions that women could and should be incorporated within such analyses, arguing that attempts to do so collapse into mere social description.[7] Practitioners in the field of intellectual history have been similarly reluctant to give due attention either to issues of women and gender or to women's roles as intellectuals in the past. Turning to an area in which I work, despite the leading edge scholarship on women and empire, mainstream histories and conceptualisations of empire are still written without incorporating consideration of women's involvement either as colonial subjects, or as agents of colonial power.[8]

It would be useful to undertake thorough research into possible explanations for the disparity between the manifest quantity and quality of work in women's history and the limited extent of its acknowledgement, let alone use, in the wider domains of historical practice. There are interesting paradoxes to consider here, since there are obvious tensions between the aspiration to integrate women's history at the core of *all* historical practice and the aspiration to ensure full recognition and analysis of the particularities of women's activities and experiences in past societies. To make particular people or issues visible is of course to identify them as specific topics for historical research, writing or teaching, and hence to separate them out for such purposes. Nonetheless it is important to make the case that one important use for such separate historical studies of women should be to inform the overall perspectives taken by historians on, say, sixteenth-century Ottoman religion, twentieth-century Italian political movements, medieval urban life, or ancient Roman slavery. Historical practice as a whole benefits most when there are practitioners who investigate and interpret women's past lives and activities as a distinctive field, and when their work is properly recognised by other practitioners in the shaping of their own particular projects and interests. The real mark of healthy influence is when there are historical conversations both among those who work on women's history (now a rich historiography) and also between such practitioners and those who take other approaches to the past (still a very limited historiography). Whether in the form of proper consideration of women's history in work centred on other themes, or the appearance of articles on women's history in journals other than those which specialise in that field, such crossovers and conversations are to be encouraged.[9]

Turning to the third question, I would argue that the heat and dust raised by the controversies which posed 'women's history' *against* 'gender history' a decade ago has now died down somewhat, and that this is a good thing. After critical reactions to the possibility that 'gender history' might once more conceal women whose lives and activities practitioners of women's history have made so much effort to make visible, explore and explain, more considered reflection suggests that the two approaches can be mutually reinforcing rather than mutually exclusive alternatives. The growth of historical scholarship which deals with men as gendered persons has become possible largely as a result of woman-centred, feminist, and queer research and theory that explore and conceptualise gender and sexuality as *constitutive elements* of human societies past and present. More specifically, one of the strengths of women's history is that it both identifies the differences and specificities of women's past lives and activities, and positions such specificities in relation to the lives and activities of men. Indeed it might be said that the very notion of 'difference' entails specifically *relational* uses of the category 'women', just as the notion of women's historical agency entails consideration of their *interactions* with men. From the analysis of industrialisation and monarchy, to histories of religion or colonial masculinity, scholarship in women's history embodies this relational and interactive approach.

A few examples from recent Anglophone scholarship on various parts of the world will illustrate this point. Leslie Peirce's path-breaking study of the women of the Ottoman court in the early modern period considers the wives, mothers, daughters and sisters of Ottoman rulers as political actors, as cultural patrons and as dynastic players.[10] It analyses royal women's exercise of these roles and their powerful agency, positioning them in relation to male relatives and court or government officials, and analysing the specificities of their position within the Ottoman elite from that relational and interactive perspective. Mrinalini Sinha's elaboration of the concept of the 'imperial social formation', which has reconstituted studies of relationships between metropoles and colonies, is also underpinned by an emphasis on the distinctive and interactive roles of men and women within that formation.[11] She explores how the dynamics of empire are articulated through differences and intersections of race and gender created through the distinctive agency of men and women. Deborah Valenze's study of women and industrialisation in nineteenth-century England, like Davidoff and Hall's foundational work, advances the study of women by situating them *analytically as well as empirically* in families, classes and communities shaped by difference and interdependence, as well as by women's distinctive experiences. Their works parallels that of Gullickson on France, Friedl on Iran, or Moitt on Antillean slavery and many more socio-political studies of women.[12] Shula Marks' analysis of relationships between a young Zulu woman, a female English Fabian educator and an African woman social worker in 1940s South Africa uses comparable strategies. It unpacks the gendered, classed and racialised interactions of these three women with one another and with the sphere of male-dominated medical and political authority, exploring the realities and limitations of their agency. Another example would be Catherine Hall's subtle and authoritative exploration of the dynamics of racialised colonialism, and gendered religious endeavour in relationships linking England and the Caribbean in the nineteenth century.[13]

My comments quite consciously include illustrations taken from a range of very diverse societies, many of which have been part of the unequal global structures of material, political, and cultural power which have shaped the world since the sixteenth century. They are my point of entry into a discussion of the fourth question about the significance of recent developments in post-colonial, imperial and cross-cultural history for the practice of women's and gender history. As noted earlier, scholars like Sinha, Najmabadi, Kandiyoti and Mohanty have been the pioneers of path-breaking conceptual and methodological work in those fields, drawing on their work in women's history and reconfiguring the fields to which they contribute.[14] This work faces in two directions, challenging the ethnocentrism of some women's history while also interrogating the neglect of women in, and gender blindness of, much work on empire and race. For feminist practitioners of women's history who had focused on the disadvantaged, exploited, unequal and disempowered position of women in western Europe and North America it has been challenging to confront histories of white women's racial and colonial power and privilege. However, that confrontation has proved to be productive as well as challenging, as seen in the critical engagement of Boydston or Najmabadi with Joan Scott's canonical discussion of gender as a category of historical analysis, or the work of Fox-Genovese and Beckles on slavery.[15] Practitioners of women's history can draw on their experience of relational and interactive approaches to the category 'women', deployed since the 1980s to address the complex interactions of gender and class in women's lives, in order to be equally attentive to women's varied positioning in colonial and racial hierarchies. From Clare Midgely's interrogations of women and empire to Few and Socilow's work on Latin America, or Antoinette Burton's sophisticated studies of the British *raj* in India there is ample evidence of the capacity of women's history for creative adaptation to the challenge of ethnocentrism.[16] There is no cause to be complacent about this issue, since ethnocentrism is a comfort zone to which it is easy to retreat, but there is visible evidence of the possibility of change.

There have also been important developments in the discussion of concepts and methods to support work on specific topics. Although it can be argued that work on African-American women has privileged their racialised situation over that of other subordinated groups in the US, it has produced valuable empirical and theoretical insights relevant for historians of women in other gendered structures of colonial or racial subordination. In particular the development of the notion of intersectionality as an analytical tool, which originated in African-American feminist thought, has also been useful to scholars working on other societies, and on concepts or comparative studies of empire and nation.[17] It allows scholars to research and analyse connections and tensions between different markers and relations of power and subordination without resorting to the construction of restrictive and un-illuminating hierarchies of oppression or exploitation. It aligns with studies of women in various African and Middle Eastern societies which analyse interactions between gender, status and age/lifecycle hierarchies, a topic also examined by a number of historians of medieval women. These hierarchies sustain relations of power and inequality whose presence significantly modifies ethnocentric western assumptions about the primacy of gender and class, and analyses of the operations of colonialism.[18] The notion of intersectionality allows practitioners of women's history to sidestep sterile arguments about the relative force of different unequal power relations without simply retreating into descriptive empiricism.

Developments in theory and method, which is a more contentious matter for those trained in historical practices than for those whose formation has been in the social sciences, is nonetheless vital if women's history is to sustain a cutting and growing edge. It becomes even more so in a context where practitioners of women's history cannot ignore critiques of ethnocentrism and cultural imperialism. Serious cross-cultural and comparative work in our field, which allows us a fuller appreciation of specificity, as well as enabling more meaningful discussion of common themes or patterns, needs the support of clear thinking about the concepts and methods which will be most relevant to that work. Knowing which ideas and analyses are 'good to think with' is an essential component of effective and discriminating women's history in the era of post-colonial thought and the recent 'provincialising' of histories of Europe **and** North America. In view of the marginalisation of women and gender perspectives in key texts on this theme, interventions which position those perspectives more centrally will be vital for the credibility of this scholarship.[19] It would diminish the potential for what could be a creative development in current historiography if older patterns of blindness and bias are replicated. For those historians who are wary of engagement with theory it is interesting to look at the arguments of Zillah Eisenstein for the notion of what she calls 'polyversality'.[20] While she undoubtedly develops a distinctive concept to aid the cross-cultural discussion of women, she grounds her work in reflections on actual history and politics, and on the need for general analyses of global patriarchies to incorporate understanding of the colonial past and on global socio-cultural diversity.

Discussion of the significance of the relevance of recent developments in imperial history and cross cultural comparison for women's history opens up the question of spaces, and networks, referred to by our final question. Imperial historians have developed an interest in the constitutive role within the imperial social formation of people's movements through 'imperial space' as migrants, missionaries, convicts, settlers and slaves, within which there is important specific work on female members of all these groups.[21] If women's history has gained by engaging with this strand in global history, it likewise has its own specific resources to offer to the making of spatial histories. One of the foundational areas in women's history has been recognition of the key role of spaces of all kinds in the construction of female/male relationships and differences. From critical engagement with Habermas's gender-blind conceptualisation of the public sphere (or space as it **is** named in French) to close studies of women in relation to household, community and other spaces, practitioners of women's history have done creative work in this area.[22] They have explored and analysed the spatial dynamics of women's roles in consumption, in faith practices, in leisure and entertainment, and as cultural and intellectual practitioners in societies across the globe. This work has deepened our understanding of the gendered character of the making of, and movement through, space in different cultures and periods and of spatial aspects shaping the activities of women as performers, activists, philanthropists, sex workers, believers and authors or artists.[23] The recent special issue of the journal *Gender and History* on the theme of 'men at home', despite its title, reveals the importance of women's history in the development of spatial histories. Covering situations ranging from modern Iran to late medieval Italy by way of Mozambique and US plantation slavery, the articles in the issue demonstrate the contribution of women's history to histories of gender, space and socio-cultural change.[24]

Indeed, one of the exciting and inspiring aspects of women's and gender history, in Anglophone scholarship and elsewhere, is its capacity to move between the dynamics of the intimate and biographical and those of the global and trans-national. The origins of these histories in strong awareness of various forms of female difference and agency has underpinned a powerful practice of studying the presence of the global in the household, of the familial in the imperial, and of the personal in political contexts small and large. Women's and gender history has also demonstrated the capacity to respond to the challenge of studying women across time and space by extending its conceptual and methodological as well as its empirical range. In the process practitioners in the field have become leading-edge conceptual and methodological contributors and innovators. While it is important to avoid complacency and to recognise the limitations and problematic aspects of our practice as historians of women and gender, we should have the confidence and the self-reflective perceptiveness to work constructively on our limitations and problems. It is on that basis that the practice of women's history can remain at the cutting edge.

Notes

1. An interesting take on the experiences of that generation is provided by G. Eley (2005) *A Crooked Line: from cultural history to the history of society* (Ann Arbor: University of Michigan Press), which gives serious consideration to the role of women's and gender history.
2. E.g. R. Lal (2005) *Domesticity and Power in the Early Mughal World* (Cambridge: Cambridge University Press); B. Bush (1990) *Slave Women in Caribbean Society 1650–1838* (Bloomington: Indiana University Press); C. Bynum (1987) *Holy Feast and Holy Fast: the significance of food to medieval women* (Berkeley: University of California Press); B. Hanawalt (1988) *Women and Work in Pre-industrial Europe* (Bloomington: Indiana University Press); J. Scott & L. Tilly (1978) *Women, Work, and Family* (New York: Holt Rinehart); L. Davidoff & C. Hall (1987) *Family Fortunes* (London: Hutchinson); I. Silverblatt, (1987) *Moon, Sun, and Witches: gender ideologies and class in Inca and colonial Peru* (Princeton, NJ: Princeton University Press).
3. D. Elson (1999) Labor Markets as Gendered Institutions: equality, efficiency and empowerment issues, *World Development*, 27 (3), pp. 611–627; A. Phillips & B. Taylor (1980) Sex and Skill: notes towards a feminist economics, *Feminist Review*, 6 (1), pp. 79–88; H. Applewhite & D. Levy (1993) *Women and Politics in the Age of the Democratic Revolution* (Ann Arbor: University of Michigan Press); J. Nelson (2007) *Courts, Elites, and Gendered Power in the Early Middle Ages: Charlemagne and others* (Northampton, Variorum); S. Kettering (1989) The Patronage Power of Early Modern French Noblewomen, *Historical Journal*, 32 (4), pp. 817–841; J. McNamara & S. Wemple (1973) The Power of Women through the Family in Medieval Europe: 500–1100, *Feminist Studies*, 1 (3–4), pp. 126–141; I. Blom,

K. Hagemann & C. Hall (Eds) (2000) *Gendered Nations* (Oxford: Berg); M. Tavakoli-Targhi (2002) From Patriotism to Matriotism: a tropological study of Iranian nationalism, 1870–1909, *International Journal of Middle East Studies*, 34 (2), pp. 217–238; A. Najmabadi (1996) 'Is Our Name Remembered?' Writing the history of Iranian constitutionalism as if gender mattered, *Iranian Studies*, 29 (1), pp. 85–109; C. Bynum (1984) *Jesus as Mother* (Berkeley: University of California Press); M. Kaplan & D. Moore (Eds) (2011) *Gender and Jewish History* (Bloomington: Indiana University Press); M. Baer (2004) Islamic Conversion Narratives of Women: social change and gendered religious hierarchy in early modern Ottoman Istanbul, *Gender and History*, 16 (2) pp. 425–458; J. de Groot and S. Morgan (Eds) (2014) *Sex, Gender and the Sacred: reconfiguring gender history* (Oxford: Wiley-Blackwell).

4. M. Erler & M. Kowaleski (Eds) (2003) *Gendering the Master Narrative: women and power in the middle ages* (Ithaca: Cornell University Press); A. Shepard & G. Walker (Eds.) (2008) Gender, Change and Periodisation, *Gender and History*, 20 (3) pp. 453–462; K. Honeyman (2000) *Women, Gender, and Industrialization in England, 1700–1870* (London: Macmillan); S. Rose (1986) Gender at Work: sex, class and industrial capitalism, *History Workshop Journal*, 21 (1) pp. 113–132; K. Canning (1992) Gender and the Politics of Class Formation: rethinking German labor history, *American Historical Review*, 97(3), pp. 736–768; J. Scott (1988) *Gender and the Politics of History* (New York: Columbia University Press); J. Boydston (2008) Gender as a Question of Historical Analysis, *Gender and History*, 20 (3) pp. 558–583; S. Morgan (2005) Rethinking Religion in Gender History: theoretical & methodological reflections, in U. King & T. Beattie (Eds) *Gender, Religion and Diversity* (London: A&C Black), pp. 113–124; J de Groot & S. Morgan (2013) Beyond the 'Religious Turn'? Past, present and future perspectives in gender history, *Gender and History*, 25 (3), pp. 395–422; J. Kelly (1986) Did Women have a Renaissance?, in J. Kelly *Women, History, and Theory* (Chicago: University of Chicago Press); P. Anagol (2008) Agency, Periodisation and Change in the Gender and Women's History of Colonial India, *Gender and History*, 20 (3), pp. 603–627.

5. For example, J. Scott (1992) Experience, in J. Butler & J. Scott (Eds) *Feminists Theorise the Political* (London: Routledge); E. Clark (1998) The Lady Vanishes: dilemmas of a feminist historian after the 'linguistic turn', *Church History*, 67 (1), pp. 1–31; S. Walby (1989) Theorising Patriarchy, *Sociology*, 23(2), pp. 213–234; A. Brah (1991) Difference, Diversity, Differentiation, *International Review of Sociology*, 2 (2), pp. 53–71; D. Kandiyoti (1988) Bargaining with Patriarchy, *Gender & Society*, 2 (3) pp. 274–290; S. Gruber & M. Szołtysek (2016) The Patriarchy Index: a comparative study of power relations across historical Europe, *History of the Family*, 21 (2), pp 1–42; V. Patil (2013) From Patriarchy to Intersectionality: a transnational feminist assessment of how far we've really come, *Signs*, 38 (4) pp. 847–867.

6. H. Bradford (1996) Women, Gender and Colonialism: rethinking the history of the British Cape Colony and its frontier zones, c.1806–70, *Journal of African History*, 37 (3) pp. 351–370; (2006) Peasants, Historians, and Gender: a South African case study revisited, 1850–1886, *History and Theory*, 39(4), pp. 86–110; also (1995) Women in the Cape and its Frontier Zones, 1800–1870: a critical essay on androcentric historiography, *Proceedings of the Biannual South African Historical Society Conference*; M. Sinha (2000) Mapping the Imperial Social Formation: a modest proposal for feminist history, *Signs*, 25 (4), pp. 1077–1082; (1997) Teaching Imperialism as a Social Formation, *Radical History Review*, 67, pp. 175–186; A. Najmabadi (2005) *Women with Mustaches and Men without Beards* (Berkeley: University of California Press); K. Babayan & A. Najmabadi (Eds) (2008) *Islamicate Sexualities: translations across temporal geographies of desire* (Cambridge MA: Harvard University Press).

7. At a conference at which I was present.

8. J. Osterhammel (1997) *Colonialism: a theoretical overview* (Princeton: Wiener); J. Osterhammel & N. Peterson (2005) *Globalisation: a short history* (Princeton: Princeton University Press); J. Burbank & F. Cooper (2011) *Empires in World History* (Princeton: Princeton University Press); M. Doyle (1986) *Empires* (Ithaca: Cornell University Press); F. Cooper (2005) *Colonialism in Question* (Berkeley: University of California Press); P. Cain & A. Hopkins (1993) *British Imperialism 1688–1990* (London: Longman); P. Cain

& M. Harrison (Eds) (2001) *Imperialism: critical concepts in historical studies* (London: Routledge); G. Eley (2010) Imperial Imaginary, Colonial Effect: writing the colony and the metropole together, in C. Hall & K. McLelland (Eds) (2010) *Race, Nation and Empire: making histories from 1750 to the present* (Manchester: Manchester University Press); J. Darwin (2009) *The Empire Project: the rise and fall of the British world-system, 1830–1970* (Cambridge: Cambridge University Press); (2008) *After Tamerlane: the global history of empire since 1405* (London: Penguin). I myself deal with this more extensively in a forthcoming article entitled 'Beyond Bias, Blindness and Marginalisation: gender and the making/unmaking of colonial and postcolonial analyses', in S. Schmolinsky et al. (Eds) (forthcoming), *Time-Space of the Imperial* (Berlin: de Gruyters).

9. Kelly, 'Did Women have a Renaissance?'; Shepard & Walker, 'Gender, Change and Periodisation'; S. Walby (1990) From Private to Public Patriarchy: the periodisation of British history, *Women's Studies International Forum*, 13 (1), pp. 91–104; J. Morgan (2016) Periodization Problems: race and gender in the history of the early Republic, *Journal of the Early Republic*, 36 (2) pp. 351–357; E. Clark (2001) Women, Gender, and the Study of Christian History, *Church History*, 70 (3), pp. 395–426; Anagol, 'Agency, Periodisation and Change'.

10. L. Peirce (1993) *The Imperial Harem: women and sovereignty in the Ottoman empire* (Oxford: Oxford University Press).

11. M. Sinha (1995) *Colonial Masculinity* (Manchester: Manchester University Press); (1994) Reading Mother India: empire, nation, and the female voice, *Journal of Women's History*, 6 (2), pp. 6–44.

12. D. Valenze (1996) *The First Industrial Woman* (Oxford: Oxford University Press); Davidoff & Hall, *Family Fortunes*; G. Gullickson (1986) *Spinners and Weavers of Auffay: rural industry and the sexual division of labour* (Cambridge: Cambridge University Press); E. Friedl (1991) The Dynamics of Women's Spheres of Action in Rural Iran, in N. Keddie & B. Baron (Eds) *Women in Middle Eastern History: shifting boundaries in sex and gender* (New Haven: Yale University Press); B. Moitt (2001) *Women and Slavery in the French Antilles, 1635–1848* (Bloomington: Indiana University Press).

13. S. Marks (1988) *Not Either an Experimental Doll: the separate worlds of three South African women* (Bloomington: Indiana University Press); C. Hall (2002) *Civilising Subjects: metropole and colony in the English imagination 1830–67* (Cambridge: Polity Press).

14. Sinha, 'Mapping the Imperial'; 'Reading Mother India'; D. Kandiyoti, Bargaining with Patriarchy; (1991) Islam and Patriarchy: a comparative perspective, in Keddie & Baron, *Women in Middle Eastern History*; also (2005) Rethinking Bargaining with Patriarchy in C. Jackson & R. Pearson (Eds) *Feminist Visions of Development: gender analysis and policy* (London: Routledge); A. Najmabadi (2004) From Supplementarity to Parasitism?, *Journal of Women's History*, 16 (2), pp. 30–35; (2006) Beyond the Americas: gender and sexuality as useful categories of analysis, *Journal of Women's History*, 18(1), pp. 11–21; C. Mohanty (1991) Cartographies of Struggle, and 'under western eyes', in C. Mohanty et al. (Eds) *Third World Women and the Politics of Feminism* (Bloomington: Indiana University Press).

15. Boydston, 'Gender as a Question'; Najjmabadi, 'Beyond the Americas'; E. Fox-Genovese (1988) *Within the Plantation Household: black and white women of the old south* (Chapel Hill: University of North Carolina Press); H. Beckles (1999) *Centering Women: gender relations in Caribbean slave society* (Princeton: Martin Riener); T. Burnard (2004) *Mastery, Tyranny and Desire: Thomas Thistlewood and his slaves in the Anglo-Jamaican world* (Chapel Hill: University of North Carolina Press); M. Elgersman (2014) *Unyielding Spirits: black women and slavery in early Canada and Jamaica* (London: Routledge).

16. C. Midgley (2007) *Feminism and Empire: women activists in imperial Britain, 1790–1865* (London: Routledge); C. Midgley et al. (Eds) (2016) *Women in Transnational History: connecting the local and the global* (London: Routledge); S. Socolow (2015) *The Women of Colonial Latin America* (Cambridge: Cambridge University Press); M. Few (1995) Women, Religion, and Power: gender and resistance in daily life in late-seventeenth-century Santiago de Guatemala, *Ethnohistory*, 42 (4), pp. 627–637; A. Burton (1998) *At the Heart of the Empire: Indians and the colonial encounter in late-Victorian Britain* (Berkeley: University

of California Press); (2003) *Dwelling in the Archive: women writing house, home, and history in late colonial India* (Oxford: Oxford University Press).

17. Early discussions are K. Crenshaw (1991) Mapping the Margins: intersectionality, identity politics, and violence against women of color, *Stanford Law Review*, 43 (6), pp. 1241–1299; D. Hine (1992) Black Women's History, White Women's History: the juncture of race and class, *Journal of Women's History*, 4 (2), pp. 125–133; later views are found in L. McCall (2005) The Complexity of Intersectionality, *Signs*, 30 (3), pp. 771–800; J. Nash (2008) Re-thinking Intersectionality, *Feminist Review*, 89, pp. 1–15; see also Brah, 'Difference, Diversity, Differentiation'; A. Brah (2004) Ain't I A Woman? Revisiting intersectionality, *Journal of International Women's Studies*, 5 (3), pp. 53–71; Patil, 'From Patriarchy to Intersectionality'.

18. Boydston, 'Gender as a Question'; Kandiyoti, 'Islam and Patriarchy'; O. Oyewùmí (2005) Visualizing the Body: western theories and African subjects, in O. Oyewùmí (Ed.) (2005) *African Gender Studies: a reader* (Basingstoke: Palgrave Macmillan), pp. 3–21; *The Invention of Women: making an African sense of western gender discourses* (St Paul: University of Minnesota Press); see also B. Bakare-Yusef et al. (Eds) (2004) *African Gender Scholarship: concepts, methodologies and paradigms* (Oxford: Oxford University Press); P. J. Goldberg (1992) *Women, Work and Lifecycle* (Oxford: Oxford University Press); K. Phillips (2003) *Medieval Maidens: young women and gender in England, c.1270–1540* (Manchester: Manchester University Press); K. Barclay *et al.* (2011) Introduction: Gender and Generations: women and life cycles, *Women's History Review*, 20 (2) pp. 175–188; P. Johnson & P. Thane (Eds) (2002) *Old Age from Antiquity to Post-modernity* (London: Routledge); A. Rowlands (2001) Witchcraft and Old Women in Early Modern Germany, *Past and Present*, 173, pp. 50–89.

19. See D. Chakrabarty (2009) *Provincializing Europe: postcolonial thought and historical difference* (Princeton: Princeton University Press); (2016) Provincializing Medieval Europe: Mandeville's cosmopolitan utopianism, in K. Lochrie (Ed.) *Nowhere in the Middle Ages* (Philadelphia: University of Pennsylvania Press); A. Dirlik *et al.* (Eds) (2000) *History after the Three Worlds: post-Eurocentric historiographies* (Latham MD: Rowman & Littlefield); A. Dirlik (2013) Thinking Modernity Historically, *Asian Review of World Histories*, 1 (1), pp. 5–44; P. Gran (1996) *Beyond Eurocentrism: a new view of modern world history* (Syracuse: Syracuse University Press); S. Conrad (2012) Enlightenment in Global History: a historiographical critique, *American Historical Review*, 117 (4), pp. 999–1027; for comment see J. Zinsser (2013) 'Women's and Men's World History? Not yet, *Journal of Women's History*, 25 (4), pp. 309–318.

20. Z. Eisenstein (2004) *Against Empire: feminisms, racism and the 'west'* (London: Zed Books), esp. pp. 34–46, 65–73, 96–101, 124–147, 181–226.

21. R. Kranidis (1999) *The Victorian Spinster and Colonial Emigration: contested subjects* (London: Macmillan); J. Clancy-Smith (2005) Women, Gender and Migration along a Mediterranean Frontier: pre-colonial Tunisia, c. 1815–1870, *Gender & History*, 17 (1), pp. 62–92; J. Bush (1994) 'The Right Sort Of Woman': female emigrators and emigration to the British Empire, 1890–1910, *Women's History Review*, 3(3), pp. 385–409; J. Myers (2001) Performing the Voyage Out: Victorian female emigration and the class dynamics of displacement, *Victorian Literature and Culture*, 29 (1), pp. 129–146; L. Chilton (2003) A New Class of Women for the Colonies: the imperial colonist and the construction of empire, *Journal of Imperial and Commonwealth History*, 31 (2), pp. 36–56; K. Ward (2009) *Networks of Empire: forced migration in the Dutch East India Company* (Cambridge: Cambridge University Press); M. Schrover (Ed.) (2008) *Illegal Migration and Gender in a Global and Historical Perspective* (Amsterdam: Amsterdam University Press); P. Williams (1999) *Illegal Immigration and Commercial Sex: the new slave trade* (Hove: Psychology Press); J. Moya (2007) Domestic Service in a Global Perspective: gender, migration, and ethnic niches, *Journal of Ethnic and Migration Studies*, 33 (4), pp. 559–579; E. Zontini (2010) *Transnational Families, Migration and Gender: Moroccan and Filipino women in Bologna and Barcelona* (Oxford: Berghahn Books); A. Bertone (1999) Sexual Trafficking in Women: international political

economy and the politics of sex, *Gender Issues*, 18 (1), pp. 4–22; T. Bastia (2006) Stolen Lives or Lack of Rights? Gender, migration and trafficking, *Labour, Capital and Society/Travail, capital et société*, 39 (2), pp. 20–47; L. Shepherd (Ed.) (2014) *Gender Matters in Global Politics: a feminist introduction to international relations* (London: Routledge); R. Parreñas (2001) *Servants of Globalization: women, migration and domestic work* (Stanford: Stanford University Press); J. Andall (2000) *Gender, Migration and Domestic Service* (Farnham: Ashgate).

22. N. Fraser (1990) Rethinking the Public Sphere: a contribution to the critique of actually existing democracy, *Social Text*, 25–26, pp. 56–80; C. Calhoun (Ed.) (1992) *Habermas and the Public Sphere* (Boston: MIT Press); S. Maza (1992) Women, the Bourgeoisie, and the Public Sphere: response to Daniel Gordon and David Bell, *French Historical Studies*, 17 (2), pp. 935–950; N. Göle (1997) The Gendered Nature of the Public Sphere, *Public Culture*, 10 (1), pp. 61–81; J. Rendall (1999) Women and the Public Sphere, *Gender & History*, 11 (3), pp. 475–488.

23. Examples include A. Firor Scott (1993) *Natural Allies: women's associations in American history* (Champaign: University of Illinois Press); B. Taylor (1983) *Eve and the New Jerusalem* (London: Virago Press); E. Rappaport (2001) *Shopping for Pleasure: women in the making of London's West End* (Princeton: Princeton University Press); M. Andrews & M. Talbot (Eds) (2000) *All the World and Her Husband: women in 20th-century consumer culture* (London: Bloomsbury); A. Bermingham & J. Brewer (2013) *The Consumption of Culture* (London: Routledge), chs 2, 3, 8, 9, 11; H. Hackel & C. Kelly (Eds) (2011) *Reading Women: literacy, authorship, and culture in the Atlantic world, 1500–1800* (Philadelphia: University of Pennsylvania Press); E. Eger (2001) *Women, Writing and the Public Sphere 1700–1830* (Cambridge: Cambridge University Press); D. Willen (1988) Women in the Public Sphere in Early Modern England: the case of the urban working poor, *Sixteenth Century Journal*, 19 (4), pp. 559–575; A. Twells (2009) *The Civilising Mission and the English Middle Class, 1792–1850* (London: Palgrave Macmillan); P. Brown & P. Parolin (Eds) (2008) *Women Players in England 1500–1660: beyond the all-male stage* (Farnham: Ashgate); J. Donawerth (2000) Poaching on Men's Philosophies of Rhetoric: eighteenth- and nineteenth-century rhetorical theory by women, *Philosophy and Rhetoric*, 33 (3), pp. 243–258; C. Jordan (2000) The Public Amateur and the Private Professional: a re-evaluation of the categories of public and private in colonial women artists' work, *Australian and New Zealand Journal of Art*, 1(2), pp. 42–60; E. Thompson (2003) Public and Private in Middle Eastern Women's History, *Journal of Women's History*, 15 (1) pp. 52–69.

24. *Gender and History*, 27 (3), November 2015.

Index